TRUMPOCRACY

ALSO BY DAVID FRUM

Patriots: A Novel

Why Romney Lost (And What the GOP Can Do about It)

Comeback: Conservatism That Can Win Again

An End to Evil: How to Win the War on Terror (with Richard Perle)

The Right Man: An Inside Account of the Bush White House

How We Got Here: The 70's, The Decade that Brought You Modern Life (For Better or Worse)

What's Right: The New Conservative Majority and the Remaking of America

Dead Right

TRUMPOCRACY

THE CORRUPTION OF THE AMERICAN REPUBLIC

DAVID FRUM

HARPER

An Imprint of HarperCollinsPublishers

HarperCollins books may be purchased for educational, business, or sales promotional use. For information, please email the Special Markets Department at SPsales@harpercollins.com.

FIRST EDITION

Designed by William Ruoto

Library of Congress Cataloging-in-Publication Data has been applied for.

ISBN 978-0-06-279673-8

18 19 20 21 22 LSC 10 9 8 7 6 5 4 3 2 1

TO MY CHILDREN,

MIRANDA, NATHANIEL, AND BEATRICE.

YOU TEACH ME MORE THAN I TAUGHT YOU. THIS BATTERED
WORLD YOUR ELDERS BEQUEATH YOU: YOU WILL MAKE IT
BETTER. IN ADMIRATION AND LOVE.

CONTENTS

INTRODUCTION

D emocracy is a work in progress. So is democracy's undoing.

Between 1975 and 2000, countries in every continent turned from repressive regimes to the rule of law, away from dictatorships of a single man or a single party toward multiparty democracy. Since then, democracy has gone into retreat. From Russia to South Africa, from Turkey to the Philippines, from Venezuela to Hungary, authoritarian leaders have smashed restraints on their power. Media freedom and judicial independence have eroded. The right to vote remains, but the right to have one's vote counted fairly may not.

Until the US presidential election of 2016, the global decline of democracy seemed a concern for other peoples in other lands; a matter for US foreign policy, yes, but not for America's internal affairs. That complacent optimism has been upended by the political rise of Donald Trump.

The crisis is upon Americans, here and now.

I write this book in the midst of that crisis. My choice of timing imposes on this project many risks of error and misunderstanding. In the rush of immediate controversies, we can overemphasize things of no lasting consequence and overlook things that will prove supremely important.

But if it's potentially embarrassing to speak too soon, it can also be dangerous to wait too long.

I sometimes wonder what would have happened if some forward-thinking member of Congress had devoted his or her career in the late 1990s to fighting for the hardening of airline cockpits against hijackers. He or she would have battled a cost-conscious industry, faced election opponents lavishly funded by airline lobbyists, and might have prevailed just in time to prevent the September 11, 2001, attacks from taking the form they did—meaning that nobody would ever have known the service that member had rendered. Instead, he or she would forever be known as that bore who droned so uselessly about a threat that never materialized.

Not all premonitions come to pass. But if we are saved, we never know for certain what we were saved from.

Even now, the severity of the Trump challenge to American democracy remains a disputed question. Some more tradition-minded Republicans will point to the Trump administration's chaotic decision making and policy failures as reassurance. "How can he be an autocrat when he botched his own agenda in Congress? He can't do anything for fifteen consecutive minutes, let alone overthrow a system of government that has lasted more than two hundred years."

The buried premise in these assurances is that the only leaders we need to fear are those who are strategic, methodical, and deft—and that the only threats a democracy need worry about are open and overt attacks on its legality. The Founders of the American republic knew better. One of the political thinkers who most influenced them, the French philosopher Montesquieu, warned that a free society must guard not only against "crimes" by powerful leaders but also against "negligence, mistakes, a certain slackness in the love of the homeland, dangerous examples, the seeds of corruption, that which does not run counter to the laws but eludes them, that which does not destroy them but weakens them."[1]

So it is now. The thing to fear from the Trump presidency is not the bold overthrow of the Constitution, but the stealthy paralysis of governance; not the open defiance of law, but an accumulating subversion of norms; not the deployment of state power to intimidate dissidents, but the incitement of private violence to radicalize supporters. Trump operates not by strategy, but by instinct. His great skill is to sniff his opponents' vulnerabilities: "low energy," "little," "crooked," "fake." In the same way, Trump has intuited the weak points in the American political system and in American political culture. Trump gambled that Americans resent each other's differences more than they cherish their shared democracy. So far, that gamble has paid off.

"Democracy," as you were taught in high school civics, is a word that traces its origin back to two Greek words: the word for "people" and the word for "rule." I call this book *Trumpocracy* because it is a study of rulership, not a study of personality. My topic is President Trump's power: how he has gained it, how he has used it, why it has not yet been effectively checked.

An American president is not some tribal chief, ruling by personal charisma and brute force. He (or someday she) works through systems: through a party in Congress and the states, through supportive media organizations, through national political networks of donors and voters, through the hundreds of staffers included in the term "the White House," and through the thousands of senior functionaries who together administer the executive branch.

This book is the story of those who enable, empower, support, and collaborate with Donald Trump. Many of those people have found ways to express their personal discomfort and disquiet with Trump. Those expressions may well be to some greater or lesser degree sincere. They may someday even become important. But as of the time of the publication of this book, they remain ineffectual.

If (when?) his enablers withdraw from Donald Trump, he will be left isolated and helpless, a dead tooth in the gums of the US government. Yet the opportunity he discovered and the danger he presented will not end with Donald Trump's career. The vulnerabilities Trump exploited will remain vulnerabilities still. Political decisions and economic trends have deeply riven the contemporary United States along lines of class, race, region, national origin, and cultural identity. Even the bonds between men and women have become attenuated. Those are not rhetorical claims; they are measurable facts. Diversity brings distrust—and the mutual distrust among Americans has been Donald Trump's most important political resource.

Since the election of 2016, much has been written about the campaign decisions that supposedly brought the United States to its present pass. Why didn't Hillary Clinton commit resources here instead of there? Why visit this state instead of that? I propose we put the spotlight on the voters rather than the candidates; on longer-term trends, not dramatic incidents; on the game as it is played, not the ballyhooed game changers who so seldom actually change anything.

Even before Donald Trump thrust himself forward as a presidential candidate, American politics had been veering toward extremism and instability. Trump seized a dark opportunity, but that opportunity had been opened and enlarged for him by others. Trump's election was a system failure, but the system did not fail out of the wild blue yonder.

Institutions do not matter for themselves. They matter because of the way they serve, or fail to serve, the people of the country. Trumpocracy has left Americans less safe against foreign dangers, has diverted their money from its proper purposes to improper pockets, has worked to bias law enforcement in favor of the powerful, and has sought to intimidate media lest they report things the public most needs to know. To shrug and say, "What does it all matter?" is not only to dismiss the poor and the vulnerable but to submit your own interests to the mercy of the greedy and unscrupulous. It is to submit to life as a subject rather than a citizen.

A human catastrophe is unfolding on the US territory of Puerto Rico as the editorial process for this book comes to its close. I do not know the ultimate toll in human life, but the whole world has caught its first glimpses of the scale of suffering on the island in the wake of Hurricane Maria. This is what it means for government to fail. Trump's government has failed not only because of indifference and incompetence, although he abounds in both, but because from the start it has been redirected from the service of the public to the aggrandizement of one domineering man and his shamelessly grasping extended family.

Every book is a journey, and the wise reader will examine the credentials of the guide. When Donald Trump entered the presidential race in the summer of 2015, I hoped for some good from him. Could he be the wake-up call that Republicans needed? Trump, you'll recall, launched his campaign not only with name-calling, but also with a fresh message. Rather than end the Medicare guarantee for people under the age of fifty-five, he would protect it. Rather than propose upper-income tax cuts, he would focus on middle-class opportunities. Rather than terminate the step toward universal health coverage in the Affordable Care Act (ACA), he would improve and enlarge coverage. Rather than propose amnesty as a solution to illegal immigration, he would secure America's borders. Perhaps as important as any of these things, Trump might at last force Republicans to confront the Iraq trauma.

Trump of course flagrantly lied about his own history with regard to the Iraq War.[2] He repeated a fantasy about opposing the war so strenuously that President George W. Bush sent representatives to Trump to beg him to be quiet. It was all utterly untrue. Yet if he is dishonest about his own history, Trump smashed the taboos that had squelched honesty in others. Perhaps now we conservatives and Republicans could talk openly about what had gone wrong and what should be learned. (I've placed my own retrospectives on Iraq on the public record for anyone interested. You can find them archived at DavidFrum.com.)

Pretty transparently, Donald Trump had no credible plans for doing any of these good things. But even to articulate such challenges to party dogma amounted to a public service of a kind. By showing that Republican voters would reward a candidate who promised to protect health care and reduce immigration, rather than the usual other way around, Trump opened the way (or so I then hoped) for some more responsible politician to adopt these issues and shove Trump aside.

I expected the good sense of Republican voters to reassert itself. I refused to allow that the party could actually nominate him, or that an unlucky bounce in the Electoral College might somehow elect him. Pro-Trump talkers cite the underestimation of Trump's chances by people like me as proof that the media "got it wrong" in 2016 and have remained "always wrong" about Trump ever since.[3]

But a wrong prediction about Trump's chances is not the same thing as an inaccurate assessment of Trump's character and behavior, or of the consequences of that character and behavior for the government of the United States. If anything, Trump's Electoral College fluke has forced a clearer and grimmer reckoning with the ominous anti-democratic forces Trump represents.

. . . rats running in the roof-beams, ants
Chewing at the foundations.
Death-beetles tick under the wall-paper, punctuate the evening
  quiet
Of families gathered at home.[4]

That haunting vision was composed almost a century ago by James Neugass, an American who fought in the Spanish Civil War. It warns that societies can dissolve into rot, as well as erupt into violence.

Trump gained the presidency thanks in great part to voters disgusted by a status quo that was ceasing to work for more and more of them. The largest and most loyal subset of those voters were men who felt devalued in the economy and disrespected in the culture, who chafed at being scolded for their "privilege" even as they succumbed to disability, drugs, and early death. Trump has not kept faith with those voters. But they have kept faith with him. For fear of them, Trump's party stays bolted to him. Members of his party may denounce him in "on background" interviews. His own staff will leak their disgust at his antics and cruelties. Yet whatever these powerful people say in private, they continue to enable him in public. It is their public actions, despite their private qualms, that sustain Trumpocracy.

President Trump has plunged the government of the United States into chaos that enhances his personal power. He has persuaded millions of Americans to ignore information they need as "fake news" from a "corrupt media." He has allowed foreign states and local politicians to tamper with the integrity of American elections to his own benefit. He demands that high officials disregard the law in favor of personal loyalty to him. He has concentrated power in the hands of military men—better men than himself, but not the right hands for the job of civilian government. He has alienated allies, appeased large enemies, and goaded small ones to the edge of war. He has brutally inflamed the ethnic and class divisions that empowered him in the first place. He has enriched himself in government in a way that disheartens every honest public official, and invites dishonest ones to imitate him.

But that cannot be the final word—and it will not be. We can choose our futures, not merely submit to them. Past generations of Americans have faced and overcome severer tests. Will this generation be found wanting in its hour on the stage of history? Someday, the time will come to write the history of that hour. I undertake this book before that time, as my contribution to ensuring that the hour's ending is one to be prouder of than its sorry opening.

TRUMPOCRACY

CHAPTER 1

PRE-EXISTING CONDITIONS

Democracy dies in darkness, opines a great American newspaper, but it would be more accurate to say that it dies by degrees. Where constitutional democracy has been lost, it has been lost because political actors have broken its rules turn by turn to achieve some immediately urgent goal. Each rule breaking then justifies the next, in a cycle of revenge that ends only in the formal or informal abrogation of the constitutional order.

Constitutional democracy is founded on a commitment first and foremost to the rules of the game. The losers in any round of play agree to accept their loss, because they believe they will soon have another turn; the winners accept limits on their gains because they anticipate that next time they may number among the losers.

"Well, here's the way I see it," said President George H. W. Bush on the night of his reelection defeat in 1992. He repeated the phrase as he continued,

Here's the way we see it and the country should see it—that the people have spoken and we respect the majesty of the democratic system. I just called Governor Clinton over in Little Rock and offered my congratulations. He did run a strong campaign. I wish him well in the White House. And I want the country to know that our entire Administration will work closely with his team to ensure the smooth transition of power. There is important work to be done, and America must always come first. So we will get behind this new President and wish him—wish him well. . . .

Now I ask that we stand behind our new President and regardless of our differences, all Americans share the same purpose: to make this, the world's greatest nation, more safe and more secure and to guarantee every American a shot at the American dream.[1]

In the years since 1992, however, the game of politics has evolved more and more into a live-fire exercise. The end of the Cold War perhaps explains the intensifying ferocity of the competition: since 1990, national security concerns have mattered less to American elites. The slowdown in economic growth since the year 2000 and the shock of the financial crisis and the Great Recession have embittered politics too; when there seems less to go around, people quarrel more ferociously over what remains. Ill feeling over the Supreme Court decision that elevated George W. Bush to the presidency over Al Gore has never healed. Accelerating ethnic and cultural diversity raises the stakes while aggravating mistrust and resentment between Americans. The failures and mistakes of government policy since 2001—from the 9/11 attacks, through the Iraq War, through the weak recovery from the Great Recession— have swung the pendulum of power more rapidly from side to side, tempting each of the two parties to grasp for more while it can, conscious that the moment of opportunity will not last long.

However you weight those causes, the record of the consequences makes grim reading.

Item:

The Republican congressional majorities elected in 2010 arrived in Washington believing they carried a mandate for radical cuts in government spending and especially the early repeal of the then-new Affordable Care Act. President Obama, elected by even more votes in 2008, insisted he retained a mandate to defend the policies enacted by Democrats in 2009–2010. Who was right? Surely both. Yet rather than bargains and compromises, all-or-nothing politics emerged as the order of the day. In the summer of 2011, frustrated by their inability to impose their will on the president, Republicans in Congress adopted a desperate tactic. Unless Obama consented to large cuts in future spending, they would not authorize a rise in the US debt ceiling. In effect, this would result in a default on the debt incurred by past spending.

Debt ceiling fights had occurred often enough in sessions past. Back in 2006, then-Senator Obama had himself voted nay on a debt ceiling increase. But in those past fights, the congressional leadership had always ensured that there were sufficient votes to pass the increase before proceeding with the demagogic speeches opposing the increase. Using the debt ceiling vote as an opportunity for crass grandstanding was a venerable congressional tradition; using it as a weapon represented something startlingly new.

Republicans threatened national bankruptcy, and they reiterated that threat until an estimated forty-eight hours before the government of the United States lost the ability to pay its bills. It was not only the payment of interest on government debt that would have been jeopardized, but also the timely payment of every salary, every government contract, every obligation of every kind. The financial and economic consequences of the stoppage of payments by the largest purchaser of goods and services on planet Earth could not be calculated, could barely even be imagined. It would be a nuclear event—and Republican Party leaders were willing to threaten it not only once, but a second time again in 2013.

Item:

President Obama tried through his two terms in office to negotiate some kind of immigration deal that would include amnesties for most or all the people illegally residing in the United States. Congress rebuffed him, even when Democrats held the majority. Advocates for immigrants pressed the president to extend some form of executive protection to this unauthorized population. Again and again, Obama replied that he lacked the legal authority to do so.

> I just want to repeat: I'm president. I'm not king. . . . I can exercise some flexibility in terms of where we deploy our resources, to focus on people who are really causing problems as opposed to families who are just trying to work and support themselves. But there's a limit to the discretion that I can show, because I am obliged to execute the law. That's what the executive branch means. I can't just make up the laws by myself.[2]

> Sometimes when I talk to immigration advocates, they wish I could just bypass Congress and change the law myself. But that's not how a democracy works.[3]

> We are doing everything we can administratively. But the fact of the matter is there are laws on the books that I have

to enforce. And I think there's been a great disservice done to the cause of getting the DREAM Act passed and getting comprehensive immigration passed by perpetrating the notion that somehow, by myself, I can go and do these things. It's just not true. . . . We live in a democracy. You have to pass bills through the legislature, and then I can sign it.[4]

In June 2012, Obama abruptly reversed himself. Facing an election in which his strategists advised that Hispanic votes would be crucial, President Obama issued the very order that he himself had so repeatedly denounced as beyond his authority. In the long history of presidential overreach, there had never been a case like it: a president asserting a power that he himself *while actually serving as president* had forcefully and repeatedly condemned as unlawful.

The 2012 action deferred enforcement of the immigration laws against people under the age of thirty who had entered the United States before age sixteen, provided they had violated no other laws. This population was estimated at about 800,000 people.[5] In November 2014, President Obama issued an even more ambitious order, this time deferring action against the parents of the beneficiaries of the 2012 order, enlarging the protected population to an estimated four million people.[6]

In June 2016, a 4–4 deadlock on the US Supreme Court would leave in place an appellate court's ruling that Obama had indeed overstepped his powers.[7] Yet Obama did not withdraw from his new assertion of power. He and his defenders argued that congressional *inaction* had left him no choice but to act alone. It's a strange version of the Constitution that says the president gains greater power to say yes when Congress tries to tell him no. Pre-2012 Obama, by contrast, recognized that if Congress declines to enact a law, then said law is not enacted, and everybody including the president must live with the consequences. Post-2012 Obama had become more impatient with restraints on his power. Or, rather, his voters had become so, as we shall see in more detail in the final chapter of this book.

Item:

American politics has often enough been poisoned by conspiracy thinking. But there was something more radical and more far-reaching about the Birther hoax of the Obama years than in conspiracy fantasies of the past. (Birthers variously argued that Barack Obama had been born in Kenya, raised a Muslim, or did not qualify as a "natural-born citizen" because his father was foreign born.[8])

1. *The hoax was accepted in some form or other by a large majority of Republican voters.* Surveys in the final year of the Obama presidency found that only about one-quarter of registered Republicans acknowledged that Barack Obama had been born in the United States. The three-quarters majority expressed either certainty that he had not (about 40 percent) or doubt that he had (about 35 percent). Highly informed Republicans were actually slightly *less* likely to accept the fact of Barack Obama's American birth than less-informed Republicans.[9]

2. *The hoax not only shaped but outright controlled the political possibilities for Republican officeholders.* When confronted on television with video of Iowa Republicans insisting that Barack Obama was hiding something about his origins, then-Speaker John Boehner had this to say to NBC's David Gregory: "It's not my job to tell the American people what to think. . . . The state of Hawaii has said that he was born there. That's good enough for me. The president says he's a Christian. I accept him at his

word." He then repeated: "The American people have the right to think what they want to think. I can't—it's not my job to tell them."[10]

You can multiply Boehner's contortions endlessly.[11] Party leaders personally rejected and derided the Birther hoax. They did not dare do so out loud where their voters and donors might hear.

3. *The hoax almost instantly became decisive in the Republican Party's presidential politics.* Donald Trump seized on the Birther hoax in 2011, shouldering aside its early promoters to emerge as the nation's preeminent denier of Obama's Americanism. People forget this now, but Republicans instantly rewarded Trump by acclaiming his as their favorite for the presidential nomination of . . . 2012! An April 2011 poll put Trump in first place among Republican presidential possibilities, by an impressive nine points over the runner-up, Mike Huckabee, and eleven points over the ultimate winner, Mitt Romney.[12]

Trump took himself out of the 2012 race in May of that year, but his early success was not overlooked. Mitt Romney sought his endorsement; other candidates emulated his methods in 2016. Asked whether Obama was a Christian at a press conference at a 2015 meeting of the National Governors Association, Scott Walker replied, "I don't know. I've actually never talked about it or I haven't read about that. I've never asked him that."[13]

Nothing like this radical denial of the Americanism of a serving president had been seen since the Civil War era, if then. The denial also revealed that as the country diversified, its conservatives would insist ever more militantly that no matter who might *reside* within the United States, the country's institutions and identity should belong only to those recognizably like them.

Item:

Supreme Court nominations have triggered political battles since the earliest days of the republic. But the rest of the federal judicial system had historically excited Americans much less. Patronage, not ideology, inspired the great majority of lower-court appointments, each party taking turns to reward friends and supporters.

That easygoing rotation has radicalized over the past two decades. The change is often dated to a 2001 article by Bruce Ackerman, a law professor at Yale. George W. Bush had been made president, Ackerman argued, only by the intervention of a conservative Supreme Court. If Bush then appointed further conservative justices, the court would be "packing itself." For that reason, "when sitting justices retire or die, the Senate should refuse to confirm any nominations offered up by President Bush."[14]

Ackerman limited his boycott idea to the Supreme Court itself, but Senate Democrats did him one better. No Supreme Court vacancies opened in George W. Bush's first term, but a great many appellate court seats did. In a closely divided Senate, Democrats successfully blocked the consideration of ten of these appointees—an unprecedented move.

Republicans struck back after gaining Senate seats in the election of 2004. They threatened to end the Senate minority's power to filibuster lower-court judicial nominations. The two parties reached a deal. The appellate-judge filibuster was preserved in theory, but with an understanding that the minority would use it only in "extreme cases." By then, the most controversial of the Bush nominees had removed themselves from consideration, so Democrats could score the exchange as a victory.

This backstory explains why Senate Republicans a decade later felt entitled to use unprecedented tactics of their own against President Obama's final nominee to the Supreme Court, Merrick Garland. Republicans refused Garland even a hearing, never mind a vote, inventing a new principle against presidents nominating Supreme Court justices in their final year. The outcome of the 2016 presidential election then allowed Republicans to claim the open seat for one of their own, Neil Gorsuch, a grab that will be regarded by Democrats as justifying whatever revenge they can exact whenever they recover a Senate majority.

Item:

Republicans had pledged and pledged again to repeal and replace Obamacare. They fought the 2012 election very largely as a referendum on that issue. After the defeat, their Congressional leadership tacitly accepted that the issue had closed. They continued the fight anyway. Donors demanded it, and it energized the rank and file. But as Eric Cantor, then the number two House Republican, conceded in an interview published in July 2017, "To give the impression that if Republicans were in control of the House and Senate, that we could do that when Obama was still in office. . . . I never believed it."[15]

But a great many others did believe it. These true-believing conservatives assumed that the party in which they had invested so much faith, energy, and money must have developed a plan to repeal and replace Obamacare, if and when the moment should arrive. So that moment did, or seemed to do, in November 2016: united Republican control of the federal government.

At which point it instantly became undeniable that the Republicans' ideas for replacing Obamacare bubbled with toxicity.

Republicans had excoriated the Affordable Care Act for presenting middle-class taxpayers with increased premiums and heightened deductibles. Their own plans would lower premiums in the individual marketplace a little, for some, by raising deductibles a lot for just about everybody. This was not malice, just arithmetic. It was arithmetic too that reducing the federal government's future contributions to Medicaid would drop millions of enrollees from the program over the next decade.

What goes around comes around. In 2017, House and Senate Republicans would try to jam through Congress a law every bit as far-reaching as the Affordable Care Act, without hearings, without debate, and (insofar as they could) without scores from the Congressional Budget Office. Ironically, while all attention was focused on President Trump's raging and bullying, the most radical attack on American norms of governance in his first year was attempted not by Steve Bannon, Jeff Sessions, Anthony Scaramucci, or any other late-night demon, but by the regular Republicans of the House and Senate. Senator John McCain vividly described the legislative method of repeal and replace:

> We've tried to do this by coming up with a proposal behind closed doors in consultation with the administration, then springing it on skeptical members, trying to convince them it's better than nothing, asking us to swallow our doubts and force it past a unified opposition. I don't think that is going to work in the end. And it probably shouldn't.[16]

Some Republicans, including John McCain, have attempted to compare the methods of ACA repeal to those with which the ACA was enacted in the first place. Yet the original ACA was lengthily debated, examined in committee, and fully scored by the Congressional Budget Office. It represented not novelty, but a somewhat more redistributionist update of the health care reform signed into law in Massachusetts by Governor Mitt Romney and originally sketched at the Conservative Heritage Foundation in the mid-

1990s, as a Republican alternative to the health care plan offered by the Clinton administration. Whatever other complaints might be brought against the ACA, nobody can say it was sprung on either Congress or the American people out of nowhere—or that senators lacked full information about its contents and consequences. ACA repeal, however, was pushed through Congress as a black box. The famous line of Nancy Pelosi's—"We have to pass the bill so that you can find out what's in it" (ripped from context in her case and distorted in its meaning by her opponents)—literally did apply to the repeal of the Affordable Care Act.

The failure of ACA repeal may deter future Congresses from repeating the smash-and-grab methods of the Republicans of 2017–18. But a sinister precedent has been set, and it will not be soon forgotten.

Item:

The twenty-first century has been an unhealthy era for political incumbents. Between November 2000 and November 2016, partisan control of the House of Representatives flipped twice; control of the Senate, four times. That's the same number of rotations, for each chamber, as in the entire fifty-five-year period from VJ Day to November 2000.

The presidency had a lower turnover rate, but even there, trouble indicators flashed. George W. Bush was reelected in 2004 with 50.7 percent of the popular vote—the lowest percentage of the popular vote in American history for any incumbent president not actually to lose. In 2012, Barack Obama won his second term by a smaller margin of the vote than he won his first, the only such drop-off since the age of Andrew Jackson.

In almost every survey since the Iraq War began to go wrong in 2004, upwards of 60 percent of Americans assessed the country as on the "wrong track." In the aftermath of the financial crisis of

2008, the wrong-track number spiked past 70 percent. It would return to that disturbing peak at intervals during the slow, weak recovery that followed.[17]

How removed from interactions with ordinary Americans did political elites have to be to plan the 2016 election as a return engagement between the two most famous political dynasties of late twentieth-century America: Bush versus Clinton? Yet the country's wealthiest citizens committed hundreds of millions of dollars to secure just that outcome. Could they not foresee trouble? Apparently not.

Rich people faced rising taxes in the Obama years, and understandably they did not like it. They had to deal with a president who seemed unusually unimpressed by their accomplishments, a sore point for a class of people accustomed to accolades and compliments. The venture capitalist Tom Perkins signed a letter to the *Wall Street Journal* in 2014 calling attention to "the parallels of fascist Nazi Germany to its war on its 'one percent,' namely its Jews, to the progressive war on the American one percent, namely the 'rich.'" Perkins warned of the possibility of a "progressive Kristallnacht."[18] Psychic alarms aside, the Obama years were actually a good time for the American affluent. Over President Obama's eight years in office, the S&P 500 gained 235 percent, more than 16 percent annually—one of the very best returns in US history.[19]

Yet through those years, one heard the pounding drumbeat of discontent: the Tea Party, Occupy Wall Street, Black Lives Matter, the Trump campaign. These movements had many points of disagreement with each other, but even more important similarities, including a rising tolerance for violence. It could still shock the nation in 2009 when one man carried a loaded rifle to an Obama political rally in Arizona.[20] Dozens of weapons were carried at the Black Lives Matter march in Dallas in 2016 that ended in the killing of five police officers and the wounding of seven more, as well as the injury of two civilians.[21] Even more and heavier weaponry would be displayed at the rallies against the removal of Confederate statues in Houston and Charlottesville in 2017.

The affluent and the secure persisted with old ways and old names in the face of the disillusionment and even the radicalization of the poorer two-thirds of American society. They invited a crisis. The only surprise was . . . how surprised they were when the invited crisis arrived.

Donald Trump did not create the vulnerabilities he exploited. They awaited him. The irresponsibility of American elites, the arrogance of party leaders, the insularity of the wealthy: those and more were the resources Trump used on his way to power.

"It's even worse than it looks," quipped a 2012 book by Norman Ornstein and Thomas Mann.[22] Such pessimism invited the reply, "That's what you said last time." Things have looked bad before without the world coming to an end. Why panic now? But it can equally be true that things were bad before, that things have gotten worse since, and that things may get even worse in the future. Like a man falling downstairs, each thump and tumble may be a prelude to the next, with the final crash still waiting for him even farther down.

Since the election of Donald Trump, the hard and painful floor seems to be rising toward us faster and faster and faster.

CHAPTER 2

ENABLERS

He did not do it by himself. Donald Trump was hoisted into office, and is sustained there by many hands:

by a conservative entertainment complex that propagandized for him;

by fellow candidates for president who appeased him in the hope they could use him;

by a Republican Party apparatus that submitted to him;

by a donor elite who funded him;

by a congressional party that protected him;

by writers and intellectuals who invented excuses for him; and

by millions of rank-and-file Republicans, who accepted him.

Even as the truth about Trump loomed ever larger and more inescapable during the presidential campaign, he drew protection and support from conservative true believers. Some of those people had opposed him in the primaries for his deviations from conservative ideology. Many more of them will rediscover that ideology after his administration ends, and condemn Trump retrospectively as "really a liberal all along."

But for now, when it matters, they are locked in. They are locked in by their cultural grievances. Donald Trump has delivered very little by way of an affirmative conservative agenda. But how much did that failure matter compared to his successful exploitation of conservative anger and alienation? The radio broadcaster Hugh Hewitt astutely explained on Twitter why so many conservatives enabled a president who achieved so little. Hewitt wrote less than a week after Trump's soft-on-Nazism response to the August 2017 white supremacist march in Charlottesville, Virginia: "I spoke to a group of influential CA GOPers tonight, long time activists, bundlers, influencers. Support for @realDonaldTrump has increased."[1] He elaborated: "Mostly this audience hates—hates—elite media. . . . It doesn't mean his supporters aren't critical. They are. Of many things. But @ealDonalTrump [*sic*] has all the right enemies."[2]

Hewitt's perception was quickly corroborated: a week after Charlottesville, a Republican pollster told Greg Sargent of the *Washington Post* that the president's defense of Confederate monuments had boosted his approval ratings among his core supporters.[3]

An even more coldly calculated manipulation of cultural grievance salvaged Donald Trump's campaign at its single most hazardous moment. In the last month of the election, Christian America heard Donald Trump confess to a lifelong practice of sexual assault.

You know, I'm automatically attracted to beautiful—I just start kissing them. It's like a magnet. I don't even wait. And when you're a star, they let you do it. You can do anything. . . . Grab 'em by the pussy. You can do anything.

Accompanying video revealed Trump behaving just as he said: snaking his arm around an actress's waist, grasping her hip, and planting an uninvited kiss on her neck. Other women came forward to complain that they too had been grabbed or groped or worse by Trump. How could Trump now deny the testimony of his own words? He did not even try. Instead, his campaign operation saved him by stoking the cultural resentments of white Catholics, exploiting raw material provided by Russian hackers and spies. You may remember the main lines of the story, but full understanding is found in the minute-by-minute timeline of events.

On October 7, 2016, at about four o'clock in the afternoon, David Fahrenthold of the *Washington Post* published an astounding story confirming a long-circulating rumor:

> Donald Trump bragged in vulgar terms about kissing, groping and trying to have sex with women during a 2005 conversation caught on a hot microphone, saying that "when you're a star, they let you do it," according to a video obtained by *The Washington Post*.
>
> The video captures Trump talking with Billy Bush, then of "Access Hollywood," on a bus with the show's name written across the side. They were arriving on the set of "Days of Our Lives" to tape a segment about Trump's cameo on the soap opera.[4]

Fahrenthold's story instantly rocketed to be the most concurrently read story in the *Post*'s history, even briefly crashing the newspaper's robust servers. For a dizzying hour, it seemed it might even decide the election.

Republican officeholders and candidates stampeded away from Trump. Reince Priebus, the chairman of the Republican National

Committee, issued a statement on October 8 saying, "No woman should ever be described in these terms or talked about in this manner. Ever."[5] Speaker of the House Paul Ryan said: "Women are to be championed and revered, not objectified" and disinvited Trump from a scheduled rally.[6] In an October 10 conference call, Ryan told fellow Republican House members that he would no longer campaign for Trump and would instead work to preserve a House majority that looked suddenly endangered.[7] "Totally inappropriate and offensive," declared Kelly Ayotte, running for reelection to the US Senate from New Hampshire.[8] "Repugnant, and unacceptable in any circumstance," said the Republican Senate majority leader, Mitch McConnell.[9] "I respectfully ask you with all due respect, to step aside. Step down," Utah's junior senator, Mike Lee, urged in a video posted on Facebook.[10] "He must step aside," agreed Alaska's senior senator, Lisa Murkowski.[11] "Donald Trump should withdraw and Mike Pence should be our nominee effective immediately," tweeted South Dakota's senior US senator, John Thune.[12] Altogether, about one-third of the Republican Senate caucus publicly called for Trump to quit the race. So did some outspoken members of the House caucus. "I'm out. I can no longer in good conscience endorse this person for president. It is some of the most abhorrent and offensive comments that you can possibly imagine," Representative Jason Chaffetz told a local Utah TV channel.[13]

Trump himself felt compelled to issue the only apology of his entire campaign, quite possibly of his entire life. He released a ninety-second video to Facebook and Twitter, in which he said the following: "I've never said I'm a perfect person, nor pretended to be someone that I'm not. I've said some things that I regret, and the words released today on this more-than-a-decade-old video are one of them. . . . I said it. I was wrong. And I apologize."[14]

But as Jimmy Stewart learns in *It's a Wonderful Life*, "No man is a failure who has friends." Donald Trump had some very useful friends indeed. Thirty-two minutes after Fahrenthold's story appeared on the *Washington Post*'s site, the Russian-backed site WikiLeaks dumped its largest email cache of the campaign: a hack of the personal Gmail account of Hillary Clinton's campaign chair, John Podesta.[15]

The Trump campaign and its media supporters knew in advance that something was coming. On Saturday, October 1, 2016, Trump's confidant Roger Stone had tweeted: "Wednesday@ HillaryClinton is done. #Wikileaks."[16] On Tuesday, October 4, WikiLeaks' founder, Julian Assange, posted a video announcement to preview his "October surprise." The *Drudge Report* bannered an openmouthed photo of Hillary Clinton headlined "ASSANGE COMES FOR HER *WIKILEAKS DANGER*."[17] Alex Jones's *Infowars* live-streamed the Assange appearance. But Assange spoke only in generalities that day, even assuring the world that he bore no personal animus against Hillary Clinton. Alex Jones fulminated, "Julian Assange is a Hillary butt plug."[18]

Instead, and with steely discipline, whoever controlled WikiLeaks awaited the perfect tactical moment. No dump Wednesday. No dump Thursday. Team Trump must have writhed in torment: Through the first week in October Hillary Clinton held a five-point lead among registered voters.[19] Then, as Republican leaders panicked and sputtered after the *Access Hollywood* tape, WikiLeaks detonated the distraction that saved the Trump campaign.

The contents of the October 7 WikiLeaks dump seemed to convict Clinton of dishonesty and two-facedness out of her own mouth. It was in one of the speeches quoted there that she said that a politician needs "both a public position and a private position."[20]

Trump's campaign had excited blue-collar white Americans by

nationalist attacks on too-permissive trade and immigration policies. It was in one of the Podesta emails that Clinton was quoted
as saying:

> My dream is a hemispheric common market, with open trade
> and open borders, some time in the future with energy that
> is as green and sustainable as we can get it, powering growth
> and opportunity for every person in the hemisphere.[21]

Trump powerfully deployed Clinton's "open borders" quote
in the third and final presidential debate on October 19, 2016.
"We have no country if we have no border. Hillary wants to give
amnesty. She wants to have open borders." The moderator, Chris
Wallace, invited Clinton to defend herself. Clinton replied, "I was
talking about energy. You know, we trade more energy with our
neighbors than we trade with the rest of the world combined. And
I do want us to have an electric grid, an energy system that crosses
borders. I think that will be a great benefit to us." Trump coun-
tered: "She wants open borders. People are going to pour into our
country." [22]

The quote about the "public position and private position" was
used by the Trump campaign to an even greater effect. Before the
WikiLeaks dump, polls showed Trump and Clinton neck and neck
when rated for "honesty and trustworthiness." By Election Day,
Trump had pulled eight points ahead as the more honest, according to the *Washington Post*/ABC News poll.[23]

No wonder Trump chortled, "I love WikiLeaks," to a Wilkes-
Barre, Pennsylvania, audience on October 10, 2016.[24] He repeated
his endorsement in Fletcher, North Carolina, eleven days later, and
altogether on 164 occasions in the last month of the presidential
campaign.[25]

Surely the greatest gift of the WikiLeaks Podesta hack to the Trump campaign, however, was the accelerant it offered to right-wing cultural grievance—and the escape valve it consequently offered to Catholics and other Christians discomfited by Trump's confessed sexual misconduct.

The October 7 WikiLeaks dump contained two email exchanges in which people connected with the Clinton campaign talked about the Catholic church. In one of the exchanges, Jennifer Palmieri, a future Clinton communications aide, replied to an email from John Halpin, a then-colleague at the Center for American Progress, a liberal think tank. The two, both liberal Catholics, were reacting angrily to news that Fox News' founder, Rupert Murdoch, had baptized as Catholic his children by his third wife, Wendi Deng. In the other exchange, Sandy Newman, a non-Catholic Clinton supporter, emailed to ask John Podesta, then the chairman of the Center for American Progress, about the possibilities for liberal reform within the Catholic church.

It's worth reading both exchanges in full.

Exchange 1, between Halpin and Palmieri, April 11, 2011:

HALPIN: Ken Auletta's latest piece on Murdoch in the New Yorker starts off with the aside that both Murdoch and Robert Thompson, managing editor of the WSJ, are raising their kids Catholic. Friggin' Murdoch baptized his kids in Jordan where John the Baptist baptized Jesus. Many of the most powerful elements of the conservative movement are all Catholic (many converts) from the SC and think tanks to the media and social groups. It's an amazing bastardization of the faith. They must be attracted to the systematic thought and severely backwards gender relations and must be totally unaware of Christian democracy.

PALMIERI: I imagine they think it is the most socially acceptable politically conservative religion. Their rich friends wouldn't understand if they became evangelicals.

HALPIN: Excellent point. They can throw around "Thomistic" thought and "subsidiarity" and sound sophisticated because no one knows what the hell they're talking about.[26]

That's it. The whole thing. Here's the second exchange, dated February 10, 2012, between Sandy Newman of a group called Voices for Progress and John Podesta. Again, I quote the totality.

NEWMAN: This whole controversy with the bishops opposing contraceptive coverage even though 98% of Catholic women (and their conjugal partners) have used contraception has me thinking . . . There needs to be a Catholic Spring, in which Catholics themselves demand the end of a middle ages dictatorship and the beginning of a little democracy and respect for gender equality in the Catholic church. Is contraceptive coverage an issue around which that could happen. The Bishops will undoubtedly continue the fight. Does the Catholic Hospital Association support of the Administration's new policy, together with "the 98%" create an opportunity?

Of course, this idea may just reveal my total lack of understanding of the Catholic church, the economic power it can bring to bear against nuns and priests who count on it for their maintenance, etc. Even if the idea isn't crazy, I don't qualify to be involved and I have not thought at all about how one would "plant the seeds of the revolution," or who would plant them. Just wondering. Hoping you're well, and getting to focus your time in the ways you want.

PODESTA: We created Catholics in Alliance for the Common Good to organize for a moment like this. But I think it lacks the leadership to do so now. Likewise Catholics United. Like most Spring movements, I think this one will have to be bottom up. I'll discuss with Tara. Kathleen Kennedy Townsend is the other person to consult.[27]

The large majority of American Catholics would agree with most of the sentiments in these exchanges. Only about one-third of American Catholics regard it as a sin to remarry without a Catholic annulment; only 17 percent agree with their church that artificial birth control is a sin.[28]

But quoted selectively and reported polemically, the Podesta exchanges provided just enough material for a counteroffensive to proclaim Donald Trump the true champion of the one, holy, catholic, and apostolic church.

On a conference call with reporters on October 12—five days (and only three weekdays) after the *Access Hollywood* recording became public—Trump's aide Kellyanne Conway seethed with indignation. She called on Clinton to "fire the staff who have engaged in this vicious anti-Catholic bigotry."[29] That same day, vice presidential candidate Mike Pence spoke at Liberty University. He urged Christians to forgive Donald Trump for his words on the *Access Hollywood* audio. "Last Sunday night, my running mate showed humility. He showed what was in his heart to the American people." But there must be no such forgiveness for those responsible for the intercepted 2011 and 2012 email exchanges. "If only on behalf of her Catholic running mate, Hillary Clinton should denounce those bigoted, anti-Catholic, anti-evangelical remarks and her campaign staff should apologize to people of faith and do it now."[30] Campaigning that same day in Florida, Trump used the same language as Conway: the email exchange showed that Clinton aides had attacked Catholics and evangelicals "viciously."[31]

Outside talkers took up the quickening complaint. Archbishop Charles Chaput of Philadelphia called the emails "ugly" and "contemptuously anti-Catholic" in his diocesan newsletter.[32] Eric Fehrnstrom, a former top aide to Governor Mitt Romney, complained in the *Boston Globe* of the "patronizing superiority that Clinton's team has for faithful Catholics in the conservative movement."[33] The *National Catholic Register* offered top billing to the Trump campaign's spin, reporting, "The chief liaison to Republican nominee Donald Trump for Catholic issues said that emails released Tuesday by WikiLeaks 'reveal the depths of the hostility of Hillary Clinton and her campaign toward Catholics.' "[34] A conservative columnist in the *Washington Post* interpreted the Podesta leaks as confirmation of the "rampant anti-Catholic bigotry that permeates Clinton World."[35]

The Podesta emails offered pro-Trump Catholics a welcome comeback after their candidate's February 2016 personal attacks on Pope Francis. The first Latin American pontiff had toured the US-Mexico border that month. Shortly before the pope's visit, Trump ripped the pope's plans in a telephone interview with Stuart Varney of Fox Business:

> So I think that the pope is a very political person. I think that he doesn't understand the problems our country has. I don't think he understands the danger of the open border that we have with Mexico. . . . Mexico got him to do it because Mexico wants to keep the border just the way it is because they're making a fortune and we're losing.[36]

On his return flight to Rome, the pope was asked about Trump's comments on the border. He replied, "A person who thinks only about building walls, wherever they may be, and not building bridges, is not Christian. This is not the gospel."[37] As ever, criticism enraged Trump. He posted his retort on Facebook:

> For a religious leader to question a person's faith is disgraceful. I am proud to be a Christian and as President I will not allow Christianity to be consistently attacked and weakened, unlike what is happening now, with our current President. No leader, especially a religious leader, should have the right to question another man's religion or faith. They [the Mexican government] are using the Pope as a pawn.[38]

This angry exchange would not seem to leave much scope for portraying Trump as the Catholic favorite in the 2016 race. But that underestimates the possibilities of outright fraud.

In June 2016, a previously unknown website designed to look like that of a local TV station—"WTOE 5 News"—began circulating a false story that the pope had endorsed Donald Trump. That first release generated about 100,000 engagements that month. WTOE 5 News vanished from the Internet soon afterward. But in late September, as if carefully timed to enhance the Podesta leaks, another previously unknown site, *Ending the Fed*, reposted the papal endorsement story. This time the fake story generated more than *one million* Facebook engagements, winning the honor as the single most circulated fake story of the entire election.[39]

Trump commands the news cycle like no American leader since Ronald Reagan. Yet he is no political giant. He and his campaign team of C-class talents stumbled from mistake to mistake, and they continue to stumble. It would not have taken a miracle to bar him from the presidency; it took a negative miracle to tumble him into it. Once in office, it was not his own cunning that enabled him to defy long-established standards of decent behavior. It was the complicity of his allies among the conservative and Republican political, media, and financial elite.

The election of 2016 popularized the political science concept of "negative partisanship."[40] The concept's authors, Alan Abramowitz and Steven Webster, observed that while many Americans do not identify as Republican or Democrat, virtually all Americans dislike one of those parties much more than they dislike the other. Trump cannily exploited negative partisanship to consolidate political support he could never have attracted for his own agenda or his own merits.

Trump campaigned as a nationalist, on the slogan "Make America Great Again." But he never spoke to or for the whole nation. The nation was too big, and he was too small. He excelled instead at discerning the grievances and angers that set American apart from American—and especially the grievances and angers of those who, like himself, felt entitled to dominate the apex of American society and now found themselves somehow occupying a place beneath their expectations.

Despite his inherited wealth and self-made global fame, the pre-presidential Donald Trump could never overcome the haunting suspicion that people laughed at him. At the time Trump clinched the New Hampshire primary in 2016, the *Washington Post* counted 103 instances since 1987 when Trump publicly referenced that sound of laughter.[41] Many Americans hear that same laughter. Trump mobilized them behind a politician who would silence the laughter if he did nothing else.

"At least he isn't politically correct." "He speaks his mind." "I'm tired of these special snowflakes." This was the last-ditch defense offered by hard-pressed Trump supporters, never mind that many of them were the most special snowflakes of them all. (Trump's counselor Kellyanne Conway once bitterly complained of the "silence and sighs" that greeted her inquiries about the admission of her children to the poshest private schools of Washington, DC.[42])

The United States was living through an epochal shift of economic power and cultural status, and Trump's supporters perceived themselves as the targets and losers in that shift. It's wrong to imagine those supporters as all displaced factory workers, all struggling coal miners. Many people solidly middle class or even rather affluent also felt that their world was turning upside down in the twenty-first century.

Many traditional Republicans too, uncomfortable as they might be with Trump's loudmouthed tweets, wondered if Trump were at least the right man for the times. A contributor to a pro-Trump website lamented:

Conservatives have won elections for decades yet despair as the country moves further and further left and every generation seems more insane than the last. Actually doing anything to confront the power of Hollywood, the mass media, or leftist corporations remains unthinkable, as doing so would clash with principles such as freedom of speech and limited government. Meanwhile, the Left presses on, destroying every last vestige of "racism," "sexism," or "homophobia." . . .

This is perhaps why Donald Trump has struck a chord with so many Republicans. Whatever his faults, at least he fights. Trump, for example, is not going to sit there and let the wife of a serial rapist tell him that he's the commanding general in a "war on women." For three-quarters of a century, conservatives have stuck to their principles as they have done nothing to challenge the power of those seeking to destroy all they hold dear. The results are clear, and more are waking up to the true nature of the modern Left.[43]

That was phrased more pungently than most, but even non-Trumpist conservatives pulsed to such emotions. Peter Augustine Lawler is a distinguished academic who served on President Bush's Council on Bioethics. Thoroughly Trump-skeptical, he nonetheless offered *National Review*'s readers some cautious praise for Trump's brutishness:

> What's wrong with gentlemen in public life? That's Trump's real question. They're losers! McCain and Romney: nice guys who looked good in going down in flames. McCain, in particular, is a loser Southern Stoic. And no gentleman, such as Jeb "low energy" Bush, could be any match for Hillary Clinton or ISIS or Silicon Valley oligarchs or emasculating political correctness.[44]

Even Trump's most ardent critics on the political Right wondered whether he was not merely symptomatic of a culture in decay, and possibly might even in his rough way offer some kind of antidote. Thus Harvey Mansfield, the noted conservative in Harvard's government department, wrote in the *Wall Street Journal* of July 30, 2016: "We are caught between distaste for a man who is not a gentleman and dislike of the political correctness that he so energetically attacks—yet whose effect he illustrates."[45]

Trump's critics loathed the president as a bully. But bullies pick on the weak. Trump's supporters saw their cultural enemies as much stronger than themselves. A revealing example made news in midsummer 2017. On June 29, President Trump tweeted a pair of harshly personal attacks on the MSNBC morning host Mika Brzezinski.

> I heard poorly rated @MorningJoe speaks badly of me (don't watch anymore). Then how come low I.Q. Crazy Mika, along with Psycho Joe, came..[46]
> ... to Mar-a-Lago 3 nights in a row around New Year's Eve, and insisted on joining me. She was bleeding badly from a face-lift. I said no![47]

The president's spokesperson, Sarah Huckabee Sanders, insisted at her press briefing later that day that it was Trump, not Brzezinski, who had been the victim of bullying.

> I don't think that the president has ever been someone who gets attacked and doesn't push back. There have been outrageous personal attacks not just on him but on everyone around him. People on that show have personally attacked me many times. This is a president who fights fire with fire, and certainly will not be allowed to be bullied by liberal media, or the liberal elites within the media, or Hollywood, or anywhere else.[48]

And although a morning show host has no army, no intelligence services, no power to issue orders and pardons, Huckabee Sanders's version of the case nonetheless resonated with many millions of conservative Americans.

Whatever else Trump may fail to do—staff a government, enact a program, safeguard US classified secrets, relieve disasters on Puerto Rico—there is one thing at which he never fails: provoking outrage among the people whom Trump supporters regard as overentitled and underdeserving: "the New York theater and arts and croissants crowd," as Rush Limbaugh calls them.[49] But don't belittle theater! Trump is the producer, writer, and star of an extravaganza performance of the theater of resentment. He summons all those who share that resentment to buy a ticket and enjoy the show.

The United States has seen many such characters before, of course. The Founding generation warned against them. They warned too of "the desire in foreign powers to gain an improper ascendant in our councils. How could they better gratify this, than by raising a creature of their own to the chief magistracy of the Union?"[50] For more than two centuries, through more than fifty presidential elections, those warnings were heeded. This time, not.

One could say the system failed. But systems are made of people with names, motives, and agency. It was not some big sputtering turbine, some grinding mass of gears and levers, that empowered and enabled Donald Trump. It was people. People with American flag pins affixed to their lapels, people who put their hands over their hearts during the pledge of allegiance, people who swear to uphold the Constitution, people who salute the military on Veterans Day and mourn the brave fallen on Memorial Day . . . people whose throats catch and whose eyes glisten when they declare their love of country and their willingness to sacrifice their all to defend its freedoms.

Those people have explanations for their actions, as we all do. "The people's business must be done." "You don't have to like the president to work with him for the public benefit." "You can support Donald Trump when he is right, and still oppose him when he is wrong." "Just shut out the noise and get to work."

Sounds pragmatic. There will be payoffs for those who do business in this way, not only in policy, but also in the form of more personal rewards. The opportunity of an all-Republican government may not last long, and the shrewd will seize the moment. More than in most administrations, the Trump White House has made celebrities of its leading personalities, and celebrity is a highly liquid currency.

But the payoffs exact a price, and that price is exacted by the megaton from American institutions and to American world leadership. For the remainder of the Trump presidency, American allies will have to make their plans on the assumption of American untrustworthiness. That kind of planning can be habit forming. For the remainder of the Trump presidency, military and intelligence leaders will work around a president who makes impulsive decisions, issues reckless statements, and cannot keep secrets. Those who serve in government will perceive that public integrity has gone out of style, polluted by a president who resents and resists the enforcement of rules. The one-third of America that identifies as "conservative" will be isolated even more profoundly within an information ghetto of deception and incitement. As in his business career, so in government, Donald Trump grabs the benefits for himself and a few associates, while offloading the costs onto those foolish enough to trust him—and anyone else who cannot wriggle away.

So let us start by looking at Trump's associates. Without them, Donald Trump would have remained what he was before 2015: a television personality, a tabloid social news presence, and the least bankable name in New York real estate.

CHAPTER 3

APPEASERS

The fix was supposed to be in. Before a single primary vote had been cast, John Ellis ("Jeb") Bush had locked up the Republican Party's big money, its top talent, and its senior leadership.

As governor of Florida, Bush had cut taxes and balanced budgets. He had challenged unions and championed charter schools. He had won accolades from Karl Rove ("the deepest thinker on our side"[1]) and Arthur Brooks, president of the American Enterprise Institute ("a top-drawer intellect"[2]).

On June 15, 2015, Bush bounded onto the stage at a Miami community college in an event carefully designed to showcase his leadership attributes: his newly trim physique, his policy knowledge, his fluency in Spanish, his deep hold on his must-win home state. That same day, he released a series of uplifting YouTube videos. Over swelling music, he hailed his record: "We led. We reformed. We got results." He saw solutions where others saw only difficulties, a nation poised to advance into its greatest century yet.[3]

Within seven weeks of that announcement, Jeb Bush's candidacy lay in smoldering wreckage.

As of June 30, 2015, Jeb Bush had raised in excess of $120 million, almost all of it in big gifts from a tiny number of wealthy families.[4] Seldom in the history of fund-raising has so much bought so little, so fleetingly. Between December 2014 and September 2015, the heir to the most successful brand in Republican politics plunged from first place in the Republican field to fifth.[5] In desperation, the Jeb Bush campaign purchased 60 percent of all political spots aired in New Hampshire in the month of October 2015. That ad barrage pushed his poll numbers in the state from about 9 percent to about 8 percent.

Donald Trump entered the presidential race the day after Jeb Bush did. He announced his candidacy in terms as grim and despairing as Bush's had been soaring and hopeful. "We got eighteen trillion in debt. We got nothing but problems . . . We're dying. We're dying. We need money . . . We have losers. We have people that don't have it. We have people that are morally corrupt. We have people that are selling this country down the drain . . . The American dream is dead."[6]

Trump had no organization, no endorsements, no plan, and no money beyond whatever of his own he was willing to spend. Within three weeks, he had surged into first place in the Republican contest. There he stayed, except for an interval in November 2015 when he was briefly overtaken by Dr. Ben Carson.[7] From Jupiter Island, Florida, to Greenwich, Connecticut; from Dallas's Highland Park to Georgia's Sea Island—not to mention from a numberless horde of pundits and reporters—the cry arose: What went wrong?

Three years earlier, Republican elites had identified Jeb Bush as the exact solution to their party's problems. They had been stunned by Mitt Romney's defeat in 2012. Despite their shock, Republican donors, talkers, and officials rapidly converged on an explanation of the loss and a prescription for the future: immigration. Everything else in the party message was working fine! A fiscal plan that ended the Medicare guarantee for people under the age of fifty-five to finance a big tax cut at the top? Repeal of the Affordable Care Act and its extension of health care to millions? No rethinking needed there at all! They attached all the blame, instead, to the one element of the Mitt Romney platform that the party's donors, elected officials, and leading ideologists had never much liked anyway: Romney's gestures toward stricter immigration enforcement.

Nobody expressed the party elites' consensus view more assuredly than the Fox News regular Charles Krauthammer. "Ignore the trimmers," Krauthammer wrote in his first postelection column. "There's no need for radical change. The other party thinks it owns the demographic future—counter that in one stroke by fixing the Latino problem. Do not, however, abandon the party's philosophical anchor. . . . No reinvention when none is needed."[8]

"We've gotta get rid of the immigration issue altogether," Sean Hannity told his radio audience the day after the 2012 election. "It's simple for me to fix it. I think you control the border first, you create a pathway for those people that are here, you don't say, 'You gotta go home.' And that is a position that I've evolved on."[9]

Fox News' principal owner agreed. "Must have sweeping, generous immigration reform," tweeted Rupert Murdoch on November 7, 2012.[10]

"It would be inhumane to send those people back, to send 12 million people out of this country," the casino mogul and Republican donor Sheldon Adelson told the *Wall Street Journal* in December of that year. "We've got to find a way, find a route, for those people to get legal citizenship."[11]

The Republican National Committee made it all official in a

March 2013 postelection report signed by party eminences. The report generally avoided policy recommendations, with a notable exception: "We must embrace and champion comprehensive immigration reform."[12]

To advance the cause, Paul Singer, one of the most open-pocketed GOP donors, made a six-figure contribution to the National Immigration Forum that spring. Almost as soon as the new Congress convened in 2013, Senate Republicans worked to strike a deal over immigration issues. A bipartisan "Gang of Eight," including Florida's ambitious young senator Marco Rubio, agreed on a plan that would create a path to citizenship for millions of illegal immigrants and substantially increase legal immigration limits for both high- and low-skilled workers.

But otherwise, the post-2012 Republican elite yielded on nothing and doubled down on everything. No U-turns. No compromises.

More passionately than any other Republican, Jeb Bush had celebrated the contributions of immigrants like his Mexican-born wife, Columba. Yet on every economic issue, no Republican adhered more strictly to party orthodoxy than Bush.

What the party elite had somehow failed to notice, unfortunately for them, was that their voters did not share the donors' and pundits' policy consensus. The Republican Party was built on a coalition of the nation's biggest winners from globalization and its biggest losers. The winners wrote the policy; the losers provided the votes. While the party elite coalesced upon more immigration, less secure health coverage, and one more Bush, the rank and file were frantically signaling: less immigration, better health coverage, and no more Bushes.

The other candidates for president in 2016 also missed the signal. Trump alone perceived it. "When do we beat Mexico at the border?" he demanded in his June 16 announcement address. "They're laughing at us, at our stupidity. And now they are beating us economically. They are not our friend, believe me. But they're killing us economically. . . . The US has become a dumping ground for everybody else's problems. When Mexico sends its people, they're not sending their best. They're not sending you. They're not sending you. They're sending people that have lots of problems, and they're bringing those problems with us [*sic*]. They're bringing drugs. They're bringing crime. They're rapists. And some, I assume, are good people."[13]

Trump's harsh language scandalized almost every pundit who commented on his words. But three weeks later, on July 5, an illegal alien from Mexico, Juan Francisco Lopez-Sanchez, gunned down Kathryn Steinle, a young American woman, on a San Francisco wharf. Lopez-Sanchez discharged a stolen weapon. It's not clear that he was aiming at Steinle. Aimed or not, Lopez-Sanchez's bullet struck the thirty-two-year-old in the back and severed her aorta in front of her horrified father. She died in the hospital two hours later. It soon emerged that Lopez-Sanchez, a repeat drug offender, had been ordered deported five times since 1993. He was at large that day in July because San Francisco's sanctuary city law forbade local police to notify federal authorities when they released him after his most recent detention. Within a week of the Steinle killing, Donald Trump skyrocketed into first place in the Republican field.

Trump's language about immigration and the American future likewise failed to impress those who had done well in the Obama years, "the coalition of the ascendant," as the *National Journal*'s Ron Brownstein called it: minorities, urbanites, new immigrants, knowledge workers, credentialed professionals, owners of capital assets.[14] Yet Trump found an audience all the same.

Polled in the fall of 2015, half of Trump's supporters within the

GOP reported having stopped their education at or before high school graduation, according to the polling firm YouGov. Only 19 percent had a college or postcollege degree. Thirty-eight percent earned less than $50,000. Only 11 percent earned more than $100,000.[15] Trump Republicans were not ideologically militant. Just 13 percent described themselves as "very conservative"; 20 percent described themselves as "moderate."[16] Nor were they highly religious by Republican standards.[17] What set them apart from other Republicans was their economic insecurity and their cultural anxiety. Sixty-three percent of Trump's supporters wished to end birthright citizenship for the children of illegal immigrants born on US soil.[18] More than other Republicans, Trump's supporters distrusted Barack Obama as alien and dangerous: Only 21 percent acknowledged that Obama was born in the United States; 66 percent of Trump voters believed that Obama was a Muslim.[19]

Trump vowed not only to get tough on undeserving outsiders, but also (and this mattered every bit as much to his rise) to protect deserving citizens from other Republicans' designs on their pensions and benefits.

> We've got Social Security that's going to be destroyed if somebody like me doesn't bring money into the country. All these other people want to cut the hell out of it. I'm not going to cut it at all; I'm going to bring money in, and we're going to save it.[20]

Trump promised a campaign independent of the influences of money that had swayed so many Republican races of the past.

> I will tell you that our system is broken. I gave to many people. Before this, before two months ago, I was a businessman.

I give to everybody. When they call, I give. And you know what? When I need something from them, two years later, three years later, I call them. They are there for me. And that's a broken system.[21]

He promised to protect the sons and daughters of farmers and factory workers from being drawn into another war in the Middle East. "If we're going to have World War III," he told the *Washington Post* in October 2015, "it's not going to be over Syria." As for the politicians threatening to shoot down the Russian jets flying missions in Syria, "I won't even call them hawks. I call them the fools."[22]

In reply, Jeb Bush, Marco Rubio, and Ted Cruz—joined by Mitt Romney from the sidelines—attacked Trump as a con man, as a pathological liar, as a cheat and swindler. Trump was blasted by outside groups as a traitor to Republican ideals and ideology. The premier conservative intellectual magazine, *National Review*, blazed the title "AGAINST TRUMP" across its February 16, 2016, issue. For good measure, NR illustrated the feature with a cartoon of Trump as a strutting Mussolini. "Sometimes you can't fix it," RNC chair Priebus resignedly acknowledged in April 2016. "Sometimes you can just take a seven-alarm fire and just make it a four-alarm fire. It's still burning, but it's not as bad as it was." But everything was fine. "I'm not pouring Bailey's in my cereal."[23]

Half the contributors to *National Review*'s "Never Trump" issue would ultimately make their peace with Trump's leadership. Some, such as Brent Bozell of the Media Research Center, reinvented themselves as his most vigorous defenders. Priebus would reach an accommodation of his own, culminating in his service as President Trump's first chief of staff. Yet as late as the Republican convention in Cleveland, most Republican officeholders and donors still regarded

Donald Trump warily. Speaker Paul Ryan's convention speech offered only the most glancing references to the party's nominee: "The next time that there's a State of the Union address . . . you'll find me right there on the rostrum with Vice President Mike Pence and President Donald Trump." "Only with Donald Trump and Mike Pence," Ryan added, "do we have a chance at a better way." Senate Majority Leader Mitch McConnell sounded barely more enthusiastic in his convention speech, omitting all personal praise of Trump, and instead itemizing bills that President Obama had vetoed and that President Donald Trump would presumably sign.

The wariness of the big donors persisted post-convention. The people who could write large checks had noticed Trump's practice of diverting campaign funds to his own businesses: $12.5 million altogether, according to a December 2016 CNN review.[24] Trump waited until the last possible minute to write off the $50 million he had loaned his campaign, leaving many donors uncertain until midsummer whether their gifts would be used to elect a president or to reimburse Trump for his takeover of their party. The reluctance of big donors to invest money in any Trump enterprise explains how Hillary Clinton outraised Donald Trump almost two to one for presidential campaign dollars. The large majority of Trump's $335 million presidential campaign take, $280 million, was given in increments under $200.

Trump's surprise win forced a hasty big-money rethink. The convention in Cleveland may have been a pinched and listless affair, but Trump's 2017 inaugural committee was easily the best funded in history, bumped by large gifts from anti-Trump Republicans seeking to make amends. (Paul Singer alone donated $1 million.[25] He was rewarded with a White House visit in February 2017.) Trump's inaugural committee collected $107 million, double the previous record of $53 million set in 2009.

Inaugurations cost money, but the largest costs are paid by tax-payers. The ceremony on the Capitol grounds is funded by Congress. The parade along Pennsylvania Avenue is paid out of the military's budget. Security is covered by the federal government. So how was Trump's record-breaking $107 million inaugural haul actually used? Good question, and one to which few will ever learn the answer. Many inaugural donors voluntarily disclose their gifts, but there is no obligation upon the inaugural committee to disclose how funds are spent. Nor are there many legal restrictions on how such funds can be used. The inaugural committee could, for example, transfer millions of dollars to pro-Trump PACs without disclosing that fact to anybody. Or it could spend huge amounts at Trump's hotels and businesses. Or it could simply hoard the money for some future secret use. The Trump inaugural committee promised that any unused funds would be donated to charity.[26] No charity ever announced receipt of any gift from this source, nor did Trump's inaugural committee offer any accounting for the money it received.

The corporations or individuals who provided the $107 million surely had few illusions about what they were buying and why. Half a million dollars bought a seat at a dinner with the vice president and his wife; a million bought lunch with the new president, congressional leaders, and incoming cabinet secretaries. These donors hoped to buy access and goodwill, even protection from a thin-skinned and vindictive president. But by writing those checks, they also bought into the Trump financial system of pelf and predation.

As did, one by one, the leading figures of the Republican Party: former presidential rivals; leaders of Congress; the party's governors, state legislators, and state party organizations; the mighty fund-raising networks of the Koch brothers and other formerly

Trump-skeptical donors. With the rarest exceptions, all came to heel.

Ohio governor and former Trump nomination rival John Kasich publicly disclosed that he had written in John McCain's name. Jeb Bush refrained from an endorsement, but his son George P. Bush reluctantly backed the ultimate Trump-headed ticket. In almost every other case, the toad was swallowed.

Senator Ted Cruz epically unloaded on Donald Trump on May 3, 2016, the eve of the Indiana primary. "This man is a pathological liar; he doesn't know the difference between truth and lies . . . in a pattern that is straight out of a psychology textbook, he accuses everyone of lying. . . . Whatever lie he's telling, at that minute he believes it . . . the man is utterly amoral."[27] Even at the Cleveland convention, Cruz declined to endorse his former rival. By Election Day, however, Cruz had submitted. He formally endorsed Trump on September 23. "If Clinton wins, we know—with 100 percent certainty—that she would deliver on her left-wing promises, with devastating results for our country."[28]

After the leak of the *Access Hollywood* video, some Republicans tried to leap off what they thought was a burning boat. Yet when Paul Ryan separated himself from Trump on October 11, 2016, it was Ryan's support—not Trump's—that cratered, dropping a net 28 points among Republicans in only ten days.[29]

The institutional Republican Party therefore had no choice but to adhere to Trump, and Trump had no choice but to rely on it. Whereas Trump's presidential fund-raising badly lagged behind Clinton's, the RNC and the other joint party committees kept pace with their Democratic counterparts: $543 million for the RNC and others versus $598 million for the DNC and its cognates. The RNC paid for Trump's field operations and much of his digital operation; the RNC and the Republican state parties took responsibility for get-out-the-vote operations. It was RNC data that powered Trump's most effective ad campaign. Titled "Hillary Thinks African Americans Are Super-Predators," the short animated video was directed via Facebook to infrequent black voters—not to win them for Trump, but to discourage them from going to the polls at all.[30]

Like Ted Cruz, Republicans overcame any distaste they felt for Trump by convincing themselves that a Hillary Clinton presidency represented an unthinkably catastrophic outcome. Every stance and principle that had seemed so important in the long run-up to 2016 was junked in order to avert the Clinton apocalypse. Entitlement reform? The party's post-2012 rethink of immigration? Judeo-Christian family values? All had to be set aside in the face of the supposedly extinction-level risk of a Clinton presidency. In the impassioned words of the radio host Mark Levin, a Trump opponent all through the primaries:

> If you believe Hillary Clinton is virtually as off-her-rocker left-wing socialist as Senator Bernie Sanders, if you believe that Hillary Clinton is in part responsible for the rise of ISIS and what took care [sic] in Benghazi . . . how the hell could you take any steps, passively or affirmatively, that would put that woman in the Oval Office? . . . As bad as the Republican may be, how could you stay home and allow that?[31]

Of all the party institutions that yielded to Trump, far and away the most important was Fox News. "Republicans used to think Fox News worked for us. Now we are discovering we work for Fox News." I first said that in 2010, and the observation held true for half a decade. Yet here too, Trump changed the rules. He bent Fox News to his will, not the other way around.

Fox did not begin the 2015–2016 cycle in the tank for Trump. The first Fox debate, in August 2015, featured the network's least ideological anchors: Bret Baier, Megyn Kelly, and Chris Wallace. The trio posed tough questions to Trump. Baier took Trump to task for refusing to commit to supporting the ultimate nominee. Megyn Kelly challenged Trump on his long history of demeaning comments about women. Chris Wallace challenged him on his habit of hurling wild, uncorroborated charges.

> Mr. Trump, it has not escaped anybody's notice that you say that the Mexican government, the Mexican government is sending criminals—rapists, drug dealers, across the border. Governor Bush has called those remarks, quote, "extraordinarily ugly." I'd like you—you're right next to him—tell us—talk to him directly and say how you respond to that and—and you have repeatedly said that you have evidence that the Mexican government is doing this, but you have evidence you have refused or declined to share.
>
> Why not use this first Republican presidential debate to share your proof with the American people?

It was Kelly's question, however, that most fiercely enraged Trump. "You've called women you don't like 'fat pigs, dogs, slobs, and disgusting animals.'" While Trump would respond to Wallace's question (which came later in the debate) with something approaching professionalism, to Kelly he retorted with a threat.

> What I say is what I say. And honestly Megyn, if you don't like it, I'm sorry. I've been very nice to you, although I could probably maybe not be, based on the way you have treated me. But I wouldn't do that.

Of course, Trump soon *did* "do that." In an August 2015 telephone interview with CNN's Don Lemon, Trump complained of Kelly:

She gets out and she starts asking me all sorts of ridiculous questions. You could see there was blood coming out of her eyes, blood coming out of her wherever. In my opinion, she was off base. . . . I just don't respect her as a journalist. I have no respect for her. I don't think she's very good. I think she's highly overrated.[32]

Trump then suggested that he would not join any more Fox debates if Megyn Kelly were involved.

That threat to Fox News opened one of the most decisively successful of Trump's repeat campaigns for dominance over his perceived foes, especially women. The next Fox debate had been scheduled for January 28, 2016, on the eve of the New Hampshire primary. Trump demanded that Megyn Kelly be excluded from the panel of questioners. Fox issued a press release mocking Trump's presumption:

We learned from a secret back channel that the Ayatollah and Putin both intend to treat Donald Trump unfairly when they meet with him if he becomes president—a nefarious source tells us that Trump has his own secret plan to replace the Cabinet with his Twitter followers to see if he should even go to those meetings.[33]

Trump persisted. He complained about Kelly on Twitter and Instagram. In a CNN interview three days before the scheduled debate, he bluntly told Wolf Blitzer: "I don't like her. I don't think she's fair to me." Kelly, Trump said, had been a nobody before the first debate. She owed all her fame to him. He wanted to attend the debate, and so warned Kelly, "She better be fair." But, he concluded pessimistically, "I don't think she can treat me fairly. I'm not a big fan of hers. Maybe I know too much about her."[34]

Fox issued a second pro-Kelly statement:

Sooner or later Donald Trump, even if he's president, is going to have to learn that he doesn't get to pick the journalists— we're very surprised he's willing to show that much fear about being questioned by Megyn Kelly.[35]

So Trump escalated. He announced a boycott of the Fox debate. Instead, he would engage in a fund-raiser "for the vets." That fund-raiser resulted in the usual shaky outcome; it would take months for Trump to be shamed into disgorging the money he raised and to honor his own million-dollar pledge.[36] Politically, though, the stunt more than delivered. The woman who was once acclaimed as the future of Fox News abruptly found herself condemned as the enemy within, a strumpet "fascinated with sex," in the accusation Newt Gingrich flung at her in an October 2016 interview.[37] Trump's allies at the *National Enquirer* gathered the salacious gossip that would provide the tabloid with a cover story in May 2017: "Megyn Kelly Exposed—Secrets of Her Rapid Rise to Power, from Her Ruthless Early Career to a Plastic Surgery Makeover." In December 2016, Kelly disclosed that after Trump's August outburst against her, she had faced death threats serious enough that she had hired armed guards to protect her three young children, all then under the age of seven.[38]

Megyn Kelly would leave Fox in January 2017. After the election, Fox's coverage descended to new sub-basements of abjectness. Fox would replace Kelly with Tucker Carlson, who filled his hour with trolling and spoofing reminiscent of white-nationalist message boards. The morning show *Fox & Friends* would dedicate itself to flattery of (and therapy for) the ego-needy president. Sean Hannity, shifted to the prime 9:00 p.m. Eastern Time slot after Bill O'Reilly's termination, lent credence to any story, no matter how wild, that might deflect attention from the Trump-Russia connection. Hannity reverentially interviewed Julian Assange and publicized the fantasy that WikiLeaks had received the Democratic emails not from Russian intelligence (as the CIA, FBI, NSA, and the Office of the Director of National Intelligence had assessed), but from a disgruntled DNC staffer, Seth Rich, who was subsequently murdered, most likely (it was heavily insinuated) at the behest of important people in the Democratic Party.[39] Fox's on-air talent abased themselves to argue that even proven collusion by the Trump campaign with Russian intelligence would be—at worst— "alarming and highly inappropriate."[40]

The steady flow of "alternative facts" from Fox News' hosts (to borrow the useful phrase of Trump's aide Kellyanne Conway[41]) would impose serious costs on the network's business. In May 2017, Fox would fall to third place among cable networks for the most desired viewing audience in weekday prime time, adults aged twenty-five to fifty-four.[42] Fox remained the largest cable network overall, but its eyeballs increasingly lacked spending power, threatening its future profitability. While the core Fox audience watches to have its prejudices ratified, many occasional Fox viewers have become impatient with a news network that distorts, misrepresents, and oftentimes outright ignores the country's most exciting domestic news story.

The predicament of Fox illustrates the larger crisis of conservatism in the Trump era. Gullibly or cynically, resentfully or opportunistically, for lack of better information or for lack of a better alternative, a great party has slowly united to elevate one man into a position of almost absolute power over itself.

Many who submitted to Trump perceived perfectly clearly what they were submitting to:

The big donors knew their money would be misappropriated.

Congressional leaders foresaw that Trump would behave outrageously and erratically.

Trump's apologists in the media world recognized his lack of principle.

They decided in favor of him anyway—expecting (or at least pathetically hoping!) that some larger good would come of it.

The Republican rank and file, however, acted on emotion, not calculus. On the night of August 25, 2017, President Trump used the cover of Hurricane Harvey to pardon Maricopa County sheriff Joe Arpaio. In July, Arpaio had been convicted of criminal contempt of court for defying a 2011 order to cease traffic patrols that profiled Hispanic drivers in his Arizona county. Through the Obama years, conservatives had reinvented themselves as "constitutionalists": upholders of law against arbitrary executive power. Ted Cruz even wrote the foreword to a book accusing the Obama administration of unprecedented lawlessness.[43] But that was then. The Arpaio pardon generated paroxysms of enthusiasm in the conservative base. A popular columnist for the conservative site Townhall.com tweeted to his 115,000 followers a pithy explanation of the justification for the about-face on arbitrary executive power:

> The main reason for President Trump to pardon Sheriff Joe was fuck you, leftists. The new rules, bitches.

followed by a smiling sunglasses-wearing emoji symbol.[44] He made a cogent point too. By August 2017, what was left of the philosophy formerly known as conservatism *beyond* "fuck you, leftists"?

President Trump may not have had policy ideas in the conventional sense. But he had a sure grasp of the emotions that impelled the Republican voting base—and how those emotions could be manipulated to empower himself and enrich his family. In 1960, a quip circulated that the Kennedy family arrived in power like the Borgias descending on some respectable Italian town. The joke did not quite work, because it did not quite apply. The Kennedys' many faults were joined to an undeniable grace and generosity of spirit, to authentic public service and a large vision of America. Not so for the Trump family. They came to loot. If rules stood in their way, the rules could go smash.

CHAPTER 4

PLUNDER

Not to injure anybody's national pride, but even before the Trump presidency, the United States ranked a not exactly reassuring eighteenth on Transparency International's corruption index, behind Hong Kong and Belgium.[1]

In modern times, however, governmental corruption in the United States has been a problem associated much more with states and localities than with the federal government, and within the federal government, with Congress more than the executive branch. In response to the Watergate scandal, Americans amended their laws and raised their expectations.

Newt Gingrich surrendered a quite legal book deal in 1994 because of public criticism that a multimillion-dollar advance to a newly elected Speaker of the House looked too much like a gift from a wealthy supporter.[2] Former Senate majority leader Tom Daschle stepped away from his nomination as secretary of Health and Human Services in 2009 because he had not paid taxes on the use of a car and driver in his business career in the mid-2000s.[3]

Candidates and presidents since Gerald Ford have followed the practice initiated by George Romney in 1968 and published their tax returns.

Politicians accepted these new stricter post-Watergate standards because they assumed everybody else accepted them. But what if somebody decided to reject them? What would happen then? Donald Trump guessed: nothing much. He not only declined to release his tax returns, but directed campaign funds to his own businesses. As late as January 2016, half a year after the launch of Trump's campaign for the Republican nomination, Trump's associates pursued a deal to license the Trump name for a Trump Tower Moscow. When the deal ran into difficulties, Trump's lawyer appealed for help to contacts in the Putin regime.[4]

A rule-of-law state can withstand a certain amount of official corruption. What it cannot withstand is a culture of impunity. So long as officials believe that corruption will usually be detected—and if detected, then certainly punished—for just that long they will believe that corruption is wrong. It is for this reason that corrupt regimes swiftly evolve toward authoritarianism, and authoritarian regimes toward corruption. Outside of the Islamic world, the twenty-first century is not an era of ideology. The grand utopian visions of the nineteenth century have passed out of fashion. The nightmare totalitarian projects of the twentieth have been overthrown or have disintegrated, leaving behind only outdated remnants: North Korea, Cuba. What is spreading today is repressive kleptocracy, led by rulers motivated by greed rather than by the deranged idealism of Hitler or Stalin or Mao. Such rulers rely less on terror and more on rule twisting, the manipulation of information, and the co-option of elites. Their goal is self-enrichment; the corrosion of the rule of law is the necessary means. As a shrewd local observer explained to me on a visit to Hungary in early 2016,

"The main benefit of controlling a modern bureaucratic state is not the power to persecute the innocent. It is the power to protect the guilty."

No president in history has burned more public money to sustain his personal lifestyle than Donald Trump. Three-quarters of the way through his first year in office, President Trump was on track to spend more on travel in one year of his presidency than Barack Obama in eight—even though Trump only rarely ventured west of the Mississippi or across any ocean.[5]

In May 2017, Congress appropriated an additional $120 million to provide security to the Trump family, half of it to reimburse local police in Palm Beach and New York City for the extra costs imposed by President Trump's weekend getaways and the decision by First Lady Melania Trump to maintain a separate residence in the first year of the Trump presidency.[6] Even this record-breaking allowance soon proved inadequate. By August 2017, the Secret Service reported it had exhausted both its budget and its agents' human capacity for overtime work. Facing a wave of resignations and retirements, the Secret Service asked Congress to raise the cap on agents' pay and overtime from $160,000 to $187,000. Kevin Johnson reported in *USA Today*:

> The president's jaunts to Mar-a-Lago are estimated to cost at least $3 million each, based on a General Accounting Office estimate for similar travel by former President Obama. The Secret Service has spent some $60,000 on golf cart rentals alone this year to protect Trump at both Mar-a-Lago and Bedminster.[7]

The annual Kushner family ski vacation in Aspen in March 2017 cost taxpayers at least $330,000.[8] An Eric Trump business trip to Uruguay in early January 2017 cost the Secret Service nearly $100,000 just for hotel rooms. It cost tens of thousands more to accompany Donald Trump Jr. to Vancouver in March 2017 and to protect Tiffany Trump, the president's youngest daughter, on a German tour and Mediterranean yachting holiday in July.[9]

Costly as the Trump family was to the presidency, the presidency was correspondingly lucrative to the Trump family. Jonathan O'Connell reported in the *Washington Post* in August 2017 that the Trump hotel in Washington, DC, collected $4.1 million more than projected in the first four months of that year.[10] Foreign governments, US corporations, and Trump's own super PAC made the Trump hotel their first choice of venue.[11] Earnings from food and drink exceeded expectations by more than 37 percent. Despite a low occupancy rate—only 42 percent—the hotel managed to extract an average room rate from the guests who did stay there of almost $660, versus an average of $495 at Washington's other ultraluxury hotels.[12]

Party funds poured into Trump's personal pockets. The Republican National Committee, Trump's 2020 reelection effort, the Republican Governors Association, and other GOP campaigns and committees together spent about $1.3 million at Trump properties in the first half of 2017.[13]

Trump's Florida clubhouse, Mar-a-Lago, doubled its initiation fee to $200,000 in January 2017.[14] Trump formed his 2020 reelection committee on his inauguration day. In its first six months of existence, the committee spent $600,000 of its donors' money at Trump-branded properties.[15] The US military spends $130,000 per month to lease space in Trump Tower, on the chance Trump might need communications equipment on a visit to his home. (The arrangement is a sublet, however, so Trump may not receive any of the money personally.[16])

These petty grifts swelled the income and enhanced the lifestyle of a family that always needed more—and was never particular about where that "more" came from. (And unlike the sad students at Trump University, whose fraud lawsuit was settled by the Trump Organization in March 2017 for $25 million,[17] the US government could bear the cost.) Yet even $600,000 here, $4 million there, hardly amounted to big money by the standards of Trump family ambition—or Trump family exigency.

Donald Trump and his Kushner in-laws are perceived as fabulously wealthy. But while they do own substantial assets, they also owe enormous debts, and it has never been clear for either family how those two figures balance. Trump has teetered on the edge of ruin again and again through his career. Over the decade since the 2008 financial crisis, his son-in-law seems to have faced ruin on an even more epic scale.

In 2007, Jared Kushner persuaded his family group to purchase an Eisenhower-era office building on New York's Fifth Avenue for a then record-setting $1.8 billion, financed by $1.215 billion in commercial mortgage bonds. The deal almost instantly went catastrophically wrong. Occupancy dropped in the wake of the financial crisis of 2008. Rents collapsed. Things did not improve for the Kushners' 666 Fifth Avenue property during the recovery. The business locus of New York shifted west and south, away from Fifth Avenue, and often out of Manhattan entirely. A post-2010 building boom offered potential tenants more attractive contemporary premises at competitive rents. The Kushner building lost $10 million in 2015 and was on track to lose considerably more in 2016.

By November 2016, the situation was becoming truly desperate. The Kushner family had refinanced the building in 2011, promising to reinvent it as a glittering new condo tower, doubling its height and adding glamorous new retail space. This additional capital came with a tough time limit. The interest rate on the loan was scheduled to double to 6.35 percent in December 2016; harsh new fees would come due as well.[18]

But in the interim, a miracle had occurred: the political rise of Donald Trump. The Kushner family very suddenly found itself attracting prospective financial partners from around the world, as Susanne Craig, Jo Becker, and Jesse Drucker reported in the *New York Times.*

> On the night of Nov. 16, [2016] a group of executives gathered in a private dining room of the restaurant La Chine at the Waldorf Astoria hotel in Midtown Manhattan. The table was laden with Chinese delicacies and $2,100 bottles of Château Lafite Rothschild. At one end sat Wu Xiaohui, the chairman of the Waldorf's owner, Anbang Insurance Group, a Chinese financial behemoth with estimated assets of $285 billion and an ownership structure shrouded in mystery. Close by sat Jared Kushner, a major New York real estate investor whose father-in-law, Donald J. Trump, had just been elected president of the United States.
>
> It was a mutually auspicious moment.
>
> Mr. Wu and Mr. Kushner—who is married to Mr. Trump's daughter Ivanka and is one of his closest advisers— were nearing agreement on a joint venture in Manhattan: the redevelopment of 666 Fifth Avenue, the fading crown jewel of the Kushner family real-estate empire. Anbang, which has close ties to the Chinese state, has seen its aggressive efforts to buy up hotels in the United States slowed amid concerns raised by Obama administration officials who review foreign investments for national security risk.

Now, according to two people with knowledge of the get-together, Mr. Wu toasted Mr. Trump and declared his desire to meet the president-elect, whose ascension, he was sure, would be good for global business.[19]

Kushner never got his Chinese loan. Anbang retreated rather than face the glare of American publicity. But Chinese money did continue to flow to the Kushner family. Even as Jared Kushner emerged as the most influential adviser to the president of the United States, his relatives marketed condominiums in China with the promise that an "investor visa" came attached. Emily Rauhala and William Wan of the *Washington Post* attended just such a marketing meeting in Beijing in May 2017. The arrival of American reporters upset the organizers, who roughly tried to eject them from the hall, explaining, "This is not the story we want." But it's the story that happened:

> Over several hours of slide shows and presentations, representatives from the Kushner family business urged Chinese citizens gathered at a Ritz-Carlton hotel to consider investing hundreds of thousands of dollars in a New Jersey luxury apartment complex that would help them secure what's known as an investor visa.
>
> The potential investors were advised to invest sooner rather than later in case visa rules change under the Trump administration. "Invest early, and you will invest under the old rules," one speaker said.
>
> The tagline on a brochure for the event: "Invest $500,000 and immigrate to the United States."
>
> And the highlight of the afternoon was [Nicole Kushner] Meyer, a principal for the company, who was introduced in promotional materials as Jared's sister.[20]

Russian banks also acquired a keen new enthusiasm for Kushner family projects. Over the course of the 2016 presidential campaign, Kushner had a number of conversations with Sergey Kislyak, the Russian ambassador to the United States. Two would be disclosed on Kushner's application for a security clearance. The rest would not—not until press reports compelled Kushner to correct the record after the fact. Kushner would also meet with the head of a Russian state-owned bank implicated in past espionage against the United States. Ned Parker and Jonathan Landy reported for Reuters on the FBI's suspicions about these meetings.

> FBI investigators are examining whether Russians suggested to Kushner or other Trump aides that relaxing economic sanctions would allow Russian banks to offer financing to people with ties to Trump, said the current U.S. law enforcement official. . . . The bank said in a statement in March that it had met with Kushner along with other representatives of U.S. banks and business as part of preparing a new corporate strategy.[21]

A very great many corporations, foreign and domestic, were preparing the same "new strategy."

Through the transition period, President-Elect Trump and his family used their new position to recognize old business associates and seek new ones. On November 14, 2016, Trump spoke for fifteen minutes to the president of Argentina, Mauricio Macri. According to reports in the Argentine media, Trump mentioned that a Trump-licensed building in Buenos Aires was stalled in the permitting process. The next day, Trump's local partners triumphantly announced that the building was moving forward. It would later emerge that not only had Trump's daughter Ivanka joined the call, but that Trump's son Eric had arranged it, at the request of Trump's lead partner in the Buenos Aires deal.[22]

Trump had licensed his name to five projects in India. His partners in those projects stopped by Trump Tower on November 17, 2016. They discussed business with Trump's three adult children, posed for a photo with the president-elect, and gave an interview afterward to an Indian publication, *The Economic Times*.[23] That's how Americans learned of the meeting: as with the Argentine discussions, the Trump transition team had provided no notice or readout of the meeting to any American media.

On November 18, 2016, President-Elect Trump would meet with Japan's prime minister, Shinzo Abe, at Trump Tower. Photographs of the encounter between the two leaders showed Trump's daughter Ivanka in attendance. Jared Kushner joined the group as well. At the time of the meeting, Ivanka Trump was in negotiations to license her clothing brand to a big Japanese retailer. That retailer was owned by a Japanese bank, which was in turn wholly owned by the Japanese government.[24] (The deal would ultimately fail.[25])

Trump tangled government, family, and business in the style of an authoritarian Third World kleptocrat. When a staffer at the National Security Council (NSC) wrote a memo denouncing H. R. McMaster, Trump's national security adviser, as one of the cultural Marxist "globalists" waging Maoist insurgency against the Trump administration, the document was brought to the president's attention by his son Donald Jr., the new CEO of the Trump Organization, and therefore someone supposedly walled off from the internal workings of the national security agencies.[26]

Authoritarian governments around the world scented possibility in an incoming Trump administration whose style so resembled theirs. Days before the 2016 election, the brutal president of the Philippines, Rodrigo Duterte, named the developer of Manila's

Trump-branded property as his special envoy to the United States.[27] Duterte would collect his reward in the form of a flattering phone call from President Trump on April 29, 2017.

TRUMP: I just wanted to congratulate you, because I am hearing of the unbelievable job on the drug problem. Many countries have the problem, we have a problem, but what a great job you are doing. I just wanted to call and tell you that.

DUTERTE: Thank you, Mr. President. This is the scourge of my nation now, and I have to do something to preserve the Filipino nation.

TRUMP: I understand that and fully understand that, and I think we had a previous president who did not understand that.[28]

In February 2017, the Trump Organization announced plans for Scion, a new lower-cost hotel line in the United States. Its first franchise, in Dallas, would be developed in partnership with a company with deep connections in Russia, Turkey, and Kazakhstan. The *New York Times* reported in May that the developer

has been quoted in the *Dallas Business Journal,* saying that the deal would be financed by his family and business associates in Turkey and Kazakhstan. In recent statements to the *Dallas Morning News* . . . he backed away from those claims and said the money would come only from him and two American partners. He declined to elaborate to The Times.[29]

The government of China approved thirty-eight Trump trademarks in the single month of March 2017. By the end of May, China had granted the president a total of seventy-seven, plus a spate more for his daughter Ivanka. The Trump Organization had applied for these marks only a year earlier. Erika Kinetz of the Associated Press reported from Shanghai:

> Dan Plane, a director at Simone IP Services, a Hong Kong intellectual property consultancy, said he had never seen so many applications approved so expeditiously.
>
> "For all these marks to sail through so quickly and cleanly, with no similar marks, no identical marks, no issues with specifications—boy, it's weird," he said. . . . Plane said he would be "very, very surprised" if officials from the ruling Communist party were not monitoring Trump's intellectual property interests. "This is just way over your average trademark examiner's pay grade," he said.[30]

Until the financial crisis of 2008, Donald Trump had almost no business interests outside the United States. That year's crisis shattered what remained of his real-estate development activity. By the fall of 2008, Trump's casino operation had staggered to its final, terminal bankruptcy. Trump Mortgage had collapsed. Trump-licensed towers in Florida and Georgia were failing. Trump companies defaulted on $334 million of debt repayment due Deutsche Bank on his last big personally directed project: Trump Tower Chicago.[31]

But Trump remained a TV star, thanks to NBC's *Apprentice*. His name had become a global symbol of ostentatious gimcrack luxe. A brand that once sought to dominate New York City settled for being big in Baku.[32] The message went forth from Pinsk to Penang, and everywhere dirty money is gained and hidden: If you are looking for someone to shine you up, you can find him in Trump Tower.

A five-bylined story for Reuters in March 2017 reported, "At least 63 individuals with Russian passports or addresses have bought at least $98.4 million worth of property in seven Trump-branded luxury towers in southern Florida."[33] In the year after Donald Trump secured the Republican presidential nomination, 70 percent of Trump's customers made their purchases through identity-shielding corporations. Trump sold $33 million worth of real estate in this concealed way in the six months after the 2016 election.[34]

Trump and his son-in-law Jared Kushner claimed to have put in place ethical safeguards against conflicts of interest. These safeguards proved utterly derisory, when not wholly fictitious. David Enrich reported in the *Wall Street Journal* in July 2017 that at a White House tech summit organized by Jared Kushner, the only start-up with a seat at the table was OpenGov.com, partly owned by Jared's brother Josh.[35]

Kushner promised to divest himself from his family's holdings. But who on earth would buy Jared Kushner's stake in the 666 Fifth Avenue project? What "divestment" meant in this case was accepting an IOU for his share from other relatives, an IOU that would acquire net value only if someone could be persuaded to rescue the Kushner family as a whole, Jared included.[36]

Trump's claims to have divested his businesses proved equally empty. Trump's sons acknowledged that they regularly reported to him on the family companies' revenues and operations.[37] Even after the supposed "separation" within the Trump family, the two sons often attended White House functions and Republican strategy sessions.[38] They acted as White House surrogates on TV and in social media, and posted photographs of themselves from within the White House precincts.[39] (Tangling the lines even more tightly, Eric Trump's wife, Lara, would take a job in May 2017 with a vendor to Trump's 2020 reelection effort.[40] She also hosted Trump campaign Facebook video spots.) Trump promised to donate all foreign profits earned by the Trump Organization to charity. But as of midyear 2017, his company had made no effort even to identify such profits, much less disgorge them.[41]

Federal conflict-of-interest statutes exempt the president and vice president from many of their strictures, partly for separation-of-powers reasons, partly for pragmatic reasons. A president's scope of authority is so vast there is almost nothing he or she could do that could not affect his or her own economic interests in some way. Even so basic a decision as proposing a budget deficit or surplus could affect the relative values of stocks versus bonds.

But these exemptions do not constitute a blank ethical check for the president. Since modern conflict-of-interest rules took form in the 1970s, presidents have volunteered near-total financial disclosure, including the publication of their tax returns. All the world can see what they have, what they earn, and what they owe, and can judge accordingly whether the president has behaved ethically or not.

Trump and Kushner—and indeed even some in his cabinet—have disregarded and defied the post-Watergate norm. Trump has told one untenable story after another about why he cannot publish his returns, finally abandoning the pretense altogether postelection, saying, "The only one that cares about my tax returns are the reporters."[42] Trump's aide Kellyanne Conway scolded journalists who continued to ask. "We litigated this all through the election. People didn't care."[43]

The disclosures required of the president by law do not convey much, because they apply only to Trump personally, not to the "upstream" corporate entities through which Trump receives his income and owes his debts.

For example, the Trump family is a part owner of a building on the Avenue of the Americas in Manhattan that carries a $950 million mortgage to the Bank of China.[44] That upstream debt weighs on Trump's income, but it need not be disclosed on a federal form. In August 2016, a *New York Times* investigation suggested that Trump owed at least $650 million, twice as much as his campaign disclosure forms acknowledged.[45] Trump's biographer Timothy L. O'Brien of *Bloomberg View* estimated to NPR early in 2017 that Trump owes in excess of $1 billion to about 150 different financial institutions, vastly more than the $310 million indicated on the first disclosure he filed as president.[46]

Trump's son-in-law and daughter also omitted enormous holdings and liabilities from their financial disclosure forms: their art collection, important investments, and exposure to as much as $1 billion in personal and corporate debt.[47]

Trump has successfully rolled back—and then some!—the ethical rules that have accreted around the presidency since Watergate. Tax disclosure refused for the first time since Gerald Ford. Conflict-of-interest rules ignored for the first time since Richard Nixon. Running a business corporation while in office for the first time since Lyndon Johnson. The first appointment of a relative to a senior government position since John F. Kennedy named his brother Robert attorney general. The first appointment of a presidential son or daughter to a senior White House position since Franklin Roosevelt's son James. The first use of presidential patronage to enrich the president's family since Ulysses S. Grant.[48] The first acceptance of substantial foreign cash flows by the president in American history. The first subordination of US foreign policy to the president's business interests in American history. The most lavish spending on the person of a president in American history.

Beyond all the many and grave evils of corruption at the top of government is the near impossibility of confining corruption within one office. Early in July 2017, the chief corporate oversight official in the Department of Justice posted a comment on her LinkedIn page explaining her recent resignation:

> Trying to hold companies to standards that our current administration is not living up to was creating a cognitive dissonance that I could not overcome. To sit across the table from companies and question how committed they were to ethics and compliance felt not only hypocritical, but very much like shuffling the deck chairs on the Titanic. Even as I engaged in those questioning and evaluations, on my mind were the numerous lawsuits pending against the President of the United States for everything from violations of the Constitution to conflict of interest, the ongoing investigations of potentially treasonous conducts, and the investigators and prosecutors fired for their pursuits of principles and facts. Those are conducts I would not tolerate seeing in a company, yet I worked under an administration that engaged in exactly those conduct. I wanted no more part in it.[49]

But while resignations in disgust are one possible response to Trumpocracy, so too is the attitude "If you can't beat 'em, join 'em."

Trump is one by one disabling the federal government's inhibitions against corruption. On March 10, 2017, Trump fired the forty-six US attorneys who had not resigned when the administration turned over. (Congress has established ninety-three US attorney positions in total.) This was more or less normal practice for a new administration. What happened next was not.

Trump left the US attorneys' jobs vacant for months. A legal expert explained the consequences to the New York *Daily News*:

While the U.S. Attorney offices will move forward without heads in place with uncontroversial cases, like ordinary fraud and white collar crimes, there are a whole bunch of crimes that, under DOJ procedures, require approval coordination between DOJ headquarters and actual Senate-confirmed U.S. Attorneys. Public corruption and international terrorism need to be coordinated with main Justice. If you don't get people in these roles, where they're supposed to be working with prosecutors on the ground, it could really slow down high profile criminal investigations.[50]

Trump did at last begin to send names forward for US attorney posts in July 2017. As he did so, it became obvious why the search for replacements had taken so long. Trump was seeking personal loyalists. Trump, normally indifferent to mid-level personnel, actually met in person with a candidate for US attorney for the District of Columbia, the US attorney with potential criminal jurisdiction over his staff and himself. In the words of CNN's Laura Jarrett, such a meeting "some former Justice Department and White House sources say sharply departs from past practice and more generally is at odds with the understood custom of insulating U.S. attorneys from political influence."[51]

Donald Trump never accepted the concept that the law should be insulated from politics. He repeatedly publicly demanded that his attorney general initiate criminal proceedings against his former opponent, Hillary Clinton.[52] His eleven-day communications director, Anthony "the Mooch" Scaramucci, bizarrely tweeted a demand on July 27, 2017, that the FBI investigate the "leak" of his financial disclosure forms.[53] Scaramucci hastily deleted the tweet after it was pointed out to him that (a) the forms were public documents, and (b) it is a serious crime for a White House staffer to attempt to order the FBI to investigate anyone. Where would the Mooch get the notion that a White House staffer could initiate such an investigation? From his boss, of course, who insisted in a July 2017 interview with Peter Baker, Maggie Haberman, and Michael Schmidt of the *New York Times* that the director of the FBI should report personally to the president:

> And when Nixon came along [inaudible] was pretty brutal, and out of courtesy, the F.B.I. started reporting to the Department of Justice. But there was nothing official, there was nothing from Congress. There was nothing—anything. But the F.B.I. person really reports directly to the president of the United States, which is interesting. You know, which is interesting. And I think we're going to have a great new F.B.I. director.[54]

Power creates temptations, and that is true even for the smallest increments of power: the power of the building inspector, of the customs official, of the cop at the traffic stop. It took a lot of work by a lot of people over a long time to build even America's highly imperfect standards of public integrity. Undoing that work would be a far easier task. Corruption is the resting state of public affairs; integrity a painstaking, unceasing struggle against cultural inertia and political gravity.

Nepotism fits naturally within authoritarian governments, poorly within republics and democracies. Shortly after entering the presidency for the first time, George Washington laid down a definitive rule against it: "I would not be in the remotest degree influenced, in making nominations, by motives arising from the ties of amity or blood."[55] Trump assigned his dubiously competent son-in-law a chair at the principals' committee of the National Security

Council, the innermost ring of American power. Among Kushner's duties: reorganizing the federal government, winning the war against ISIS, and negotiating Israeli-Palestinian peace. Kushner also took it upon himself to attempt to create a clandestine back channel to the Russian leadership, using the facilities of the Russian embassy to elude detection by US security services.

On President Trump's visit to Israel in May 2017, the president brought Jared Kushner into his meeting with Prime Minister Benjamin Netanyahu—leaving his national security adviser, H. R. McMaster, waiting outside the door of his suite in the King David Hotel, according to the gossipy but usually reliable *Kafe Knesset* (an account uncontradicted by the Trump White House).[56] It was on Kushner's advice too that Trump abruptly reversed his position on legal status for young illegal aliens, without prior notice to either the attorney general or the White House chief of staff.

At the G20 summit in Hamburg, Trump invited his daughter Ivanka to fill his chair when he exited the room. The theory of American government is that official role, not blood relationship, determines who does what. If the president dies in office, he is succeeded by the vice president, not the first lady. There is no such role as "first daughter," despite Ivanka Trump's sometime use of that title. Yet at Hamburg, Ivanka posed with her father in group photographs with the chancellor of Germany, the prime minister of Canada, and other leaders—none of them joined by spouses or children.[57]

On the first day of his new administration, President Trump sought and got from his Justice Department an interpretation of the 1967 anti-nepotism law that allowed him to bring his daughter and son-in-law aboard. It held that the 1967 law applied only to members of "executive agencies"—and that the White House staff did not count as such. The DOJ's opinion acknowledged that this permission represented a new interpretation of the law, but it argued that under the circumstances innovation was warranted. Was it not better to bring informal advisers into the government, where they would be subject to conflict-of-interest rules and other federal ethics laws?[58]

The deputy assistant attorney general who wrote that opinion soon proved sadly naive in his expectations. The Kushners accepted the prestige, power, and perks of the White House, but not its ethical obligations. It was just as Thomas Jefferson had warned after leaving the presidency, a bookend to Washington's injunction against nepotism two decades earlier:

> Towards acquiring the confidence of the people the very first measure is to satisfy them of [the president's] disinterestedness, & that he is directing their affairs with a single eye toward their good, & not to build up fortunes for himself & family: & especially that the officers appointed to transact their business, are appointed because they are the fittest men, not because they are his relations.[59]

The satisfying assurance that the president is appointing the fittest individuals—and not seeking "to build up fortunes for himself and his family"—is precisely what is most lacking under Trumpocracy.

CHAPTER 5

BETRAYALS

Trump's former press secretary Sean Spicer took his Catholicism seriously. So when the attendance list for President Trump's May 2017 meeting with Pope Francis was released, reporters were startled to see Spicer's name missing. First Lady Melania Trump would attend, as would Jared Kushner and Ivanka Trump. The secretary of state would join, as would the national security adviser. Then the list took a detour down the protocol hierarchy. Trump's communications adviser Hope Hicks made the list. So did his bodyguard and factotum Keith Schiller. So did Dan Scavino, Trump's social media manager, famous for retweeting alt-right memes (sometimes with a sharp anti-Semitic edge). No Spicer.

Even the White House press corps, its members frequent targets of Spicer's rages and victims of his manifold untruths, felt a pang of sympathy for their tormentor. "That planners of this trip couldn't or wouldn't get @seanspicer into the Vatican speaks to a small-mindedness I find incredibly depressing," tweeted the *New York*

Times' Glenn Thrush.[1] His colleague Maggie Haberman agreed: "This seems needlessly harsh—when else is Spicer likely to meet the Pope, and it mattered to him?"[2]

Anyone who follows President Trump's Twitter feed has perceived Trump's unstable temperament: his self-pity, his tantrums, his blame shifting. The reporters who cover him struggle to convey the ritual humiliations he inflicts, the rancor he incites. "He's the meanest man I've ever met," a reporter who traveled on the Trump campaign remarked to me in the spring of 2017. Trump has created a snake pit working environment, seething with hatreds and perforated by mutually vindictive leaks. He extracts groveling flattery in public and private, but never requites even the most abject loyalty.

To work for Donald Trump, you must ready yourself to lie and lie. Remember Trump's doctor Harold Bornstein? In August 2016, Bornstein put his signature to a medical assessment that Donald Trump's health was "astonishingly excellent." The assessment concluded, "If elected, Mr. Trump, I can state unequivocally, will be the healthiest individual ever elected to the presidency."[3] In fact, Donald Trump would become the oldest man to enter the presidency, and most likely the third most obese, after William Howard Taft and Grover Cleveland.

Those who work for and with Trump must accept that he reserves the right to embarrass or denigrate them at any moment for any reason, or for no reason at all, just impulsive whim. Here's one of dozens of examples, chosen because it involved the aide Trump has praised more volubly and publicly than any other, Kellyanne Conway.

There is no den she will not go into. When my men are petrified to go on a certain network I say, "Kellyanne, will you go?" Then she gets on and she just destroys them. So anyway, thank you, baby. Thank you. Thank you. Be careful.[4]

Trump thrust upon this lavishly praised aide the duty to appear on CNN on the day of the firing of FBI director James Comey to deny the obvious. She said,

This has nothing to do with Russia. Somebody must be getting fifty dollars every time [Russia] is said on TV. . . . [This] has everything to do with whether the current FBI director has the president's confidence and can faithfully execute his duties.[5]

Two days later, of course, President Trump would himself appear on NBC with Lester Holt and acknowledge that the firing *was* driven by his exasperation at Comey's refusal to exonerate him of "the Russia thing."

And in fact when I decided to just do it, I said to myself, I said "You know, this Russia thing with Trump and Russia is a made-up story, it's an excuse by the Democrats for having lost an election that they should have won."[6]

Conway—and the rest of the Trump talkers—were abandoned to make the best they could of that, as of so many things. In one mad Twitter moment, Trump actually formally alerted the whole country not to rely on those who spoke for him. "As a very active President with lots of things happening, it is not possible for my surrogates to stand at podium with perfect accuracy!"[7]

Trump's vice president, Mike Pence, has been obliged to deliver untruth after untruth on Donald Trump's behalf. On January 15,

2017, Pence confronted a carefully phrased question from CBS's John Dickerson on *Face the Nation.*

Dickerson asked, "Did any adviser or anybody in the Trump campaign have any contact with the Russians who were trying to meddle in the election?"

Pence replied:

Of course not. And I think to suggest that is to give credence to some of these bizarre rumors that have swirled around the candidacy and—the fact that a few news organizations, not this one, actually trafficked in a memo that was produced as opposition research and associated that with intelligence efforts I think could only be attributed to media bias. And I said this week at the press conference, the American people are tired of it.[8]

At the time Pence spoke, the flagrant falseness of those words was known to President Trump himself, to the president's son, to the president's son-in-law, to the president's former campaign manager, and (it seems likely) to the president's newly designated chief of staff. Yet nobody set the poor vice president straight—and the highly forgiving vice president seems not to have objected at all to being left in the dark in this way.

During the Russia inquiry, the country got to know Trump's so-called legal adviser Jay Sekulow. Sekulow ran a pair of nonprofit Christian advocacy groups from which he directed some tens of millions of dollars to himself, his family, and their businesses. Between 2011 and 2015, Sekulow collected $230 million in charitable donations, the *Washington Post* reported in June 2017.

Through a complex arrangement involving [the two charities], $5.5 million was paid directly to Sekulow and five family members in salary or other compensation, tax records covering those years show. Another $7.5 million went to businesses owned by Sekulow and his sister-in-law for producing and consulting on TV, movie and radio shows, including his weekday program, "Jay Sekulow Live!" And $21 million went to a small law firm co-owned by Sekulow, records show.

These arrangements were approved by a board of directors entirely made up of Sekulow's family members, all of them paid via the charities.

"It's more like a family business than a public charity," said Daniel Borochoff, president of the American Institute of Philanthropy, which runs CharityWatch. "You would have to have a lot of trust in this family in order to want to give them your money."[9]

The most troubling of all of Trump's hires, however, was his principal national security adviser during the campaign, the former lieutenant general Michael Flynn. Books could and will be written about the tragic arc of the heroic battlefield commander who dwindled into shabby dishonor (and perhaps much worse) after failing at the capstone job of his to-then impressive career, director of the Defense Intelligence Agency. Flynn turned to extremist anti-Muslim ideologues, accepted money from Russian and Turkish clients, failed to disclose as the law required, and made himself the face of some of the Trump campaign's mob outbursts. In normal presidential campaigns, the national security team keeps well away from the more contentious forms of politicking. Condoleezza Rice, for example, spoke at the 2000 Republican convention—but she had not one single negative word to offer about any living person. The closest she approached to invective was this:

> The first Republican that I knew was my father, John Rice. And he is still the Republican that I admire most. My father joined our party because the Democrats in Jim Crow Alabama of 1952 would not register him to vote. The Republicans did.[10]

Here, by contrast, is Michael Flynn. He took the stage at the Cleveland convention to wild chants of "Lock her up! Lock her up!" Flynn repeated the chant, as he had so often done while campaigning for Trump.

> That's right. Lock her up. That's right. Lock her up. I'm going to tell you what, it's unbelievable; it's unbelievable. Yes; I use—I use #neverHillary; that's what I use. I have called on Hillary Clinton, I have called on Hillary Clinton to drop out of the race because she, she put our nation's security at extremely high risk with her careless use of a private email server.

(The crowd resumed chanting "Lock her up!" and Flynn repeated the phrase.)

> Lock her up. Lock her up. You guys are good. Damn right; exactly right. There's nothing wrong with that.

(More chanting of "Lock her up!")

> And you know why; and you know why? You know why we're saying that? We're saying that because if I, a guy who

knows this business, if I did a tenth, a tenth of what she did, I would be in jail today. So—so, Crooked Hillary Clinton, leave this race now![11]

Two months after that "if I did a tenth" comment, Michael Flynn reportedly joined a conversation with top Turkish ministers to discuss the kidnapping and forcible removal to Turkey of a US permanent resident sought by the Ankara government for political offenses.[12] Flynn surely knew of the notorious Trump Tower meeting in June 2016 at which Donald Trump Jr. was offered Russian state materials "incriminating" of Hillary Clinton. As a former DIA director, Flynn had to understand what Donald Jr. would later claim he did not appreciate: that he was witnessing—and being invited to participate in—a Russian espionage attempt against the US political process. Flynn would later neglect to disclose his Russia contacts on the relevant forms, forms signed under the penalty of felony.

Enabling the bad people in the Trump orbit were the weak people. As White House counsel and as White House chief of staff, Trump appointed two of the least experienced, least commanding holders of either job in recent history. Counsel Don McGahn learned two weeks before Inauguration Day that Flynn was being investigated by the FBI. He did not or could not stop Flynn's appointment.[13] Chief of staff Reince Priebus allowed Trump's favorites to build self-aggrandizing empires of a kind never before seen in the West Wing. Jared Kushner has—and Trump's former political adviser Steve Bannon had—his own full-time press aide. Ivanka Trump and Kellyanne Conway each has her own "chief of staff." Bannon even acquired a perk otherwise awarded only to the president and vice president, his own personal "body man" to follow him wherever he went. Sarah Huckabee Sanders answered a reporter querying the unprecedented entourages of Bannon, Kushner, Conway, and Ivanka Trump as follows:

> It's a great thing that staffers are so engaged at such a high level and have created very ambitious portfolios within the president's agenda. We are shaking things up, and it's a great thing for which the results will ultimately speak for themselves.[14]

Empire building by subordinates is made possible by Trump's disengagement from management, policy, and lawmaking. In late June 2017, President Trump convened Republican senators in hopes of rallying support for the leadership's version of Obamacare repeal. According to an account of the meeting published in the *New York Times*:

> A senator who supports the bill left the meeting at the White House with a sense that the president did not have a grasp of some basic elements of the Senate plan—and seemed especially confused when a moderate Republican complained that opponents of the bill would cast it as a massive tax break for the wealthy, according to an aide who received a detailed readout of the exchange. Mr. Trump said he planned to tackle tax reform later, ignoring the repeal's tax implications, the staff member added.[15]

Trump had one big idea to gain passage of the health care bill: the intimidation of holdouts, like Nevada senator Dean Heller. Heller ranked as the most vulnerable of the Republican senators facing reelection in 2018. He shied from supporting the very unpopular Republican bill. Trump threatened to run seven figures' worth of attack ads against Heller if he did not yield. McConnell complained to Reince Priebus that attacking Heller would be "beyond stupid." As reported by Glenn Thrush and Jonathan Martin in the *New York Times*:

> "They didn't check in with anybody," said Josh Holmes, Mr. McConnell's former chief of staff. "There was no clearing of channels, no heads-up, nothing."[16]

In this instance, Trump relented. But Trump would return to attack other members of his party who vexed him. He fixed all the blame for the failure of Obamacare repeal on Majority Leader Mitch McConnell. He waged Twitter battles with Arizona's two US senators, John McCain and Jeff Flake, as well as with Tennessee's Bob Corker, chairman of the Senate Foreign Relations Committee, after each criticized him, never quite grasping that their support was at least as essential to him as his was to them.

Over the course of 2017, the Trump White House one by one extruded its wild men and gradually assumed something more like orderliness under Chief of Staff John Kelly and National Security Adviser H. R. McMaster. But even as the courtiers evolved toward higher professionalism, their king's madness raged hotter and fiercer. I close the editing of this book on the weekend that President Trump responded to a post-hurricane humanitarian catastrophe on the US territory of Puerto Rico by plunging into hours of Twitter abuse of the mayor of San Juan for not being nice to him. "The Mayor of San Juan, who was very complimentary only a few days ago, has now been told by the Democrats that you must be nasty to Trump."[17] "Such poor leadership ability by the Mayor of San Juan, and others in Puerto Rico, who are not able to get their workers to help. They want everything to be done for them when it should be a community effort. 10,000 Federal workers now on Island doing fantastic job."[18] "We have done a great job with the almost impossible situation in Puerto Rico. Outside the Fake News and politically motivated ingrates, people are now starting to realize the amazing work that has been done by FEMA and our great military."[19]

Trump would not take advice. He would not behave "presidentially," insisting rather that his behavior was perfect just as it was.

My use of social media is not Presidential—it's MODERN DAY PRESIDEN-TIAL. Make America Great Again![20]

After he nearly lost his top economic adviser, Gary Cohn, by seeming to condone Nazis and white supremacists on the rampage in Charlottesville, Virginia, Trump doubled down at a rally in Phoenix, Arizona:

Dishonest people. So here is—here is me—I hope they're showing how many people are in this room, but they won't. They don't even do that. The only time they show the crowds is when there's a disrupter or an anarchist in the room. I call them anarchists. Because, believe me, we have plenty of anarchists. They don't want to talk about the anarchists. . . . If you're reading a story about somebody, you don't know. You assume it's honest, because it's like the failing *New York Times*, which is like so bad. It's so bad.

[Booing]

Or the *Washington Post*, which [I] call a lobbying tool for Amazon, OK, that's a lobbying tool for Amazon.

Or CNN, which is so bad and so pathetic, and their ratings are going down.

[Booing]

Right?

CROWD: CNN sucks! CNN sucks! CNN sucks!

But all the networks—I mean, CNN is really bad, but ABC this morning—I don't watch it much, but I'm watching in the morning, and they have little George Stephanopoulos talking to Nikki Haley, right? Little George. And—and he talks about the speech I made last night, which, believe it or not, got great reviews, right? . . .

But they also said that he must be a racist because he never mentioned the driver of the car, who is a terrible person, drove the car and he killed Heather, and it's a terrible thing. But they said I didn't mention, so these are my words. "The driver of the car is a murderer, and what he did was a horrible, inexcusable thing." They said I didn't mention it.

And then they asked me, just to finish it, they asked me, what about race relations in the United States? Now I have to say they were pretty bad under Barack Obama, that I can tell you.[21]

("Heather" is a reference to Heather Heyer, the young woman who was run over and murdered by a white nationalist at the August 2017 demonstration in Charlottesville; this was Trump's only mention of her in his entire Phoenix rally speech, which took place ten days after her death.)

As in his previous business career, President Trump reacted explosively to any attempt to subject him to anything like normal political or even human limits.

White House officials and informal advisers say the triggers for his temper are if he thinks someone is lying to him, if he's caught by surprise, if someone criticizes him, or if someone stops him from trying to do something or seeks to control him.

Thus Nancy Cook and Josh Dawsey reported for *Politico* in August 2017. They were reporting after the Charlottesville fiasco, a political crisis aggravated by Trump's refusal ever to acknowledge error or change course.

"In some ways, Trump would rather have people calling him racist than say he backed down the minute he was wrong," one adviser to the White House said on Wednesday about Charlottesville.[22]

It's for that reason that Trump filled his White House and administration with the deferential, even servile. He appointed his former personal bodyguard Keith Schiller to direct "Oval Office operations." On the campaign trail, Schiller and his team gained an ugly reputation for violence against lawful protesters. In maybe the most dramatic instance, Schiller snatched a protester's banner, then smacked the protester in the face after he tried to seize it back.[23] It was Schiller who would deliver to James Comey the notice of his termination as FBI director.

Donald Trump entrusted his online presence to a former golf caddy, Dan Scavino. It was Scavino who oversaw the retweeting from accounts like @WhiteGenocideTM (located in "Jewmerica") and the scavenging of message boards for images like that of Hillary Clinton's face atop a pile of money and alongside a Star of David bannered "Most corrupt candidate ever!" (The Star of David was later amended to a circle.)

Trump hired a former manager at the Trump hotel in Washington, DC, as chief usher of the White House.[24] He named Omarosa Manigault, a former contestant on *The Apprentice*, to the White House staff. He appointed the former wedding planner of his son Eric Trump to oversee federal housing programs in New York City, a post in which loyalty matters even more than usual to Trump, since his company collects millions of dollars of revenue every year from that program.[25] (Interestingly, that program was the only one to be exempted from the draconian cuts to housing spending in Trump's first budget request.[26])

Trump hates criticism and expects huge, heaping servings of flattery. The flattery mostly occurs behind closed doors. On June 12, 2017, however, the country was given a televised view, when Trump invited cameras to record the opening moments of a cabinet meeting. Vice President Pence set the tone: "The greatest privilege of my life is to serve as vice president to the president who's keeping his word to the American people." (By that point, Trump had already broken his campaign promise to build a wall and have Mexico pay for it. Two weeks later, the Carrier furnace plant in Pence's home state of Indiana supposedly "saved" by Trump's efforts would close, and all its manufacturing jobs would move to Mexico.[27]) Chief of Staff Reince Priebus continued, "On behalf of the entire senior staff around you, Mr. President, we thank you for the opportunity and the blessing that you've given us to serve your agenda." One by one, like members of the Soviet Politburo addressing Comrade Stalin, they paid their more or less fulsome tributes. "I am privileged to be here—deeply honored—and I want to thank you for your commitment to the American workers," said the secretary of labor. "It was a great honor traveling with you around the country for the last year and an even greater honor to be here serving on your cabinet," gushed the secretary of the treasury. "Mr.

President, what an incredible honor it is to lead the Department of Health and Human Services at this pivotal time under your leadership. I can't thank you enough for the privileges you've given me and the leadership that you've shown," said the head of that department.[28]

A normal cabinet would balk at such self-abasement. A normal president would gag at it. (President George W. Bush, for whom I worked, especially distrusted flattery and flatterers. His eyes would narrow and a cynical smile would form, as if to say, "Now I see what you are.") Donald Trump expects and rewards it. Such behavior is profoundly shameful, and honorable people will not do it. This fact forces a president who wishes to do it to hire dishonorable people—and to thrust honorable people into irretrievably dishonorable situations.

No American military man of his generation commanded more universal admiration than did Lieutenant General H. R. McMaster. A combat veteran of Iraq, Afghanistan, and the Gulf War, and also the author of an acclaimed book about civilian-military relations, McMaster embodied the high ideal of the soldier-intellectual, a man who excelled in both thought and action. When President Trump named McMaster to replace the Russia-compromised Michael Flynn as national security adviser, the wise people of national security breathed their relief. "An outstanding choice!" exulted Senator John McCain.[29]

In the spring of 2017, this fine public servant faced a serious challenge. He had consented to serve a president elevated to power in some considerable part by clandestine help from Russia, an unfriendly power. The exact degree of collusion between the Trump team and Russia remained shadowy at that time; President Trump had not yet fired FBI director James Comey, and Donald Trump Jr.'s "I love it!" email welcoming Russian help would not come into public view until July 2017.[30] Yet the odor of treason already hung heavy in April. The allies worried about Trump's incessant praise of Vladimir Putin and about his campaign statements raising doubts about America's NATO obligations, statements seconded by important campaign surrogates like Newt Gingrich, the former Speaker of the House.[31] America's allies wanted reassurance, and McMaster believed he had found the perfect way to deliver it.

At the newly built headquarters of the North Atlantic Treaty Organization in Brussels, a monument had been erected to the spirit of Article 5, the treaty's mutual-defense guarantee. A NATO summit was scheduled for May 25, 2017. There Trump would personally dedicate the Article 5 monument—and reaffirm America's pledge to defend its allies.

The appropriate words were written, circulated, revised, and approved, in a process overseen by McMaster personally.[32] The day before the speech, a senior administration official (most likely McMaster himself) briefed the *New York Times* that Trump's NATO speech would explicitly endorse Article 5.

President Trump is expected to publicly endorse NATO's mutual defense commitment at a ceremony on Thursday at the alliance's headquarters, an administration official said, breaking months of silence about whether the United States would automatically come to the aid of an ally under attack.

Mr. Trump will make the promise in Brussels at the start of three days of meetings with European heads of state, according to the official.[33]

The agreed language remained in place as late as the morning the speech was to be delivered, according to Susan Glasser of *Politico*.[34]

Then, at the last second, Trump balked. He stood in front of the monument. He read the speech. He omitted the pro–Article 5 language. Why? Ideology? Russian influence? Truculent resistance to the advice of others unless swaddled in extravagant flattery? Who knows? Whatever the reason for the language's disappearance, it fell to McMaster to undo the damage. Standing before the traveling press corps in Taormina, Sicily, on May 27, 2017, two days after the NATO speech, McMaster expostulated that nothing untoward had happened. On the record this time, he said:

> I think it's extraordinary that there would be an expectation that the president would have to say explicitly that he supports Article 5. Of course he does. He did not make a decision not to say it. It was implicit in the speech. There was no decision to not put it in there. It is a matter of fact that the United States, the president, stands firmly behind our Article 5 commitments under NATO.[35]

One of the most honorable soldiers of his generation felt obliged to speak untruths to protect the United States' global interests from the consequences of the president's willfulness.

When good men do bad things, they usually have good motives. McMaster, like many other national security experts and veterans, joined the Trump administration in the hope of protecting the country. Perhaps there was ambition mixed in, or some other lesser motive—we are all human—but they could fairly assure themselves that they dealt with the devil for the noblest of reasons.

In the months after Trump's surprise Electoral College victory, many conscientious people wrestled with the question "Should I take a job in the Trump administration?" A week after the election,

Eliot Cohen—an anti-Trump Republican who had served at senior levels in past administrations—eloquently advised those facing this dilemma to answer yes.

It seems to me that if they are sure that they would say yes out of a sense of duty rather than mere careerism; if they are realistic in understanding that in this enterprise they will be the horse, not the jockey; if they accept that they will enter an administration likely to be torn by infighting and bureaucratic skullduggery, they should say yes. Yes, with two conditions, however: that they keep a signed but undated letter of resignation in their desk office (as I did when I was in government), and that they not recant a word of what they have said thus far. Public service means making accommodations, but everyone needs to understand that there is a point where crossing a line, even an arbitrary line, means, as Sir Thomas More says in *A Man for All Seasons*, letting go without hope of ever finding yourself again.

It goes without saying that friends in military, diplomatic, or intelligence service—the career people who keep our country strong and safe—should continue to do their jobs. If anything, having professionals serve who remember that their oath is to support and defend the Constitution—and not to truckle to an individual or his clique—will be more important than ever.[36]

Scarcely a week later, Cohen changed his mind.

My about-face began with a discreet request to me from a friend in Trumpworld to provide names—unsullied by having signed the two anti-Trump foreign policy letters—of those who might be willing to serve. My friend and I had agreed to disagree a while back about my taking an uncompromising anti-Trump stand; now, he wanted assistance and I willingly complied.

After an exchange about a senior figure who would not submit a résumé but would listen if contacted, an email exchange ensued that I found astonishing. My friend was seething with anger directed at those of us who had opposed Donald Trump—even those who stood ready to help steer good people to an administration that understandably wanted nothing to do with the likes of me, someone who had been out front in opposing Trump since the beginning.

The problem, as Cohen now perceived it, was less Trump himself than the "mini-Trumps" with whom Trump surrounded himself.

One bad boss can be endured. A gaggle of them will poison all decision-making. They will turn on each other. No band of brothers this: rather the permanent campaign as waged by triumphalist rabble-rousers and demagogues, abetted by people out of their depth and unfit for the jobs they will hold, gripped by grievance, resentment and lurking insecurity. Their mistakes—because there will be mistakes—will be exceptional.

Nemesis pursues and punishes all administrations, but this one will get a double dose. Until it can acquire some measure of humility about what it knows, and a degree of magnanimity to those who have opposed it, it will smash into crises and failures. With the disarray of its transition team, in a way, it already has.[37]

Deals with the devil seldom end as good bargains, and so it has been for all who signed the Mephistophelean pact with Donald Trump. Rather than constraining Trump, they have been, if not outright corrupted by him, at least tainted by him. McMaster's lie in Taormina was an eminently pardonable one, but a lie it remained. Those less exquisitely honorable than McMaster—and serving in less indispensable roles—found themselves called on to abase themselves much deeper. Trump's communications director Anthony Scaramucci inaugurated his brief moment in the national spotlight with an outburst of grotesque flattery.

> I've seen this guy throw a dead spiral through a tire. I've seen him at Madison Square Garden with a topcoat on. He's standing in the key and he's hitting foul shots and swishing them, okay? He sinks three-foot putts.[38]

(The official White House transcript improved the compliment by amending "three-foot putts" to "30-foot putts."[39])

Treasury Secretary Steven Mnuchin recited the same cringing script in a March public forum with *Axios*'s Mike Allen: "This guy's got more stamina than anybody I've ever met," Mnuchin said of Trump. "I mean, I thought I was in good shape. . . . I mean, it's unbelievable. He's constantly doing things." Asked how that was possible, given Trump's bad diet and abhorrence of exercise, Mnuchin answered perfectly straight-faced, "He's got perfect genes. He has incredible energy, and he's unbelievably healthy."[40]

It was behaviors like this that I foresaw when I delivered my own answer to Eliot Cohen's question in January 2017.

> Good people can do the right thing even under pressure. But be aware: The pressure to do the wrong thing can be intense—

and the closer one approaches to the center of presidential power and prestige, the more intense the pressure becomes. It's easy to imagine that you'd emulate Walters [the IRS director who refused to release political opponents' tax returns to the Nixon White House] when reading the book he wrote four decades after the fact. But in the moment? In the Oval Office? Face to face with the president of the United States?

So maybe the very first thing to consider, if the invitation comes, is this: How well do you know yourself? How sure are you that you indeed would say no?

And then humbly consider this second troubling question: If the Trump administration were as convinced as you are that you would do the right thing—would they have asked you in the first place?[41]

One thing was clear: everyone who entered the Trump administration for nonselfish motives would sooner or later find himself or herself betrayed by a president who demanded loyalty in its most servile form, but who never returned it.

Trump equally betrayed those who had believed his campaign promises and election pledges. Isolationists and anti-interventionists had lauded Trump as the candidate who would stay clear of the Syrian Civil War and wind down America's overseas commitments. In the words of the venture capitalist Peter Thiel, one of Trump's few high-profile supporters from the technology industry:

Trump's agenda is about making America a normal country. A normal country doesn't have a half-trillion dollar trade deficit. A normal country doesn't fight five simultaneous undeclared wars. In a normal country, the government actually does its job.[42]

Instead, Trump plunged deeper into the Syria conflict than Barack Obama had ever dared, firing cruise missiles at Syrian government airfields and shooting down Syrian government aircraft. Trump escalated the tempo of violence in Yemen and approved a surge of additional troops to Afghanistan. Trump mused aloud about military intervention in Venezuela and did not halt the US military buildup in Poland and Romania. He threatened preemptive war upon North Korea and edged toward military confrontation against Iran.

Tough on terror? Trump promised to "bomb the shit out of [ISIS]"—and, less colloquially, to deliver a plan within thirty days of taking office to finish the terror group once and for all.[43] The plan was never presented. Instead, the US military continues to execute Obama-era plans against ISIS in Iraq, capturing Mosul on exactly the timetable Trump had once derided as too slow and "so dumb."[44] Trump's distinctive change to US counterterrorism policy has been to mock terrorism's victims. After the murder of a French police officer in Paris on April 20, 2017, Trump chortled on Twitter that the attack would likely help his French cognate, Marine Le Pen.[45] It didn't. In May, Trump got into a Twitter feud with Sadiq Khan, the mayor of London, hours after an ISIS-inspired terror attack that killed seven and wounded forty-eight.[46] (Some British observers attribute Labour's electoral surge in London in the 2017 UK general election to Trump's obnoxious comments four days before the vote.)

Compel allies to contribute more to their defense? Days before the 2017 South Korean presidential election, Trump reneged on his own deal to install missile defenses in the peninsula, demanding an additional $1 billion from Seoul toward the system's costs.[47] He threatened to rip up the US–South Korea Free Trade Agreement in an interview given only a week before the election.

Trump's ill-timed words helped elect the more soft-line candidate, who promptly disregarded Trump's policy and sought negotiated agreements with North Korea.[48]

Strong advocates for Israel choked back their revulsion against the Trump campaign's appeals to anti-Semitism in order to support a candidate who pledged to move the US embassy to Jerusalem and abrogate Barack Obama's Iran deal. Within weeks of taking office, Trump defaulted on both commitments.[49]

The most famous and electorally important of Trump's campaign pledges was his vow to "build the wall and make Mexico pay for it." There will be no wall, and Mexico will pay for nothing. The first budget proposed by the supposed great builder-president allowed for nothing but some prototype extensions to existing fencing near San Diego. As of midsummer 2017, no work had begun.[50]

Of all the Fausts to Trump's Mephistopheles, none paid higher prices—and received less in return—than Trump's supposed partisan allies in Congress.

The unexpected 2016 Electoral College result offered Republicans an opportunity they had experienced only once since the Great Depression: united control of all the elected branches of the federal government. That previous opportunity, many Republicans felt, had been squandered by the George W. Bush administration. The Iraq War had consumed the administration's energy and political credit. Its most enduring domestic policy legacy was a deviation from orthodoxy: the prescription drug benefit, which by 2016 was adding almost $100 billion per year to the cost of Medicare. Conservatives took no more joy in Bush's signature education reform, No Child Left Behind. His temporary tax cuts had mostly lapsed since 2013. In retrospect, the years before the loss of Congress in November 2006 looked to conservatives at best like a series of unprincipled improvisations, at worst an active sellout. Even Jeb

Bush felt obliged to criticize George W. Bush's record. Asked in New Hampshire in May 2015 about differences between the two, the younger Bush answered, "I think that in Washington during my brother's time, Republicans spent too much money. I think he could have used the veto power—he didn't have line-item veto power, but he could have brought budget discipline to Washington, DC. That seems kind of quaint right now given the fact that after he left, budget deficits and spending just like lit up astronomically. But having constraints on spending across the board during his time would have been a good thing."[51]

Republicans resolved not to waste the opportunity if it ever recurred. They would cut taxes and spending, roll back regulations, undo Obama-era programs. All that was required from the next Republican president, the antitax crusader Grover Norquist jested, was enough working digits to sign their bills into law.[52]

But when that wish was finally granted, it was incarnated in the weird form of Donald Trump. Unlike the automaton president of Norquist's dreams, Trump very much had a mind of his own: a mind uninterested in, and in fact barely cognizant of, the hyper-ideological program of his party. What Trump did care about was personal wealth, power, and domination.

"Paul Ryan, I don't know him well," said candidate Trump at a press conference after his streak of Super Tuesday wins on March 1, 2016, "but I'm sure I'm going to get along great with him. And if I don't, he's going to have to pay a big price."[53] Trump attempted to exact that price in August of that election year. Paul Ryan faced a primary challenge that month from a Trump wannabe: a wealthy Wisconsin businessman with provocative views on trade, immigration, and minority groups. That challenger, Paul Nehlen, publicly flattered Trump—even backing him in his bizarre dispute with the family of the fallen war hero Humayun Khan. Trump thanked and praised Nehlen for his "good campaign." Trump for weeks refused to endorse Ryan, even mockingly using the same language ("I'm just not quite there yet") Ryan had previously used about him.[54] Trump eventually reversed course, as it became evident that Nehlen would lose (ultimately by a margin of 68 points). Three days before the primary, Trump leaped to the side of the certain winner.

Trump never did extract from Ryan the formal surrender he craved. Yet Trump had discerned that the balance of power between the two men favored Trump, not Ryan. Normal presidents arrive in Washington with an ambitious policy agenda they seek to enact through Congress. They propose; Congress disposes. Trump had no such agenda, but Republicans in Congress did: a big, ambitious, and radical agenda. They wanted to undo the health care changes of the Obama years and outright reverse them, to slow the projected growth of Medicare and Medicaid. They wanted to rewrite the corporate tax code, overturn Obama-era rules on greenhouse gases, and return trillions of dollars of redistributed income. They wanted to federalize gun policy, compelling states like California and Illinois to accept within their own borders the concealed-carry permits issued by more permissive states. They wished to bestow regulatory favors on favored industries and firms.

All those actions and many others would require the signature of a president who neither understood nor cared about most of them. What he needed in return from Congress was not action, but inaction: inaction on ethics, inaction on disclosures, and above all inaction on allegations that Russia manipulated the election to help him—and them.

We'll protect your business if you sign our bills. That was the transaction congressional leaders offered Trump. They failed to appreciate until too late that Trump, not they, had the stronger hand in this bargaining.

Two perverse factors strengthened Trump against the congressional Republicans.

The first factor was the stark unpopularity of much of what the congressional Republican leadership wished to do. Speaker Ryan, a true believer, would willingly hazard his political career to finish off Obamacare once and for all. But Ryan could not trust Donald Trump to do the same. At the first affront to his ego, Trump might defect, as he did on debt-ceiling negotiations in September 2017. Trump betrayed the Republican demand for a twelve-month extension in favor of the Pelosi-Schumer offer of three months' reportedly because he was peeved at that moment with Republican congressional leaders. Or as when he reversed his position on deferred action for young illegal aliens reportedly to punish his attorney general for failing to protect him against the appointment of a special counsel. Congressional Republicans dared not impose any restraint or even oversight on Trump lest he wreck all their plans out of peevish spite or simple loss of interest.

The second unlikely factor enhancing Trump's power over Congress was Trump's *own* unpopularity. In June 2010, the Gallup organization reviewed all the House elections since World War II. Gallup found that when a president polls above 50 percent approval, his party loses an average of thirteen seats in midterm elections, but thirty-seven seats when he polls below 50 percent. (Adding the two Obama midterms of 2010 and 2014, losses of sixty-three and thirteen respectively, does not change the math.)[55] With Trump polling below 40 percent through his first months in office and a margin of only twenty-three seats, House Republicans had to assume that their majority might not have long to last. That made it all the more urgent to get Trump's signature on laws *fast*— and to protect Trump from damaging investigations that might push his popularity deeper into the danger zone. The one postwar president to poll below 35 percent during a midterm election—Harry Truman in 1946—suffered the staggering loss of fifty-five seats.

The worse Trump behaved, the more frantically congressional Republicans worked to protect him.

The chairman of the House Intelligence Committee entangled himself in a bizarre sequence of misconduct and untruths in an effort to sabotage the investigation of Trump's Russia connections.

Republican leaders in Congress kept silent when Trump's designated attorney general, Jeff Sessions, testified inaccurately about his Russia connections during his confirmation hearing—and silent again as it emerged that Trump's son-in-law and most powerful aide, Jared Kushner, had lied about his Russia contacts on his application form for a security clearance.

Congressional committees that exhaustively investigated the deaths of US personnel at the Benghazi consulate in 2012, and the Internal Revenue Service's scrutiny of the tax-exempt status of conservative groups that strayed too close to electoral politics, yawned away the ethical infractions of the Trump White House. "I think the people who voted for Donald Trump went into it with eyes wide open," Jason Chaffetz, the chair of the House Oversight Committee, told my *Atlantic* colleague McKay Coppins in March 2017. "Everybody knew he was rich, everybody knew he had lots of different entanglements. . . . These other little intrigues about a wealthy family making money is a bit of a sideshow."[56]

"He's a businessman, not a politician," said Mike Pence in October 2016, defending Donald Trump after the *New York Times* published a 1995 tax return in which Trump took a nearly $1 billion deduction for losing other people's money.[57]

"He's learning the job," said Senate Majority Leader McConnell to *Newsmax* TV in April 2017, assuring viewers that Trump had come to appreciate NATO—six weeks before the NATO summit at which Trump demonstrated he had not.[58]

"The president's new at this. He's new to government." That was Paul Ryan's excuse for Trump's attempt to pressure the FBI into halting its investigation into the Russia matter.[59]

"It does no good for me to comment on his Twitter behaviors," said Utah senator Mike Lee on the morning of Trump's "body slam CNN" tweet, a video originating from a racist and anti-Semitic account that showed an image of Trump wrestling and punching a man with a CNN logo in place of a head.[60]

What did these party loyalists receive in return for their indulgence and protection? In the end, not much. The "enough working digits" theory of the presidency proved wrong. Absent effective presidential leadership, Congress could not organize itself to enact a bold reform agenda. House members from ultra-secure districts could not agree with senators from competitive states. Leaders in the House and Senate could not cajole or coerce straying votes. No effective communication strategy could be agreed on, nor did anyone have the authority to absorb feedback from the communicators and revise the reform program in ways that responded to criticism. The only criticism that mattered was criticism from the activist base, never from the reachable center. As much as any crank on Facebook, the Republican majority in Congress had locked itself within a closed information system. A party that listens only to itself, and speaks only to itself, deprives itself of the power to persuade anybody else.

Yet, whatever sordid things Republicans in Congress did for Trump, it was never enough for Trump's voting base. In August of 2017, a George Washington University poll asked Republican voters in Republican-held districts what they thought of their member of Congress. Was he or she doing enough to support President

Trump, too little, or too much? Only 35 percent answered "just enough." A majority, 53 percent, said "too little." (A defiant 4 percent said "too much.")[61]

So the time ticked down, month by month, with scant domestic legislation to show for it. Some individual members of Congress did receive highly personal returns for their indulgence of Trump's use of power. Representative Tom Price of Georgia, one of Congress's most active traders of stocks under the jurisdiction of his committee, was appointed secretary of Health and Human Services. Price resigned in September 2017, after incurring almost $1 million in charter jet costs in less than eight months. Representative Mick Mulvaney, a Tea Party radical who had pushed the United States to default on its obligations in the debt-ceiling battles of 2011 and 2013, was named the director of the Office of Management and Budget. The former Montana congressman Ryan Zinke, a hunting companion of Donald Trump Jr., got the Interior Department. Elaine Chao, the wife of Senate Majority Leader Mitch McConnell, returned to head the Labor Department, resuming a post she had held under President George W. Bush.

The supply of such tangible rewards is finite, however. Appointments of House members to executive branch jobs generate special elections, with all their political risks. Although the GOP retained the seats opened by Trump's appointments, it did so by worryingly narrowing margins: only four points in Georgia's Sixth District special election, for example, down from twenty-three points in the election of November 2016. This kind of patronage could be safely distributed only to representatives of the reddest seats in the reddest states. It might seem more prudent to reward members of Congress by promoting their aides to executive branch jobs. That method bumped into another problem: the slow Trump staffing process. There are many explanations for that slowness, but at the bottom of them all seems to be Trump's own profound and incorrigible distaste for organization.

The Trump Organization had habitually lived in chaos, careening from crisis to crisis. Trump's biographers have reported with amazement that his companies did not generate balance sheets or profit-and-loss reports, in large part because Trump could not or would not read them.[62] "It surprised me how much of a family-type operation it was, instead of a business kind of orientation where there is a structure and there is a chain of command and there is delegation of authority and responsibility." That assessment of Trump's business style was delivered in 1989 by the CEO of Trump's brief and disastrous venture into the airline business. "I don't think he *manages*," said the head of a construction company that worked on Trump Tower. "I think he lets it all just happen."[63]

Trump never built a proper transition team. New Jersey governor Chris Christie, Vice President Mike Pence, Jared Kushner—each headed his own effort, each canceling out the work of the others. The head of the office of presidential personnel in the new administration, Johnny DeStefano, had headed the data operation of the Trump presidential campaign. A former congressional aide, DeStefano had no executive branch experience, no experience in recruiting in either the private or public sector, and limited authority anyway to make hiring decisions. Trump himself insisted on reviewing the résumé of every candidate for every sub-cabinet and sub-sub-cabinet job—a process that held the entire staffing process hostage to Trump's short attention span, weak work ethic, and ferocious demand for abject personal loyalty. Yet it would be wrong to regard the irregularity of Trump's White House and administration as a story of failure. Trump the president, like Trump the businessman and Trump the candidate, plunged his working environments into chaos because he intuited that chaos enhanced his power. "We can't do that, sir, it's against the rules" are words Trump never wanted to hear.

Trump did not merely fail to organize his government. He actively sabotaged organization wherever it began to take form. He let his former personal secretary schedule his telephone calls, subverting the accustomed role of the White House chief of staff.[64] He staffed his National Security Council with sinister oddballs. He mocked the stature of the chairman of the Senate Foreign Relations Committee and questioned the IQ of the secretary of state. He conducted public business on his insecure personal cell phone.[65] He made political speeches to agents of the Central Intelligence Agency, exhorted captive military audiences to call their members of Congress to support his agenda, and delivered an address to the National Scout Jamboree so vituperatively partisan that the organization felt obliged to apologize to attendees.[66] Most catastrophically of all, he exposed his hurts, rages, fears, and schemes for all to see on his personal Twitter account.

Speaking at the Conservative Political Action Conference (CPAC) in February 2017, Trump's senior presidential aide Steve Bannon listed "the deconstruction of the administrative state" as one of the three supreme goals of the new administration.[67] Deconstruction would involve repealing laws and eliminating agencies. This was the kind of work President Carter did when he deregulated passenger air travel and commercial freight traffic in the 1970s; that President Reagan did when he freed oil and natural gas prices in the 1980s; that President Clinton did—for better or worse—when he scrapped the New Deal regulation of the financial services industry in the 1990s. It's hard work, built on serious economic analysis, requiring approval by Congress and support from public opinion.

The Trump administration settled for an easier project: *paralyzing* the state either by failing to staff it in the first place or else by filling its ranks with incompetents and self-seekers, by trashing ethical rules, and by abdicating the responsibility of the president and White House to set policy and then confirm that policy is in fact executed.

Trumpocracy as a system of power rests not on deregulation but on nonregulation, not on deconstructing the state but on breaking the state in order to plunder the state.

CHAPTER 6

————

ENEMIES OF THE PEOPLE

Generally speaking, do you favor or oppose permitting the courts to shut down media outlets that are biased or inaccurate—or haven't you heard enough yet about that to say?"

The YouGov polling agency put that question on behalf of the *Economist* to a robustly large sample of 1,482 Americans in July 2017. A plurality of Republicans and Trump supporters endorsed the idea: 45 percent of both said they favored permitting courts to shut down media organizations.[1]

That seems a pretty extreme result. Yet the poll was no freak.

In March 2017, Pew Research Center asked, "Is it very important in maintaining a strong democracy in the United States to . . . " followed by a list of rights. Only 49 percent of Republicans defended "the freedom of news organizations to criticize political leaders" as "very important" to democracy, as opposed to 76 percent of Democrats.[2]

A July Marist poll for NPR-PBS asked a series of questions about whether certain rights had gone "too far." Asked about freedom of the press, 42 percent of Republicans surveyed said yes, versus only 11 percent of Democrats.[3]

Donald Trump has not had many successes as president. Convincing his supporters to regard honest media as "fake news" must rank high among them.

No American president in history—no national political figure of any kind since at least Senator Joe McCarthy—has trafficked more in untruths than Donald Trump. He owed the start of his political career to the Birther hoax. He falsely insisted that he lost the popular vote only because of somewhere between three and five million ballots cast by illegal aliens. He falsely claimed that his was the largest inaugural crowd in history. He repeated false stories about New Jersey Muslims cheering the 9/11 attacks. He recited false statistics about the majority of terrorists since 9/11 entering the United States from foreign countries. He falsely denied that his campaign communicated with Russia about hacking the Hillary Clinton campaign. He falsely boasted that he enacted more bills in his first one hundred days and first six months than any previous president. He even told a false anecdote about an imaginary friend named "Jim" who never visits Paris anymore because "Paris is no longer Paris."[4]

And yet at the same time as Donald Trump's mouth and iPhone were propagating falsehoods, fictions, and fantasies to a vast global audience, he convinced himself that it was *he* who was the victim of a vast media campaign of defamation and falsehood.

"Dishonest media says Mexico won't be paying for the wall if they pay a little later so the wall can be built more quickly. Media is fake!" Trump tweeted those words on January 8, 2017.[5] Three weeks later, Trump signed an executive order that called for funding the wall from future federal budget requests.[6] When asked in March whether there was any possibility that Mexico would pay for the wall, Senate Majority Leader McConnell tersely replied, "Uh, no."[7] By June, Trump had retreated to a hope that the hypothetical wall could be paid for with revenues from solar panels on its surface.[8]

"Totally biased @NBCNews went out of its way to say that the big announcement from Ford, G.M., Lockheed & others that jobs are coming back . . . to the U.S., but had nothing to do with TRUMP, is more FAKE NEWS. Ask top CEO's of those companies for real facts. Came back because of me!"[9] Thus Trump tweeted January 18, 2017. But of course NBC was right. Trump was taking credit for decisions by Ford and GM to cancel planned expansions in Mexico because of waning demand for the small cars produced there, the Ford Focus and the GM Cruz, respectively. There would be no "return" of jobs to the United States. The cars were not wanted, so they would not be manufactured anywhere.[10] In June, Ford would announce termination of all North American production of the Focus and the shifting of all future Focus production to China.[11]

Trump tweeted literally dozens of variants on the claim that "the Russia story" was "fake news" "invented by the Democrats." Here's just one, from February 26, 2017: "Russia talk is FAKE NEWS put out by the Dems, and played up by the media, in order to mask the big election defeat and the illegal leaks!"[12] By July, the "FAKE NEWS" had become real even to the Trump Twitter feed. "Just out: The Obama Administration knew far in advance of November 8th about election meddling by Russia. Did nothing about it. WHY?"[13]

March 18: "Despite what you have heard from the FAKE NEWS, I had a GREAT meeting with German Chancellor Angela Merkel. Nevertheless, Germany owes. . . . ."[14] Ten days after that "GREAT" meeting, Angela Merkel gave her famous Munich speech warning that Europe could no longer rely on the United States to defend its interests and must henceforward take its future into its own hands.[15]

Enraged by negative coverage of conditions on Puerto Rico, Trump tweeted eight separate fulminations against "fake news" over the weekend of September 30–October 1, 2017.

Trump's grandiosity led him to escalate his allegations against the press. They were not merely "unfair" or "fake"—they were outright enemies. Not merely personal enemies either. A president of the United States who gratefully welcomed campaign assistance from a hostile foreign spy agency denounced America's free press as enemies of the nation.

"The FAKE NEWS media (failing @nytimes, @CNN, @NBCNews and many more) is not my enemy, it is the enemy of the American people. Sick!"[16] President Trump tweeted those words on February 17, 2017.

He repeated the phrase in his February 2017 speech to CPAC. "A few days ago I called the fake news the enemy of the people, and they are—they are the enemy of the people." He threatened, "We're going to do something about it."[17]

Trump fired off tweet after tweet intimating retaliation against Amazon to punish its founder, Jeff Bezos, for his investment in the *Washington Post*. Trump knocked $9 billion off Amazon's stock valuation on August 16, 2017, with this tweet:

> Amazon is doing great damage to tax paying retailers. Towns, cities and states throughout the U.S. are being hurt—many jobs being lost![18]

Against the even more hated CNN, Trump's staffers plotted a yet larger-scale revenge. Michael Grynbaum reported for the *New York Times* in July 2017:

White House advisers have discussed a potential point of leverage over their adversary, a senior administration official said: a pending merger between CNN's parent company, Time Warner, and AT&T. Mr. Trump's Justice Department will decide whether to approve the merger, and while analysts say there is little to stop the deal from moving forward, the president's animus toward CNN remains a wild card.[19]

Threats were the habitual and natural language of Trump's staffers too. In a postinaugural interview on *Meet the Press*, Trump's aide Kellyanne Conway warned Chuck Todd that unwelcome questioning would provoke some unspecified reprisal.

> **CHUCK TODD**: All right, Kellyanne, let me stop you here because . . . you make a very reasonable and rational case for why crowd sizes don't matter. Then explain, you did not answer the question, why did the president send out his press secretary, who's not just the spokesperson for Donald Trump. He could be—He also serves as the spokesperson for all of America at times. He speaks for all of the country at times. Why put him out there for the very first time in front of that podium to utter a provable falsehood? It's a small thing. But the first time he confronts the public it's a falsehood?
>
> **KELLYANNE CONWAY**: Chuck, I mean, if we're going to keep referring to our press secretary in those types of terms I think that we're going to have to rethink our relationship here.[20]

Yet if Trump and his aides pondered more carefully, they might have realized that there was no need for retaliation. Much as Donald Trump would have enjoyed a world in which all media were reduced to the sycophancy of *Fox & Friends* and *Hannity*, the tactical lobe of Trump's brain surely recognized the superior usefulness of the media as an enemy.

In the early days of the Trump transition, Nic Dawes, a journalist who has worked in two authoritarian-trending countries, India and South Africa, delivered a warning to the American media about what to expect from a figure like Trump. "Get used to being stigmatized as 'opposition,'" he wrote. "The basic idea is simple: to delegitimize accountability journalism by framing it as partisan."[21]

Donald Trump is often praised for "not speaking like a politician." What that means in practice is that Trump never equivocates. Peter Bull, a specialist in political communication, has rightly observed:

> We all equivocate in certain situations but politicians are particularly prone to it. That's not necessarily because they are devious, slippery or evasive, but because conflict is endemic to politics, and politicians get asked a lot of questions that cause communicative conflicts. These conflicts occur especially when all the main forms of response may make the politician look bad or threaten their future freedom of action.[22]

To be unequivocal, however, is not the same as to be honest. Politicians equivocate precisely to avoid lying. Trump lies without qualm or remorse. If necessary, he then lies about the lie. (The Hillary Clinton campaign made a powerful online ad that contrasted repeated instances of Trump insisting, "I never said that" followed immediately by a clip of him saying precisely that thing.[23]) But whatever Trump says, he says without qualification, deceiving the inattentive into regarding him as a truthful man, rather than the most shameless liar in the history of the presidency.

The Russia-born journalist Masha Gessen has astutely noted the commonality of the dishonesty of Donald Trump and the man he admires so much, Vladimir Putin. *"Lying is the message,"* she wrote. "It's not just that both Putin and Trump lie, it is that they lie in the same way and for the same purpose: blatantly, to assert power over truth itself."[24]

The normal politician calculates that lying is counterproductive over the long term. Lie too often, and you develop a reputation as a liar. Donald Trump gained just such a reputation in his pre-political career. "I wouldn't believe Donald Trump if his tongue were notarized," said a deputy mayor of New York. Innumerable investors, lenders, customers, and graduates of Trump University would say the same. In national politics, however, Trump benefited from the hesitation of reporters and journalists to call a lie for what it is. In a CNN interview in September 2016, Kellyanne Conway shut down a searching inquiry about Trump's tax returns by Alisyn Camerota with the taunting challenge, "Are you calling him a liar?"[25] Trump's explanations for not releasing his returns were indeed blatant and untenable lies. But to say so outright on TV? It violated every instinct in a responsible and fair-minded TV interviewer's being.

Sometimes lying is unavoidable in government. During the Cuban missile crisis, the Pentagon's chief spokesman, Arthur Sylvester, said things that were later exposed as untrue. Summoned before a congressional committee to explain himself (in those bygone days, official lying was thought to require congressional action!), Sylvester replied that a government had the "right, if necessary, to lie to save itself when it's up into a nuclear war."[26] Responding to the criticism those words touched off, Sylvester later elaborated what he meant:

As the Defense Department's spokesman I espoused the the-
sis that the indisputable requisite of a government information program was that it be truthful. But I also stated that on
occasions (such as the Cuban missile crisis) when the nation's
security was at stake, the Government had the right, indeed
the duty, to lie if necessary to mislead an enemy and protect
the people it represented.[27]

Whatever you may think of Sylvester's position, it has nothing in common with Donald Trump's. Trump's lies were never
deployed for national security purposes—or often for any public
purpose at all. They were deployed to soothe his ego and protect
him from his own incessant wrongdoing.

A CNN analysis released on June 29, 2017, counted 770 presidential tweets since Inauguration Day. Twenty-seven tweets mentioned veterans, his third most common subject. The runner-up
subject, "jobs," was mentioned sixty-seven times. Far in first place:
attacks on the press, eighty-five tweets.[28] Negative media coverage
became a powerful resource for Trump—in fact, his only resource,
as actual accomplishments eluded him. By inflaming antipress feeling, Trump could wall his supporters within an alternative information system controlled by him.

Evidence of the Trump campaign's collusion with Russia could
not be refuted or suppressed. But Trump's supporters could be
manipulated into disregarding it. As of July 2017, only 9 percent
of Republicans accepted the unanimous assessment of US intelligence agencies—including Trump's own appointees—that Russia
intervened in the 2016 election to help Trump.[29] One-third of Republicans refused to believe the uncontested fact, acknowledged (if
condoned) by Trump himself, that Donald Trump Jr. had met with
Russian agents to seek information harmful to Hillary Clinton.[30]

Supporters could be fed "alternative facts" and extenuating excuses. Did Trump falsely imply that he had "tapes" of his conversations with FBI director James Comey? "That was a smart way to make sure [Comey] stayed honest in those hearings," gushed *Fox & Friends'* cohost Ainsley Earhardt.[31] Had Trump improperly demanded that the FBI director pledge personal loyalty to him? "If you're a CEO or a leader, that's what you want your team to be, a bunch of people who are loyal to the team," explained *Fox & Friends'* lead host, Steve Doocy.[32] As noted in chapter 2, Trump falsely claimed that the MSNBC morning host Mika Brzezinski had paid court to him at Mar-a-Lago bleeding from a face-lift. Sean Hannity justified Trump's harshly personal untruth. "The destroy-Trump media—they're a bunch of crybaby whiners. They can't handle return fire. Oh, it only goes in one direction in their world."[33]

Trump and his supporters hoped to drive independent media out of business altogether. As early as November 2016, Sean Hannity demanded on Twitter that the Trump administration refuse to engage any independent media organizations. "If I were @realDonaldTrump NO ACCESS!"[34] Former House Speaker Newt Gingrich exceeded Hannity, urging President Trump to bar CNN and other independent media organizations from entering the White House briefing room.[35] Press Secretary Sean Spicer would experiment in February 2017 with Hannity's and Gingrich's advice, by punitively barring the *New York Times*, CNN, and the BBC from a briefing open to their competitors.[36]

Trump's attacks on the media ventured beyond criticism to outright incitement of violence. His campaign rallies triggered furious audience outbursts at members of the media—and the strategic mobilization of antimedia rage defined the Trump presidency as well. "I really think they don't like our country. I really believe that," Trump said of journalists at an August 22, 2017, rally in Phoenix, Arizona.[37] His supporters responded exactly as Trump hoped and anticipated they would. Mark Landler and Maggie Haberman reported for the *New York Times*:

> Pointing repeatedly to the cameras in the middle of a cavernous convention center, Mr. Trump whipped the crowd into fevered chants of "CNN Sucks." Members of the audience shouted epithets at reporters, some demanding that the news media stop tormenting the president with questions about his ties to Russia.[38]

Verbal violence can turn real. When it did so, Trump supporters loudly cheered. In the final hours of the May 26, 2017, special election for Montana's single congressional seat, the Republican candidate, Greg Gianforte, was asked a question he did not like by a reporter, Ben Jacobs of the *Guardian*. Gianforte, a large man, body-slammed Jacobs and then punched him. Gianforte's campaign spokesperson immediately issued a statement blaming Jacobs for initiating the confrontation. Within hours, audio and videotape of the encounter—including a police recording of the ambulance call—contradicted that statement.[39] Gianforte was charged with assault. Three Montana newspapers that had endorsed him withdrew their support. And then . . .

Then the conservative world rallied to condone Gianforte's entirely unprovoked violence. A local Fox news team had witnessed the attack and provided crucial corroboration of Jacobs's version of events. Its members were never invited onto Fox's national programs to tell their story. Instead, a Fox panel cheered Gianforte and jeered Jacobs. From *Fox News' Specialists* program, May 25, 2017:

GUEST 1: What happened there in Montana, apparently the snowflake reporter invaded Gianforte's safe space. We have a saying up there, "You mess around, you mess around, you might not be around."

GUEST 2: This guy was not a reporter looking for a fair story. He was obviously doing a takedown on him. And this guy got his back up—he got a little bit of Montana justice.[40]

That same day, the radio host Rush Limbaugh added his own endorsement of "Montana justice." (The reference to Limbaugh's laughing is from the Limbaugh program's own transcript of the monologue.)

Ladies and gentlemen, I must do something. I must join the chorus of people condemning what happened out there. This manly, obviously studly Republican candidate in Montana took the occasion to beat up a pajama-clad journalist, a Pajama Boy journalist out there.

The story is he grabbed his neck and threw the guy to the ground because the journalist was being insolent and disrespectful and whiny and moany and accusatory. And the manly, studly Republican simply didn't realize that on the big stage you can't do this kind of stuff and kicked the guy's ass to the ground. This cannot be accepted. This must be condemned. I wonder how many people in Montana are now gonna vote for the guy, though? [*Laughing*][41]

Limbaugh was not wrong that many conservatives liked Gianforte better after the assault than they did before. In the twenty-four hours after the attack, on the actual election day in Montana, Gianforte received $116,000 in donations—more than his total in the previous week. The haul was even more startling since election-day donations are by definition useless to influence the outcome of the vote.[42] The proceeds of Gianforte's attack were so lucrative that two days later the National Republican Campaign Committee used Gianforte's name and signature in a mass-mailing to fund-raise for the Republican candidate in a special election in Georgia's Sixth District. "I know with your support, [name], we can defeat Pelosi and the liberals in Georgia and the remaining special election. Can I count on you to continue your support before the last crucial FEC deadline before Georgia and the other special elections?"[43]

Gianforte's violence against a member of the press had become a monetizable asset.

The term "fake news" entered common speech to describe a very real phenomenon: manufactured disinformation then disseminated by click-maximizing hucksters, racist trolls, and foreign intelligence agencies to susceptible users of social media. As discussed in chapter 3, the most trafficked of these stories was the claim that the pope had endorsed Donald Trump. Prominent others: that Hillary Clinton was suffering from Parkinson's disease; that her aides were running a pedophile sex ring out of a pizzeria in northwest Washington, DC; that she was somehow responsible for the murder of a Democratic staffer victimized by an attempted robbery.

This kind of fake news was often concocted and then propagated with help from Russia's huge social media disinformation infrastructure. Adrian Chen offered a close-up view of this infrastructure in the *New York Times Magazine* in June 2015, well before anybody imagined how it could sway American politics:

> One Russian newspaper put the number of employees at 400, with a budget of at least 20 million rubles (roughly

$400,000) a month . . . creating content for every popular social network: LiveJournal, which remains popular in Russia; VKontakte, Russia's homegrown version of Facebook; Facebook; Twitter; Instagram; and the comment sections of Russian news outlets. One employee estimated the operation filled 40 rooms.

Chen described the artistry behind the highest-priority trolling:

While other workers churned out blandly pro-Kremlin comments, [this] department created appealing online characters who were supposed to stand out from the horde. [Chen's source] posed as three of these creations, running a blog for each one on LiveJournal. One alter ego was a fortuneteller named Cantadora. The spirit world offered Cantadora insight into relationships, weight loss, feng shui—and, occasionally, geopolitics. Energies she discerned in the universe invariably showed that its arc bent toward Russia. She foretold glory for Vladimir Putin, defeat for Barack Obama and Petro Poroshenko. The point was to weave propaganda seamlessly into what appeared to be the nonpolitical musings of an everyday person.[44]

This industrial disinformation project would exert its power for Donald Trump in 2016. Massimo Calabresi reported for *Time* on how it was done:

In one case last year, senior intelligence officials tell TIME, a Russian soldier based in Ukraine successfully infiltrated a U.S. social media group by pretending to be a 42-year-old American housewife and weighing in on political debates with specially tailored messages. In another case, officials say, Russia created a fake Facebook account to spread stories on political issues like refugee resettlement to targeted reporters they believed were susceptible to influence. . . .

Moscow's agents bought ads on Facebook to target specific populations with propaganda. "They buy the ads, where it says sponsored by—they do that just as much as anybody else does," says the senior intelligence official.[45]

Facebook has since confirmed that Russian customers did indeed purchase at least $100,000 of advertising on its site, which was seen by at least ten million people in carefully targeted states and districts. Altogether, Russian messages reached 126 million Facebook users.

The 2016 presidential campaign introduced Americans to fake news as a tool of power. A term that had originated to describe intentional lying was redefined by Trump to dismiss honest reporting.

Trump deployed the term as a weapon against everything from errors made in good faith and promptly corrected (like a mistaken report that a bust of Martin Luther King Jr. had been removed from the Oval Office)[46] to the most meticulously documented truths. Trump's aide Sebastian Gorka called it "fake news" to describe the Muslim travel ban as a travel ban even after President Trump himself had resumed using the term.[47] Sean Hannity blamed CNN for staging a "fake news" incident even as he acknowledged that the incident was a hoax and CNN was blameless.[48] Increasingly, Trump's supporters use "fake news" as an epithet to mean any reporting not wholly subservient to pro-Trump messaging.

Trump's press spokeswoman Sarah Huckabee Sanders said on June 27, 2017, "I think it's the constant barrage of fake news that is directed at this president, probably, that has garnered a lot of his frustration." In the *very next sentence* she promoted the latest release by a notorious producer of fraudulently edited polemical videos: "There's a video circulating now—whether it's accurate or not, I don't know—but I would encourage everyone in this room and, frankly, everybody across the country to take a look at it."[49] To shift in under a minute from denouncing as "fake" news that is true, and then to promoting as true "news" that is fake—well, there is the Trump White House, captured and revealed.

Russian-originated fake news is not a uniquely American problem. Centrist leaders across the continent of Europe have been beset by it. One striking example was deployed in the 2017 French presidential election. The Moscow-disliked candidate Emmanuel Macron had taken part in a campaign event that featured him skillfully gutting an eel— obviously an important credential for any would-be president of France. Eel gutting is messy work, and so after the job was completed, Macron washed himself before shaking hands with local voters. Somebody edited the eel-gutting video to create the false impression that Macron had washed his hands in snobbish disgust *after shaking hands with working-class voters*. The doctored news was then spread by pro-Putin and pro–Le Pen French-language sites.[50]

Days before the French vote, hackers dumped a ten-gigabyte trove of emails stolen from the Macron campaign. A Trump-friendly social media troll named Jack Posobiec somehow got advance notice of the impending dump. (Posobiec—then affiliated with Canada's *Rebel Media*—was issued White House press credentials in April 2017.) According to security experts quoted by Dustin Volz of Reuters, Posobiec was the very first person to use the hashtag #MacronLeaks.[51]

Yet even this kind of non-US fakery doubled back on the Trump administration. Emilio Ferrara of the University of Southern California observed the overlap between pro-Trump and anti-Macron social media accounts. In an academic paper reported by Jordan Pearson for Vice Media, Ferrara concluded: "Of the nearly 100,000 users in the sample who participated in the MacronLeaks discussion on Twitter, 18,000 were bots," many of which had previously tweeted anti-Clinton materials in 2016. Ferrara speculated that perhaps there existed a black market for bot accounts, but it's surely at least equally plausible that the relationship is political rather than monetary.[52]

You can expect to see more and worse of this stuff in future elections. Technology already exists—and will soon be commercialized—that will enable Internet trolls to create fake video clips of politicians and celebrities that will look and sound exactly like the impersonated original. Meanwhile, the line between fake-news trolling and ordinary right-of-center journalism is blurring.

The fake-news troll Mike Cernovich—a propagator of the hoax that people associated with the Clinton campaign were running a pedophile sex ring out of a Northwest DC pizzeria—not only got access to the White House press briefing room, but began regularly receiving White House tips and leaks. It was to Cernovich that Trump officials leaked their complaint that Obama's former national security adviser Susan Rice had "unmasked" their Russian ties.[53] The trolls at *Gateway Pundit*, who had assiduously promoted Russian-invented disinformation about the supposed detention of 1,500 US service personnel at Turkey's Incirlik Air Base, among many other fantasies, were accredited to the White House press corps by the Trump administration in February 2017.[54]

On the other side of the podium, disregard for truth amounted to a positive job qualification in the Trump White House. Sarah Huckabee Sanders's mulish denials, Sean Spicer's guilty squirming, Kellyanne Conway's brazen non sequiturs, made TV celebrities of each. But outright lying is a high-risk media strategy. Among the things that made the early Trump White House press briefings such fascinating viewing was the ever more open disdain of the assembled journalists for Sean Spicer, and the ever tarter sarcasm of their follow-up questions. Rather than contest this battle, the Trump administration increasingly avoided it. White House press briefings were taken off camera, then closed even to recording devices, then cut to less than a quarter of an hour. Secretary of State Rex Tillerson refused to allow journalists to travel with him, creating an absurd situation in which the American public often learned about the actions of the secretary of state from the controlled media of foreign authoritarian governments.[55]

The avoidance strategy, however, also had its limits. It is not as if the press vanishes when an administration declines to speak. The press continues to ask—and sooner or later somebody will answer. The Trump administration, among the least intentionally communicative presidential administrations in history, also quickly proved the leakiest. An AP report of May 13, 2017, wonderfully conveyed the irony:

> Trump is said to be seething over the flood of leaks pouring out of the White House and into news reports. He's viewed even senior advisers suspiciously, including Bannon and Priebus, when stories about internal White House drama land in the press. A dozen White House officials and others close to Trump detailed the president's decision-making and his mood on the condition of anonymity in order to discuss private conversations and deliberations.[56]

All presidents chafe against their press coverage. Donald Trump actually has less to complain about than almost any of his predecessors.

No president—not Barack Obama, not John F. Kennedy—has benefited more from slavish and sycophantic coverage from the media organizations that influence his supporters the most: Fox News, Breitbart, *Newsmax*, and the English-language propaganda outlets of the Russian state, Sputnik and RT. It often seems that, like Stalin's cabinet ministers, Fox News' hosts compete to offer the most abject flattery to a president who watches more TV than any other in history.

Even with more independent-minded media, Trump got better coverage than he might have expected. The practices and taboos of traditional media forbade them to report on many things discreditable to Trump but deemed by them not of legitimate public interest. Much that might have been embarrassing in Trump's personal and family life went unreported for these reasons.

The traditional media's commitment to "both sides of the story" created within them an insatiable internal demand for positive comments about a president about whom there was otherwise so little good to say. On cable and on prestigious op-ed pages, nothing was a surer path to prominence than devising some—any!—praise or defense of Trump. Hence the desperate hunt by CNN for pro-Trump talking heads; hence the weird participation trophies that even Trump-skeptical commentators awarded the president when and if he behaved in a relatively normal way for a few consecutive hours.

"This was presidential, this was big-league stuff," said CNN's David Gergen after Donald Trump's first face-to-face meeting as president with Vladimir Putin.[57] "He became president of the United States in that moment, period. There are a lot of people who have reason to be fearful of him, to be mad at him. But that was one of the most extraordinary moments you have ever seen in American politics," said CNN's Van Jones after Trump paid tribute to the widow of a Navy SEAL in his first speech to a joint session of Congress.[58]

President Trump, however, did not notice or appreciate this bias in his favor. He raved and raged and seethed in self-pity. His claque at Fox and on talk radio agreed with and amplified him.

The United States used to champion rights and liberties around the world. In his July 2017 trip to Warsaw, however, Donald Trump stood side by side with Polish president Andrzej Duda and joined him in a joint attack on press freedom. Trump opened with an attack on CNN and NBC ("Despite the fact that I made them a fortune with *The Apprentice*, but they forgot that"). He then turned to the Polish president and asked him, "Do you have that also, Mr. President?"[59] Duda smiled and agreed. Duda's party had politicized Poland's state broadcaster, converting it into a propaganda outlet for the governing party, and then banned independent media organizations from reporting inside the Polish parliament. The outright ban had to be abandoned in the face of public protests, but stringent restrictions on the coverage of both parliament and the courts remained in place.[60]

CNN's Tom Kludt asked a White House spokesperson for comment on this apparently unprecedented attack on the free media by an American president on foreign soil—and received the following answer:

> This is a president who was elected by the American people for telling it like it is and he will do that no matter the setting, unlike many in the media and political circles who change their messaging based on the audience and venue. Furthermore, the media certainly has no problem attacking the President on the global stage.[61]

Elected leaders normally accept press criticism as part of the job. Trump could not endure even a taste of it, a vulnerability mockingly commented upon by Vladimir Putin at their first post-election face-to-face meeting. The journalist-murdering Russian leader jerked a thumb at the American press corps and slyly asked Trump, "Are these the ones who have hurt your feelings?"[62]

Restrictions on media freedom are an early warning sign of de-democratization in declining democracies. Turkey, once the great hope for democratization in the Islamic world, detained hundreds of journalists during the April 2017 referendum campaign to concentrate power in the hands of its authoritarian leader Recep Tayyip Erdoğan.[63] Hungary's Viktor Orbán politicized his country's state broadcaster and used government advertising to bring privately owned print media under his party's control. South Africa's state broadcaster refuses to cover protests against the governing African National Congress and has fired journalists who defy its ban.[64] India's Narendra Modi forced a liberal TV channel off the air for twenty-four hours in November 2016 to punish it for allegedly compromising national security.[65]

More than on any other issue—more than on taxes, or health care, or immigration, or trade, or anything else he supposedly cares about—President Trump has made it his supreme and highest priority to defame those who responsibly and accurately report his tenure of his high office. What Donald Trump wants is more bias, not less; more fake news, not less. What he demands from the media is not objectivity, but complicity.

And from the right-of-center media, complicity is what Trump is getting. Trump is doing all this with the acquiescence of the institutional Republican Party and the support of conservatives across the country. What we are seeing here is not merely one man's petty ego needs on display, although we are certainly seeing that.

What we are seeing is a grant of permission from millions of people to the president of the United States to diminish, discredit, corrode, and ultimately subvert what the authors of the US Bill of Rights listed among the very first freedoms necessary to their great experiment in self-government.

CHAPTER 7

RIGGED SYSTEM

A record 137.5 million Americans voted in 2016," reported the Pew Research Center after the fact.[1] That achievement, however, was marred by some odd discrepancies.

African American electoral participation has steadily risen over the past decades, reaching a peak of more than 65 percent of those eligible in the presidential election of 2012. Four years later, only 58 percent of eligible black Americans cast a ballot, a decline unprecedented in modern times for any American ethnic group.

Perhaps black voters were uninspired by Hillary Clinton's candidacy. "Young Black Voters Voice Doubts About Clinton," reported the *New York Times* on September 5, 2016.[2] On the other hand, similar headlines could surely have been reported about John Kerry in 2004. Yet African Americans turned out for Kerry in greater percentages than for Hillary Clinton.

Something else happened to dampen African American participation in the election of 2016, and that something was the surge of Republican victories at the state and local levels during the Obama presidency. Republicans entered the 2016 cycle controlling all elected branches of government in half the states in the country, their best showing since the 1920s. Democrats controlled only seven states, their worst showing since Reconstruction.

Among the first uses to which Republicans put their ascendancy was revising state voting procedures. Between 2010 and 2016, some twenty states rewrote their laws in ways that made voting more difficult, often with blatantly partisan effect. For example, six states cut back on early and weekend voting. Early voting encourages participation by minority voters, who tend to have less control over their working hours. By contrast, mail-in ballots—preferred by the elderly and by military personnel, and historically the most fraud-prone element of the American electoral system—went untouched. Ten states instituted new voter identification rules, again often with partisan effect. Texas, for example, allowed only seven forms of identification: a concealed-carry permit was acceptable; a photo ID from the state university system was not.[3]

Of the twenty states that raised new difficulties to voting during the Obama years, only six did so in time for 2012; fourteen in time for 2016. One of the most consequential of the pre-2016 changes occurred in Wisconsin, a must-win state for Republicans: the abolition of the state's "special registration deputies," individuals certified by the state to check proofs of eligibility and add names to the voter rolls. These deputies had played a critical role in minority registration drives in the city of Milwaukee. In their stead, Wisconsin instituted a system of online registration more convenient to those with computer access and savvy—and a stark impediment to those who lack either or both.[4]

Mike Pence's Indiana did not lag far behind. An August investigation led by Fatima Hussein of the *Indianapolis Star* found that

Republicans used their control of state and local government to reduce early voting options in center-city Indianapolis and expand them in the Republican suburbs to the northeast. Early voting stations in GOP-leaning Hamilton County were multiplied from one to three; in Democrat-favoring Marion County, they were cut from three to one. Result: while early absentee voting rose by 63 percent in Hamilton between 2008 and 2016, it tumbled by 26 percent in Marion. Options were expanded in other Republican counties as well, helping to shift the state from Obama's Democratic column in the presidential election of 2008 back to Romney and Trump in 2012 and 2016.

Enabling many of these changes was a 2013 Supreme Court decision, *Shelby County v. Holder,* that put an end to the most biting section of the 1965 Voting Rights Act. That section required nine states (Alabama, Alaska, Arizona, Georgia, Louisiana, Mississippi, South Carolina, Texas, and Virginia) as well as some forty counties (in states including California, Florida, New York, and North Carolina) to gain preclearance from the federal Department of Justice for changes to their voting rules.

At the time Republican-led states adopted their new voting rules, Donald Trump's candidacy for president was imagined by virtually nobody. Wisconsin's governor, Scott Walker, hoped that the 2016 Republican presidential nominee might be himself. But the new system was positioned for Trump to use—and to weaponize with some special measures all his own.

Throughout their existence as members of a self-governing republic, Americans have fused a deep conviction that "here, the people rule" with a deep ambivalence about who exactly should be enumerated among "the people." This ambivalence has never been resolved, and if anything seems to have become more intensely felt over the past quarter century. The same Marist poll quoted in the previous chapter that showed that 43 percent of Republicans thought the country had "gone too far" in protecting the rights of the media also showed that a quarter of them believed the United States had gone "too far" in protecting the right to vote.[5]

As the country has become polarized between rich and poor, and as the white majority in the United States has dwindled, a mood of anxiety has gripped those who feel themselves vulnerable to new demands on the state. This anxiety was eloquently expressed by Paul Ryan's 2011 "tipping point" speech:

> America is drawing perilously close to a tipping point that has the potential to curtail free enterprise, transform our government, and weaken our national identity in ways that may not be reversible.
>
> The tipping point represents two dangers: first, long-term economic decline as the number of makers diminishes and the number of takers grows . . . and second, gradual moral-political decline as dependency and passivity weaken the nation's character.[6]

The same thought was expressed more crudely the next year by Donald Trump Jr., who in October 2012 tweeted, "The American republic will endure until the day Congress discovers it can bribe the public with the public's money," a remark he (spuriously) attributed to Alexis de Tocqueville.[7]

The elder Trump articulated the same apprehension for the future in a September 2016 interview with the Christian Broadcasting Network's David Brody.

> I think this will be the last election if I don't win. I think this will be the last election that the Republicans have a chance of

winning because you're going to have people flowing across the border, you're going to have illegal immigrants coming in and they're going to be legalized and they're going to be able to vote and once that all happens you can forget it. You're not going to have one Republican vote. And it's already a hard number. Already the path is much more difficult for the Republicans. You just have to look at the maps.[8]

It was not out of the ether that Donald Trump confected his postelection claim that he lost the popular vote only because "millions" voted illegally.[9] Such claims have been circulating in the Republican world for some time, based in some cases on purported statistical evidence.[10] Beyond the evidence, however, was fear: fear that the time would soon come, and maybe already had come, when democracy would be turned against those who regarded themselves as its rightful winners and proper custodians. That fear can legitimize actions that once would have seemed utterly unacceptable, antidemocratic, un-American, verging on the treasonable.

Through the 2016 campaign, Trump had denounced American democracy as a "rigged system": rigged against him, specifically, by a "small handful of global special interests." Trump's final campaign ad, released on November 6, 2016, showed three faces to illustrate those "global special interests": the financier George Soros; the chair of the Federal Reserve, Janet Yellen; and the CEO of Goldman Sachs, Lloyd Blankfein. A voice-over intoned:

It's a global power structure that is responsible for the economic decisions that have robbed our working class, stripped our country of its wealth, and put that money into the pockets of a handful of large corporations and political entities.[11]

The Anti-Defamation League issued a worried statement about this closing appeal:

> Whether intentional or not, the images and rhetoric in this ad touch on subjects that anti-Semites have used for ages. This needs to stop. In the final days before the election, tensions are extremely high. It's a time when all candidates need to be especially responsible and bid for votes by offering sincere ideas and policy proposals, not by conjuring painful stereotypes and baseless conspiracy theories.[12]

But for some Republicans, Trump's "rigging" claims represented an opportunity rather than an embarrassment. Trump followed up his ungrounded claims of widespread illegal voting by forming a presidential advisory commission on electoral integrity under Vice President Mike Pence. The commission's strongest personality, Kansas's secretary of state, Kris Kobach, had long argued that US elections were corrupted by illegal voting—and that the proper remedy was the frequent and aggressive purging of voter registration rolls.

Duplication of voter registration is an endemic feature of American life. A young person born in one state who attends college in another, finds a first job in a third, and then settles down in a fourth could leave a trail of registrations behind her, because nobody invests much energy removing people from registration rolls when they leave a state. On the other hand, there's very scant evidence that this duplication of registration leads to duplication of *votes*. While it's theoretically imaginable that our itinerant young person could fraudulently request absentee ballots from states one, two, and three, the lawbreaking would require considerable effort. Absentee ballots are typically sent by US mail only to the recorded street addresses, so the fraud-minded voter will have to arrange some kind of multi-state collection service.

To ascertain whether a Juan Garcia Gomez who cast a ballot in Kansas is the same person or different from a Juan Garcia Gomez who voted in Nebraska requires much more specific information, such as a Social Security number. State law, however, typically protects individual voter information. For that reason, fifteen states refused to cooperate with the Pence commission, contending that its requests for voters' names, birth dates, and Social Security numbers violated state law; those states were Arizona, California, Connecticut, Delaware, Kentucky, Massachusetts, Minnesota, Mississippi, New Mexico, New York, Pennsylvania, South Dakota, Tennessee, Virginia, and Wyoming. Others signaled negative responses soon to come: Arkansas, Hawaii, Illinois, Louisiana, Maryland, Montana, and Rhode Island. The majority of the states that did offer cooperation with the commission insisted that they would provide only publicly available information, not including Social Security numbers, for example.[13] (Wisconsin added that it would provide the federal government publicly available information only on the same terms it provides voter information to political parties: on payment of a fee of $12,500.)

But of course the publicly available information would not advance the commission's case very far. Vexed, President Trump angrily demanded in a July 1, 2017, tweet:

> Numerous states are refusing to give information to the very distinguished VOTER FRAUD PANEL. What are they trying to hide?[14]

The answer to that presidential question quickly became obvious, as the White House was forced to acknowledge that it lacked a secure means to store voters' information. It would be too grimly ironic if a White House project to stop voter fraud instead created a centralized database of voter information that hackers could access . . . to enable voter fraud.

This fear is not at all a hypothetical concern. The Russian effort to subvert the 2016 information did not stop at "fake news." Hackers attacked state voting systems too: 150,000 attempts just in the state of South Carolina.[15] Like the invading Martians in H. G. Wells's *War of the Worlds*, who are ultimately laid low by humble earthly diseases, the Russian hackers were impeded by the decentralized chaos of American voting systems. If election-critical information is centrally stored, however, it will have to be effectively secured. The competence record of a White House that routinely misspells names, bungles titles, and makes crude factual errors in the course of wrongly accusing others of factual errors is not reassuring.[16]

I write this book, and perhaps you read it, at a time when many details of the Trump-Russia collusion remain unsettled. Yet the essential elements of the transaction have been apparent since the summer of 2016: Russia mounted a costly and aggressive espionage campaign to help elect Donald Trump and congressional Republicans and to defeat Hillary Clinton and congressional Democrats.[17] Donald Trump's son, son-in-law, and campaign manager privately met with Russian spies offering damaging information about Hillary Clinton. "If it's what you say I love it especially later in the summer," replied Donald Trump Jr. to the offer of Russian aid, an offer that specifically referenced "Russia and its government's support for Mr. Trump."[18]

Trump's team of foreign policy advisers in 2016 was led by people who had received pay from the Russian state or state-controlled businesses.[19] Most troublingly—and without overstepping what has yet been proved—it certainly *looks* as if the Trump campaign coordinated its strategy and messaging with Russian-sponsored hacking and disinformation efforts.[20]

But the culpability does not stop with Donald Trump, his family, or even his campaign.

In December 2016, the *Washington Post* reported on what had happened when congressional leaders were briefed on the Russian hacks earlier that year.

> In September, during a secret briefing for congressional leaders, Senate Majority Leader Mitch McConnell (R-Ky.) voiced doubts about the veracity of the intelligence, according to officials present. . . .
>
> In a secure room in the Capitol used for briefings involving classified information, administration officials broadly laid out the evidence U.S. spy agencies had collected, showing Russia's role in cyber-intrusions in at least two states and in hacking the emails of the Democratic organizations and individuals.
>
> And they made a case for a united, bipartisan front in response to what one official described as "the threat posed by unprecedented meddling by a foreign power in our election process."
>
> The Democratic leaders in the room unanimously agreed on the need to take the threat seriously. Republicans, however, were divided, with at least two GOP lawmakers reluctant to accede to the White House requests.
>
> According to several officials, McConnell raised doubts about the underlying intelligence and made clear to the administration that he would consider any effort by the White House to challenge the Russians publicly an act of partisan politics.

Some of the Republicans in the briefing also seemed opposed to the idea of going public with such explosive allegations in the final stages of an election, a move that they argued would only rattle public confidence and play into Moscow's hands.[21]

The Obama administration observed increasingly assertive Russian attacks on European political systems as early as 2014. For reasons we will learn from the memoirs its members write, the Obama administration hesitated to respond. Was it to protect its Iran diplomacy? A hope it could mollify Russia into ending aggression against Ukraine? A more general aversion to forceful foreign policy? Overconfidence in the robustness of democratic political systems, including its own? Whatever the motive, the results are as we have seen: warnings were issued to Russia, but no action was taken during the election, and only very limited penalties applied afterward, most notably the seizure of two Russian diplomatic compounds.

By then it was too late. A president beholden to Russia had been installed in the Oval Office: the most successful foreign espionage attempt against the United States in the nation's history. And from beginning to end, the president's political party rallied to protect him—and itself—from investigation, exposure, and consequences.

"I'll be the first one to come out and point to Russia if there's clear evidence," declared House intelligence chair Devin Nunes in December 2016.[22] Instead, over the following months, Nunes actively collaborated with the Trump White House to sabotage his committee's investigation, to the point where he was forced to recuse himself from further involvement. House Speaker Ryan issued multiple statements viewing Russia's behavior with alarm in 2016. But Ryan took a firm stance from the beginning against anybody digging too deep into what had happened. "As we work to protect our democracy from foreign influence," Ryan said in a written statement of December 12, 2016, "we should not cast doubt on the clear and decisive outcome of this election."[23] When in June 2017 the Senate voted 97–2 to limit President Trump's ability to lift sanctions on Russia, Ryan whipped votes in the House to block the measure.[24] (An amended version of the June sanctions bill did pass both houses at the end of July and was signed by President Trump in August.[25] The sanctions remained unimplemented as of November 1, 2017.)

Even supposed Russia hawks like Senator Marco Rubio came to Trump's aid when it counted. At the June 8, 2017, public hearing for the fired FBI director James Comey, Rubio used his public airtime to try to extract admissions that would discredit Comey and exculpate the president. Remember, Trump himself had acknowledged in an interview with NBC's Lester Holt on May 11 that he had fired Comey precisely in order to put an end to the "made-up story" that Russia helped him win the election. Trump's motive for firing Comey was no longer a matter in dispute. Yet it was Rubio more than any other senator on the committee who endeavored to distract from that undisputed fact.

> **RUBIO**: But the specific ask was that you would tell the American people what you had already told him, what you had already told the leaders of Congress, both Democrats and Republicans: that he was not personally under investigation. . . .
>
> **COMEY**: Yes, sir, that's how I . . .
>
> **RUBIO**: In fact, he was asking you to do what you have done here today. . . .
>
> **RUBIO**: So, in essence, the president agreed with your statement that it would be great if we could have an investigation,

all the facts came out and we found nothing. So he agreed that that would be ideal, but this cloud is still messing up my ability to do the rest of my agenda.

RUBIO: So are those the other—are those the only two instances in which that sort of back-and-forth happened, where the president was basically saying, and I'm paraphrasing here, it's OK, do the Russia investigation. I hope it all comes out. I have nothing to do with anything Russia. It'd be great if it all came out, if people around me were doing things that were wrong.

RUBIO: You know, this investigation is full of leaks, left and right. I mean, we've learned more from the newspapers sometimes than we do from our open hearings, for sure. You ever wonder why, of all the things in this investigation, the only thing that's never been leaked is the fact that the president was not personally under investigation, despite the fact that both Democrats and Republicans in the leadership of Congress knew that, and have known that for weeks?[26]

That last sentence, it should be noted, was the single most often heard pro-Trump talking point of the period. Rubio dutifully reprised it for the watching world.

The truth outed, as truth tends to do, especially with Trump's stumblebum crew. The line written into the script of *All the President's Men* about Watergate applies even more forcefully to the Trump family and its entourage: "The truth is, these aren't very bright guys, and things got out of hand." But it is also true that the wrong actions of Donald Trump and his family were protected before the fact, and condoned after the fact, by the larger Republican and conservative world. I jokingly tweeted at the end of May that after all the excuses condoning Greg Gianforte's assault on Ben

Jacobs, we would next be called on to explain why treason is bad.[27] That joke all too quickly proved prophetic.

Geraldo Rivera opened the excuse making on the May 10, 2017, *Hannity* show.

> If the Russian KGB chief is talking to Paul Manafort and the chief says, "You know, I've got this dirt here that says Hillary Clinton was this or that," and Paul Manafort says, "Next Wednesday, why don't you release that, that'd be great for us." That's not—I don't know that that's a crime at all. What's the crime?[28]

In a conversation with me on the May 21, 2017, edition of CNN's *Fareed Zakaria GPS*, the pro-Trump author Ronald Kessler said, "There's no violation of law if, in fact, the campaign colluded with Russia, whatever that means."[29] The conservative radio host Michael Reagan said the same thing in a CNN discussion on May 31: "Collusion is not breaking the law."[30]

On his June 22, 2017, television program, Sean Hannity and former Speaker Newt Gingrich agreed that it would be a positive benefit to the United States if Trump had worked with the Russians against Hillary Clinton. "If I worked for President Trump and his campaign, and I thought the Russians had information that would expose Hillary for being a liar, and I said, 'Could you release that?' Is that a crime?"[31]

Hannity returned to the theme on his radio program the next day:

> What was the collusion? That maybe somebody in the Trump campaign talked to somebody in Russia because Russia supposedly had the information that Hillary Clinton had destroyed on her server when she committed a felony and tried

to cover up her crimes? Is that a crime, to say, "Release it?"
To show the truth? To show damaging information?[32]

The former Fox anchor Brit Hume similarly absolved the Trump
campaign on the June 25 *Fox News Sunday*. "While it obviously
would be alarming and highly inappropriate for the Trump campaign to—of which there's no evidence, by the way, of colluding with
the Russians—it's not a crime."[33] Some went further still, wondering
why anybody need worry about Russia at all. "The news media in
the West pose a far greater danger to Western civilization than Russia does," tweeted the radio host Dennis Prager on July 14, 2017.[34]

Whether collusion with a Russian espionage agency would violate US election laws raises complex issues of legal interpretation.
The national security implications, however, are straightforward
and grim. A candidate who had received help from a hostile foreign power would depend hugely on that power's goodwill. What
if they released evidence against him? They could wreck his presidency, provoke an impeachment crisis, possibly send him to prison.
He would have to govern himself very circumspectly, even at political risk to himself at home. Collusion between a US president and
a hostile foreign power would constitute the gravest espionage crisis
in American history—and one of its blackest pages of treason.

The below timeline of relevant events was compiled by NBC
News, abridged by me with some interpolations in bold type.

June 9, 2016: Donald Trump Jr.—along with Jared Kushner
and Trump's former campaign chair Paul Manafort—meet
with the Kremlin-connected lawyer Natalia Veselnitskaya.
  June 9: Trump tweets for the first time about Clinton's
missing 33,000 emails.

July 18: The *Washington Post* reports on the first day of the GOP convention that the Trump campaign changed the Republican platform to ensure that it didn't call for giving weapons to Ukraine to fight Russian and rebel forces.

July 21: **Trump gives an interview to David Sanger and Maggie Haberman of the *New York Times* in which he repeatedly refuses to commit to defending NATO's Baltic allies Latvia, Lithuania, and Estonia against Russia.**

July 22: WikiLeaks releases emails stolen from the Democratic National Committee.

July 27: In the final news conference of his 2016 campaign, Trump tells Russia: "If you're listening, I hope you're able to find the thirty thousand emails that are missing."

August 4: Obama's CIA director, John Brennan, confronts his Russian counterpart about Russia's interference.

October 4: WikiLeaks' Julian Assange says his organization will publish emails related to the 2016 campaign.

October 7: The Department of Homeland Security and the director of national intelligence release a statement directly saying that Russia is interfering in the 2016 election.

October 7: **The *Washington Post* reports the *Access Hollywood* video.**

October 7: WikiLeaks begins releasing emails stolen from Clinton's campaign chair, John Podesta, **less than one hour after the *Washington Post* report.**

October 31: "This WikiLeaks is like a treasure trove," Trump says on the campaign trail.

November 4: "Boy, I love reading those WikiLeaks," Trump says from Ohio.[35]

All this may be coincidence, a sequence of misunderstandings. But it does not look good for the integrity of the American political system. The authoritarians of older times abolished elections altogether or falsified them so outrageously as to render them meaningless. Modern authoritarian states do not so explicitly renounce the democratic idea. Even Vladimir Putin's Russia has elections in which millions of people vote, and it's not at all obvious that Putin cheats very much in the counting of that vote. In the Russian parliamentary elections of September 2016, Vladimir Putin's party won a perfectly plausible 54 percent of the vote, on the basis of a turnout that the regime candidly described as the lowest since the end of communism.[36] In Putin's system, if you have to cheat in the vote counting, you've left things far too late. And Putin's is the most repressive of the world's de-democratizing states. The others—places such as Hungary, the Philippines, South Africa, Turkey, and so on—distort the election processes even less, although just enough to preclude unwelcome results.

In modern authoritarian states, unapproved candidates are deterred from running; disfavored people are discouraged from voting. Votes may be counted honestly enough, but voting systems are tilted in favor of the party of the leader. In the Hungarian elections of 2014, for example, the party of the prime minister won 133 out of 199 parliamentary seats, with only 44.9 percent of the vote. In such states, state resources are directed in ways that support the party of the leader. State-owned and state-influenced media spread disinformation and defamation about opponents. Rather than discuss issues, ethnic grievances are stoked—and when outsiders report on what is happening, the regime exploits the opportunity to denounce a hostile external world for defaming the nation.

Americans regard their democracy as beyond comparison to such sad international cases. Yet here too the democratic system was and is harshly contested. The right of all adult citizens to vote is no longer seriously debated by Americans, but the universal ability to vote seems to encounter new obstacles with every passing year. If Donald Trump entrenches himself in power, those obstacles will rise higher and proliferate more numerously across the American political landscape.

The fear that the younger Donald Trump inserted into Tocqueville's mouth—that a democracy can last only until citizens discover they can vote themselves benefits—actually originated nearer to home. "A democracy cannot exist as a permanent form of government. It can only exist until the majority discovers it can vote itself largess out of the public treasury. After that, the majority always votes for the candidate promising the most benefits with the result that democracy collapses." Those oft-quoted words, also sometimes attributed to Aristotle and Thomas Babington Macaulay, seem to have originated in a 1951 op-ed in the *Daily Oklahoman* by a retired Wisconsin state senator.[37] What's interesting about those words is not how prescient they are, but really how opposite to the truth.

In the United States as in other countries, the great threat to constitutional democracy has not been the demands for largesse by the many, but the fears for their property of the few. The most successful antidemocratic movement in American history—the reduction of voting rights after Reconstruction—was intended precisely to thwart local majorities voting themselves such benefits as schooling and paying for it by higher taxes on the rich. The rollback worked too. Only 50,752 ballots were cast by the 1.7 million people of South Carolina in the election of 1924, half as many as cast by 700,000 South Carolinians in 1872. (Connecticut, with 300,000 fewer people than South Carolina in 1924, cast eight times as many votes).

Now in the 2010s, the integrity of American democracy is challenged again—and again the challenge is backed by threats of armed violence. In June 2017, a rumor spread via Facebook that protesters planned to rally at a park in Houston, Texas, to demand the removal of a statue of Sam Houston. Hundreds of supporters of the statue rallied, a large number of them carrying rifles, some wearing body armor.

Hermann Park, the site of the Sam Houston statue, is one of the city of Houston's most visited parks. The Houston Zoo is located within it; the Children's Museum of Houston stands just a few blocks away. On weekends, the park is typically crowded with young families. Yet some dozens of Texans decided that this would be an appropriate place to plan a gunfight. And of course they were entirely within their rights, as those rights are understood in twenty-first-century America. Texas law forbids citizens to carry deadly weapons "in a manner calculated to alarm." Otherwise, long arms may be shouldered by virtually anyone in almost any place. It might be thought that bringing a rifle into a playground is itself "calculated to alarm." But over the past generation, gun carriers have become much more assertive and the authorities much more accommodating.

Gun carriers at the so-called Unite the Right rally in Charlottesville in August 2017 acted more like a paramilitary force than as individual demonstrators. They wore pseudo-military outfits, including body armor. They took tactical formations to surround the site of the expected confrontation—although when murder was done, it was done ISIS-style, by ramming a car into a crowd of demonstrators.

The City Council of San Antonio, Texas, met in August 2017 to debate removal of a Confederate monument from that city's Travis Park. Ten men bearing assault rifles and wearing Kevlar vests took positions outside the council's chambers.[38]

The open display of military-style weapons at public meetings is not an ancient right cherished by Americans through the centuries. "Among free men," Abraham Lincoln famously wrote, "there can be no successful appeal from the ballot to the bullet; and that they who take such an appeal are sure to lose their case, and pay the cost."[39] Yet just such a threat is what is being issued in Houston and Charlottesville and San Antonio—and more places yet to come.

The following happened in Loudoun County, Virginia, on Election Day 2016.

A man wearing a Donald Trump shirt and carrying a weapon stood outside a voting location in Loudoun County, Virginia. . . . "I had my 9-year-old son with me. I felt intimidated," [Erika] Cotti said. "And I had to explain to my 9-year-old why a man with a 357 magnum is standing outside the polling station."

Cotti said the man offered her a Republican sample ballot, which she declined.

"He's like, 'Who are you going to vote for, crooked Hillary?' And I was like, 'That's really none of your business,'" Cotti said, adding that the man was standing in the sidewalk outside of the office when they left and blocking their path.[40]

Will there be more such incidents in 2018 and 2020? It's all quite legal. In many Americans' minds, the right to carry arms is now the master right of American law, to which all other rights must yield. In 1994, the average gun-owning household owned four weapons; by 2015, the average gun-owning household owned eight.[41]

At a press conference in the lobby of Trump Tower two days after the violence in Charlottesville, Trump channeled the feelings of the men who carried guns to prevent an elected government from putting lawful decisions into effect. "You had people in that group that were there to protest the taking down of, to them, a very, very important statue and the renaming of a park from Robert E. Lee to another name."[42] (The new name to which Trump objected was "Emancipation Park.") A week later still, at an August 22, 2017, rally in Phoenix, Arizona, Trump again identified himself with those defending Confederate monuments by force of arms: "Yes, by the way, they are trying to take away our history and our heritage. You see that."[43]

Through the 2016 campaign, Trump had condoned political violence by his supporters against protesters in their midst: "You know what they used to do to guys like that when they were in a place like this? They'd be carried out on a stretcher, folks."[44]

Back then, however, the cause was purely personal: his own election, unconnected to any larger movement in American society or culture. As Trump's personal popularity sagged, he sought larger and bigger forces to sustain him. Speaking to police officers in Long Island, Trump endorsed intentional police brutality against members of Salvadoran gangs, whom he condemned as "animals."

> They kidnap. They extort. They rape and they rob. They stomp on their victims. They beat them with clubs, they slash them with machetes, and they stab them with knives. They have transformed peaceful parks and beautiful quiet neighborhoods into bloodstained killing fields. They're animals.[45]

When dealing with such subhumans, the police should dispense with legal niceties, urged the president.

When you see . . . these thugs being thrown into the back of a paddy wagon, you just see them thrown in, rough, and I said, "Please don't be too nice." Like when you guys put somebody in the car and you're protecting their head, you know, the way you put their hand over, like, don't hit their head and they've just killed somebody, don't hit their head, I said, "You can take the hand away, OK?"[46]

Those remarks drew what was described as "wild applause" from the police attending.[47] And even though the president's words were promptly repudiated by senior police leaders across the nation, those who shared a national origin or a skin tone or a last name with the people Trump regarded as "animals" must wonder: *Has the president of the United States authorized such actions against me as well?*

The American economic system might feel "rigged" against Trump supporters. But the American political system of 2016 had in important ways been rigged in Trump's favor. Yet as Trump and his supporters looked to the future, how secure could they feel? Their hold on the electorate was weak. Foreign governments' hold over them was possibly very strong. Maybe the answer—the only answer—was not to rig less, but to rig much more.

CHAPTER 8

AMERICA ALONE

merica First doesn't mean America alone." Gary Cohn and H. R. McMaster, President Trump's highest-ranking economic and national security aides, offered that assurance in an op-ed for the *Wall Street Journal* at the end of May 2017.[1] They were too sanguine. Month by month through the Trump presidency, the United States found itself more isolated from its former friends and allies.

Through the spring and summer of 2017, President Trump escalated his rhetoric against North Korea. The escalation culminated in a bloodcurdling interview with Reuters on April 27. "There is a chance that we could end up having a major, major conflict with North Korea."[2] "North Korea best not make any more threats to the United States. They will be met with fire and fury like the world has never seen," he told television cameras in the Cabinet Room on August 9.[3] "The United States has great strength and patience, but if it is forced to defend itself or its allies, we will have no choice but to totally destroy North

Korea," Trump told the United Nations General Assembly on September 19.[4]

Yet even as he pushed toward conflict, Trump himself was gratuitously threatening and insulting the single country whose cooperation would seem most obviously necessary to any tough policy on North Korea: South Korea. It would be South Korea that would do most of the fighting, most of the dying, most of the suffering, and most of the paying in the "major, major conflict" Trump spoke of so lightly. And yet in the *very same Reuters interview* in which Trump menaced North Korea, he embarked on an angry rampage against the South.

He announced intentions to cancel the US–South Korea Free Trade Agreement. "It's unacceptable. It's a horrible deal made by Hillary. It's a horrible deal. And we're going to renegotiate that deal, or terminate it." He demanded an additional $1 billion payment from South Korea for a missile defense deployment already negotiated, reneging on a deal stipulating that the United States would provide the weapon system if South Korea provided the land.

> I said, "Why are we paying? Why are we paying a billion dollars? We're protecting. Why are we paying a billion dollars?" So I informed South Korea it would be appropriate if they paid. Nobody's going to do that. Why are we paying a billion dollars? It's a billion-dollar system. It's phenomenal. It's the most incredible equipment you've ever seen—shoots missiles right out of the sky. And it protects them and I want to protect them. We're going to protect them. But they should pay for that, and they understand that.

It should surprise nobody that neither of these complaints had much truth to it. South Korea is threatened less by North Korean missiles than by the thousands of North Korean artillery tubes aimed at Seoul. Military experts believe the North could reduce the South's capital to rubble within twenty-four hours. The Terminal High-Altitude Aerial Defense (THAAD) system over which Trump haggled in public with South Korea is positioned south of Seoul, primarily to protect US bases in the Korean Peninsula. Hillary Clinton had little to do with the US–South Korea Free Trade Agreement. A framework inherited from the George W. Bush administration was revised in 2009 and 2010 by President Obama's trade negotiators to provide more protection for the US automobile industry against Korean imports.

What happened next should also surprise nobody: the South Korean presidential election ten days after the Reuters interview was decisively won by the more US-skeptical candidate—who promptly suspended deployment of the THAAD system for which Trump had tried to shake his country down.

Only two weeks before, the Trump administration had stumbled into a farcical embarrassment. Interviewed on Fox Business on April 12, 2017, Trump had announced that he was sending "an armada, very powerful" into Korean waters to warn the North against making trouble. Six days later, the US Navy posted online a photograph of the fleet in question—the aircraft carrier *Carl Vinson* and four other warships—3,500 miles away and heading in the opposite direction: southwestward through the Sunda Strait into the Indian Ocean. The most conservative and America friendly of the three Korean presidential candidates, Hong Joon-pyo, ventilated the fiercest anger against his false-tongued ally: "What Mr. Trump said was very important for the national security of South Korea. If that was a lie, then during Trump's term, South Korea will not trust whatever Trump says."[5] Trump had already irritated Koreans by credulously repeating to the *Wall Street Journal* the chauvinist claim by China's president that "Korea actually used to be a part of China."[6] For reasons nobody in Korea could discern—and nobody in the United States either—President Trump seemed intent on belittling, deceiving, and making public fools of them. But if they could not guess his motives, they could still resent his treatment. At the end of President Obama's term, according to the Pew survey, 88 percent of South Koreans expressed confidence that the US president would do the right thing in world affairs. In June 2017, only 17 percent of South Koreans expressed such confidence in President Trump.[7]

South Korea reacted more angrily than many other allied countries, but not radically so. Among citizens of other Asia-Pacific allies, 78 percent of Japanese had expressed confidence in Obama; only 24 percent in Trump. Eighty-four percent of Australians trusted Obama; only 29 percent Trump. (That latter number might have been even worse for Trump if the poll had been conducted after the August 3, 2017, leak of a January telephone transcript in which Trump told Australian prime minister Malcolm Turnbull that he found it more "pleasant" to talk to Vladimir Putin than to the leader of America's truest and most militarily capable Asia-Pacific ally.[8])

Only in the Philippines did a majority, 69 percent, trust Trump—and even there, a higher percentage (94 percent) had trusted Obama.

America's southern neighbors have long mistrusted the power of the United States. "Poor Mexico! So far from God, so close to the United States," goes the saying usually attributed to the Mexican ruler Porfirio Díaz. In 2013, 38 percent of adult Mexicans described US power as a potential threat to their country; in the first year of the Trump presidency, that number vaulted to 61 percent.[9]

The European numbers looked even more dismal. In a span of months, trust in the US president to do the right thing dropped by forty-three points in Italy, fifty-seven points in the United Kingdom, seventy points in France, and seventy-five points in Germany.

The Trump-Germany relationship started bad, and got worse. November 9 is the most portentous date in the German calendar: the day the kaiser abdicated in 1918, of Kristallnacht in 1938, and of the opening of the Berlin Wall in 1989. On that morning in 2016, the German government awoke to the news that its American partners and protectors had elected to the presidency an authoritarian nationalist of an all-too-familiar stamp. German chancellor Angela Merkel released as faint and hedged a message of congratulation to President-Elect Donald Trump as one ally has perhaps ever offered another:

> Germany and America are bound by common values—democracy, freedom, as well as respect for the rule of law and the dignity of each and every person, regardless of their origin, skin color, creed, gender, sexual orientation, or political views. It is based on these values that I wish to offer close cooperation, both with me personally and between our countries' governments.[10]

Note two things about this message: its offer of cooperation is conditional, and Germany will be the judge of whether the conditions have been met.

America's allies around the world always have preferences in US elections. In 2004, Germany's Gerhard Schröder and France's Jacques Chirac did not conceal their hope that George W. Bush would lose to John F. Kerry. In 2012, Israel's Benjamin Netanyahu visibly yearned to see the back of Barack Obama. Still, once it's all over, allies disappointed in the result swallow their chagrin and get down to business.

The year 2016 was different.

Donald Trump made clear from the very start that there was no doing business with the vaunted dealmaker. He demanded everything; he offered nothing. "Trump was upset at the notion that allies' interests should be taken into account."[11] So Tracy Wilkinson and Brian Bennett reported in the *Los Angeles Times* in July 2017 about Trump's review of the Iran nuclear deal. The phrase could be applied to almost any foreign policy matter. Foreign leaders quickly perceived that Trump could easily be manipulated, but never reasoned with.

On June 5, 2017, four American Arab allies—Bahrain, Egypt, Saudi Arabia, and the United Arab Emirates—abruptly cut diplomatic ties with a fifth, Qatar. The Saudi bloc accused Qatar of support for terrorism. They suspended Qatar's overflight rights and restricted trade and travel. Iranian president Hassan Rouhani seized the opportunity to wedge apart the pro-American Gulf states, saying, "Iran's airspace, sea, and ground transport links will always be open to Qatar, our brotherly and neighbor country."[12] Qatar's regional ally Turkey reinforced its troop presence in the peninsular emirate.

US intelligence services soon confirmed that Qatar had been the victim of a disinformation campaign by the United Arab Emirates. Karen DeYoung and Ellen Nakashima reported in the *Washington Post* on July 16, 2017:

> The United Arab Emirates orchestrated the hacking of Qatari government news and social media sites in order to post incendiary false quotes attributed to Qatar's emir, Sheikh Tamim Bin Hamad al-Thani, in late May that sparked the ongoing upheaval between Qatar and its neighbors, according to U.S. intelligence officials.
>
> Officials became aware last week that newly analyzed information gathered by U.S. intelligence agencies confirmed

that on May 23, senior members of the UAE government discussed the plan and its implementation. The officials said it remains unclear whether the UAE carried out the hacks itself or contracted to have them done.[13]

Given Qatar's importance to Western regional strategy—it houses the largest American base in the Gulf, from which the Pentagon flies anti-ISIS air strikes—the Qatar matter called for utmost delicacy. Only . . . his head turned by Saudi flattery and gifts, President Trump had already taken a vehement public stand against Qatar.

"During my recent trip to the Middle East I stated that there can no longer be funding of Radical Ideology. Leaders pointed to Qatar—look!" he tweeted at 8:06 a.m. on June 6, 2017. At 9:36 Trump posted, "So good to see the Saudi Arabia visit with the King and 50 countries already paying off. They said they would take a hard line on funding . . ." adding at 9:44, ". . . extremism, and all reference was pointing to Qatar. Perhaps this will be the beginning of the end to the horror of terrorism!"

As Marc Champion and Marek Strzelecki together reported for Bloomberg News on July 19:

> United Arab Emirates Foreign Minister Anwar Gargash confirmed this week that Trump's "very, very successful" trip to the Gulf in May had helped trigger the decision by his country—together with Saudi Arabia, Egypt, and Bahrain—to launch a political and economic assault on Qatar.[14]

President Trump may well not have known Qatar's importance to America's regional military strategy. He surely did know that Qatar's national airline had once been a tenant in New York's Trump

Tower, and that it had let the lease lapse in 2014. Worse, Qatar had unwisely held its December 6, 2016, national day celebration in Washington in the National Portrait Gallery. By contrast, Qatar's rival Bahrain had correctly sited its December 7, 2016, national day celebration in Trump's Washington, DC, hotel. Lobbyists for Saudi Arabia had spent $270,000 in the hotel between October 2016 and March 2017.[15] Whatever the motive, the result badly damaged the US strategic position—and intensified the world's distrust of America's undisciplined and self-dealing president.

The increasingly authoritarian leaders of Poland likewise exploited Trump's inattention and indifference. In chapter 7, I described Trump's strange indulgence of that government's crackdown on press freedoms during his visit to Warsaw. After Trump departed, the governing party seems to have interpreted his praise for Poland as "safe, strong, and free," as permission for another outrage, this time against Poland's courts.[16] The government crammed through two houses of parliament a bill summarily retiring the entire Polish Supreme Court and empowering the governing party's justice minister to name all their successors. Only by mobilizing demonstrations larger than anything since the end of communist rule in 1989 did the liberal opposition compel Poland's president to veto his own party's legislation.

The Trump presidency empowered dictators worldwide, by dimming American ideals and by hobbling American power. In the first six months of 2017, the government of Vietnam arrested fifteen people for antistate activities, more than in any year since 2011. Matthew Tostevin reported for Reuters:

> Every activist and analyst that Reuters interviewed mentioned a perceived shift in U.S. priorities under Trump as a new factor in reducing pressure on Vietnam's government.

Not only was Washington paying less attention to the region or to human rights, but Trump gave Vietnam less reason to show willingness to address human rights issues when he dropped the [Trans Pacific Partnership] trade deal, in the name of an "America First" policy.[17]

No foreign leader manipulated Trump more adeptly than Vladimir Putin. "Why should I tell Putin what to do?" Trump had demanded at a July 27, 2016, press conference.[18] Yet it often seemed that Putin had found a way to tell Trump what to do.

Trump's deference to Putin reverberated through the western alliance. Countries that relied on the United States to protect them from Russia worried that they could rely on America no longer. The leaders of the European allies knew early about Donald Trump's long and disreputable financial connections to Russia. The British had direct access to the US collection of Russians cackling and chortling over their successful penetration of the American election system. The French and Germans and Poles had sources of their own. All could recognize in Donald Trump something much graver than a merely difficult partner. Trump seemed intent on a diplomatic revolution. At the core of this revolution: a presidentially led assault on the cohesion of the European Union.

George W. Bush observed in 2003, "Since the end of World War II, the United States has strongly supported European unity as the best path to European peace and prosperity."[19] That was a precisely accurate statement. From Truman through Obama, America's European policy has been strikingly consistent: the United States has supported a democratic and united Europe joined to Canada and the United States by NATO.

"We recognize we will benefit more from a strong and equal partner than from a weak one."[20] Those words happen to have been pronounced by Bill Clinton. They could as easily have appeared in a speech by any of his predecessors or successors. Until Trump. Trump has more than once dismissed NATO as "obsolete." In an interview at the time of the Republican convention, he repeatedly and forcefully expressed uncertainty about whether, as president, he would honor America's NATO obligations to small countries threatened by Russia.[21] He cheered Britain's exit from the European Union. Trump and his chief campaign strategist, Steve Bannon, made common cause with populist nationalists working to end the European Union outright. President-Elect Trump received Nigel Farage, the former leader of the UK Independence Party, before he met British Prime Minister Theresa May. Before Bannon joined the Trump campaign, he promoted the Dutch politician Geert Wilders and France's Marine Le Pen on his Breitbart.com website. Hungary's authoritarian prime minister, Viktor Orbán, claimed to have been granted a call with President-Elect Trump in November before the president of France.

As president, Trump sharpened his hostility to the European allies. Reuters reported in February on an encounter with Steve Bannon that persuaded Peter Wittig, Germany's ambassador to the United States, to prepare for a policy of "hostility towards the EU."[22] Ambassador Wittig proved prescient.

"You have to think about it this way: We are in a trade war. We have been for decades." So said Trump's secretary of commerce, Wilbur Ross, on CNBC on March 31, 2017.[23] Secretary Ross did not specify America's enemies in that war, but his frequent coauthor Peter Navarro—appointed by President Trump to head a newly created "National Trade Council"—identified Germany as one of them. "Germany is one of the most difficult trade deficits that we're going to have to deal with but we're thinking long and hard about that," said Navarro in a March 6, 2017, speech.[24]

Trump's diplomacy reserved its smiles for nondemocracies that offered commercial opportunities, not only in the Persian Gulf and the Philippines, but even in the case of as bad an actor as Recep Erdoğan's Turkey, also home to a major Trump-branded project in Istanbul. Secretary of State Rex Tillerson visited Turkey on July 15, 2017, the one-year anniversary of an attempted coup that the Erdoğan regime had used as an excuse for mass roundups of political opponents, and especially journalists. In April 2017, a fraud-stained referendum had approved constitutional amendments that would empower Erdoğan to rule for life. Yet Tillerson had this to say at Erdoğan's self-honoring anniversary ceremony:

> We're all here in Istanbul at a momentous time. Nearly a year ago, the Turkish people—brave men and women—stood up against coup plotters and defended their democracy.[25]

New friendships sought among dictatorships; old friendships burned among democracies. That was the product of "thinking long and hard."

The key element of this long and hard thought: a new refusal by the Trump administration to respect the European Union's 2007 treaty agreement to adopt a common external trade policy. In consequence, EU member nations no longer field their own trade negotiators—a fact that President Trump steadfastly refused to acknowledge. "The negotiators for Germany have done a far better job than the negotiators for the United States," Trump said at a March 18, 2017, joint press conference in Washington. "But hopefully we can even it out."[26] Merkel reminded him at that same press conference: "The European Union is negotiating those agreements for all of the member states."[27]

Trump often revealed ignorance of basic facts about the international order, but something more than ignorance was at work here. In his March speech, Navarro had explicitly cited Germany's EU treaty commitments as a flimsy excuse the United States would ignore under President Trump. "I think that it would be useful to have candid discussions with Germany about ways that we could possibly get that deficit reduced *outside the boundaries and restrictions that they claim that they are under*" (my italics).

President Trump returned to the theme on Twitter on May 30, 2017, writing, "We have a MASSIVE trade deficit with Germany, plus they pay FAR LESS than they should on NATO & military. Very bad for U.S. This will change."[28] By then, though, something else had changed too. At a major speech in Munich on May 28, 2017, ten days after her first bilateral meeting with Trump, Merkel had brought down the curtain on an epoch in US-Germany relations. Speaking in her characteristically careful style, the chancellor delivered a warning to Germans and Americans alike:

> The times when we could completely rely on others are, to an extent, over. I experienced that in the last few days, and therefore I can only say that we Europeans must really take our fate into our own hands, of course in friendship with the United States and in friendship with Great Britain and as good neighbors wherever it is possible, also with Russia and also with all the other countries. But we need to know that we have to fight for our own future and destiny as Europeans.[29]

This is precisely what Trump rejected. Past American presidents heralded a more united Europe as a counterweight to the Soviet Union and then Russia. A united Europe would be a superpower in its own right, with a population more than triple that of Russia and an economy more than twelve times as large. Trump resented European unity because it also enhanced European power as against the United States. Trump interpreted international affairs as he interpreted everything: as a struggle for dominance, never cooperation among equals.

In his February 2017 CPAC address, Trump expressed plainly his vision of a world economy in which America domineered over a subservient planet. "We are going to make trade deals, but we're going to do one-on-one, one-on-one. And if they misbehave, we terminate the deal. And then they'll come back and we'll make a better deal. None of these big quagmire deals that are a disaster."[30]

The beauty of one-on-one deals, from Trump's point of view, is that in such deals the United States for the foreseeable future will almost always overawe its counterparty. It can impose one-sided terms, act as judge and jury in its own cause, demand endless revisions in its own favor.

The Americans and friends of America who built the post-1945 world order foresaw the temptation to abuse American dominance. They had fought a terrible war against would-be global empires. They repudiated constructing one of their own. They keenly appreciated America's unique power and unrivaled wealth. They understood that these advantages would diminish over time. They deliberately built a world system that accorded large and small states more equality of respect than ever before in world history. They designed trade and treaty systems governed by rules, rules to which the United States would submit like any other country. Indeed, they intended exactly the things that Donald Trump now complains about: that the United States would have to make concessions to smaller partners, that it would not act as judge in its own cases, that it would subordinate its parochial and immediate national interests to the larger and more enduring collective interest. America would find its own security by working for the security of others.

Americans accepted a new world order that constrained their own power in part because they were accustomed to such constraints at home. The US Constitution likewise overweights smaller states and rural minorities against urban majorities. But they had also learned from the catastrophes of world history. It is dangerous for any state, no matter how strong, to attempt to subordinate all others. Selfish hegemons from the Habsburg emperor Charles V to the Soviet dictator Joseph Stalin summoned up coalitions to topple them—and no single state could ever prevail against so many adversaries. In the world as at home, systems that serve the interests of all endure better than systems that oppress many to serve a few.

Upholding that system has become even more challenging since the end of the Cold War. American allies feel less frightened of Russia, more attracted by the opportunities of a rising China, and less accepting of American actions they dislike, from the Iraq War to electronic surveillance. (Germans acclaim Obama now, but after the Snowden revelations of 2014 the German government expelled the CIA station chief in Berlin, a shocking action by a NATO partner.[31]) Whoever became president in 2016 would need extraordinary vision and tact to manage a more refractory world system, one in which year by year the United States and its core allies counted for less, and China, India, and other emerging economies counted for more. Instead, the United States stumbled into a presidency determined to smash that system. Trump hoped that an unconstrained America could grab more power for itself (and thereby for him). He never understood that America's power arose not only from its own wealth and its own military force, but from its centrality to a network of friends and allies.

During the election cycle, external observers of American politics often wondered—and sharply pressed anyone they regarded as a DC insider—whether there might be some method to Trump's madness. Did his outbursts and tirades, disconcerting as they were, perhaps follow some shrewd strategy? After Election Day, the hunt for Trump's logic naturally intensified.

It did not take long for that search to be abandoned as futile. Receiving Sergey Lavrov, the Russian foreign minister, in the Oval Office in mid-May, Trump blurted a crucial counterterrorism secret entrusted to the United States by a regional ally. Greg Miller and Greg Jaffe reported for the *Washington Post* on May 15, 2017:

> In his meeting with Lavrov, Trump seemed to be boasting about his inside knowledge of the looming threat. "I get great intel. I have people brief me on great intel every day," the president said, according to an official with knowledge of the exchange.
>
> Trump went on to discuss aspects of the threat that the United States learned only through the espionage capabilities of a key partner. He did not reveal the specific intelligence-gathering method, but he described how the Islamic State was pursuing elements of a specific plot and how much harm such an attack could cause under varying circumstances. Most alarmingly, officials said, Trump revealed the city in the Islamic State's territory where the U.S. intelligence partner detected the threat.[32]

From that point, speculation about Trump's secret strategy almost entirely ceased. "More and more, he looks like a complete moron," a veteran of Trump's presidential campaign groused to the *Daily Beast*.[33]

Moron or no, Trump remained the president and still wielded the vast power of that office—or anyway could do so on days he bothered to show up, pay attention, and make decisions. This fact could not be ignored or elided. If a Donald Trump presidency could happen, anything could happen. American words could no longer be trusted, American reactions no longer predicted. If, as seemed increasingly possible, Trump had been helped into the presidency by a Russian intelligence operation, then the ultimate guarantor of the whole world order had revealed a system-shaking vulnerability—as if the Red Cross could not manage a blood bank, as if the Federal Reserve had run out of dollars. Every international actor, benign or malign, had to take the new information into account. America's friends might hope that the Trump presidency would prove short, its activities limited and ineffectual. They could count the months and minutes until a return to something more like normal. But things could never wholly return to normal again, could they?

Long after Donald Trump retires to the great golf club in the sky, prudent allies will remember what the Trump presidency revealed about the American political system, and not just the single man who held that office.

In a 2014 speech, Trump's future political adviser Steve Bannon proposed Vladimir Putin as the true leader of a new kind of global conservative movement. Bannon is a vague and discursive talker who habitually attributes his own thoughts to unnamed others, so it's necessary to quote him at some length.

> At least Putin is standing up for traditional institutions, and he's trying to do it in a form of nationalism—and I think that people, particularly in certain countries, want to see the sovereignty for their country, they want to see nationalism for their country. They don't believe in this kind of pan-European Union or they don't believe in the centralized government in the United States. They'd rather see more of

a states-based entity that the founders originally set up where freedoms were controlled at the local level.

We the Judeo-Christian West really have to look at what he's [Putin] talking about as far as traditionalism goes—particularly the sense of where it supports the underpinnings of nationalism—and I happen to think that the individual sovereignty of a country is a good thing and a strong thing. I think strong countries and strong nationalist movements in countries make strong neighbors, and that is really the building blocks that built Western Europe and the United States, and I think it's what can see us forward.

You know, Putin's been quite an interesting character. He's also very, very, very intelligent. I can see this in the United States where he's playing very strongly to social conservatives about his message about more traditional values.[34]

The conservative journalist Chris Caldwell articulated a more lucid explication of Bannon's 2014 message at Hillsdale College in February 2017:

So why are people thinking about Putin as much as they do? Because he has become a symbol of national self-determination. Populist conservatives see him the way progressives once saw Fidel Castro, as the one person who says he won't submit to the world that surrounds him. You didn't have to be a Communist to appreciate the way Castro, whatever his excesses, was carving out a space of autonomy for his country.

In the same way, Putin's conduct is bound to win sympathy even from some of Russia's enemies, the ones who feel the international system is not delivering for them. Generally, if you like that system, you will consider Vladimir Putin a menace. If you don't like it, you will have some sympathy for him. Putin has become a symbol of national sovereignty in its battle with globalism. That turns out to be the big battle of our times.[35]

In that battle—if a battle is the right metaphor—Donald Trump has aligned with Putin against almost all of America's most important allies, and the US national security apparatus has demonstrated an incapacity to constrain or moderate him. Vivian Salama of the Associated Press reported in mid-July 2017:

Deep divisions are increasingly apparent within the administration on the best way to approach Moscow in the midst of U.S. investigations into Russian meddling in the American presidential election. Trump has repeatedly cast doubt on the conclusion of U.S. intelligence agencies that the Russian government sought to tip the election in his favor and has dismissed investigations into the possibility of collusion between his campaign and Moscow as a "witch hunt."

Meanwhile, he has pushed for cooperation between Moscow and Washington on various matters including the raging conflict in Syria.

But some top aides, including National Security Adviser Gen. H.R. McMaster, have been warning that Putin is not to be trusted. . . .

[One US official said] diplomats and intelligence officials were "dumbfounded" by the president's approach.[36]

The dumbfounding only accelerated from there.

Days previous to that AP report, Greg Jaffe and Adam Entous

broke the news in the *Washington Post* that the Trump administration had terminated aid to CIA-backed anti-Assad forces inside Syria.[37] The Trump administration had signaled this decision in late March 2017, when it announced that it would no longer demand the ouster of the Syrian dictator Bashar al-Assad—a reversal not only of Obama administration policy, but of a long-standing Republican congressional demand.[38]

Assad must go, insisted Senate Majority Leader Mitch McConnell at a press conference in April 2017. "I don't see how there can possibly be any settlement in Syria that includes Bashar al Assad. I just can't imagine after all the butchering of his own people that he's been doing now for four or five years that there could be any successful conclusion to this chaos with him still there."[39]

"Assad must go," read the headline on an April 2017 press release from Ed Royce, the Republican chair of the House Foreign Affairs Committee. "With more than 480,000 people killed by the regime, and 14 million driven from their homes, it is clear there is no hope for real peace in Syria until Assad is held accountable."[40]

Assad must go, had declared a group of Republicans on the Senate Foreign Relations Committee: Florida's Marco Rubio, Colorado's Cory Gardner, Oklahoma's James Lankford, and Tennessee's Bob Corker, the committee's chairman.[41] Assad must go, agreed two Republicans on the Senate Armed Services Committee: John McCain and Tom Cotton.[42]

"Assad's crimes against humanity cannot go unanswered," declared House Speaker Paul Ryan in a May 2017 statement.[43] "The United States of America should be prepared to use military force to strike military targets of the Assad regime," intoned Mike Pence in the October 2016 vice presidential debate.[44]

Against this overwhelming party consensus, Trump imposed a policy about-face. "This is a momentous decision. Putin won in

Syria," said one of the *Washington Post*'s sources on the policy reversal.

The regulars lost on staffing too.

The former national security adviser Michael Flynn had chosen as his deputy K. T. McFarland, a Fox News host who had last served in government in the 1980s as a speechwriter to Secretary of Defense Caspar Weinberger. Bloomberg reported in early April that Flynn's replacement, H. R. McMaster, had forced McFarland out, banishing her 9,700 miles and eight time zones away to the ambassadorship to Singapore.[45] Three months later, McFarland was still in Washington, still coming to work at the NSC.

Trump appointed as a counterterrorism adviser Sebastian Gorka, a Breitbart blogger who pleaded guilty in August 2016 to attempting to board a flight at Reagan Airport with a gun in his carry-on bag.[46] It took almost nine months for H. R. McMaster and Chief of Staff John Kelly to dispense with Gorka's services to the United States.

The most disturbing personality in the Trump national security system, however, was always Trump himself. Enraged by information that law enforcement agencies had surveilled his campaign chairman, Paul Manafort, President Trump emitted a bizarre sequence of tweets on March 4, 2017. Trump alleged that former president Obama had ordered listening devices installed to monitor Trump himself. "How low has President Obama gone to tapp [*sic*] my phones during the very sacred election process. This is Nixon/Watergate stuff. Bad or sick guy!"[47] In an effort to substantiate Trump's wild and false claims, press secretary Sean Spicer repeated at the White House briefing podium an assertion by a Fox News personality that Britain's signal agency GCHQ had carried out the "tapping" at Obama's behest. That assertion was in turn based on rumors circulated on Russian television and pro-Moscow websites. An obviously embarrassed Spicer raced through a mumbled reading of the allegation. However miserably Spicer felt about it, he dutifully hurled the false and alliance-damaging accusation from behind the Great Seal of the United States.[48] In a September 1, 2017, court filing the Trump Department of Justice would formally acknowledge that the president's accusation of "tapps" had been baseless from the start. "Both FBI and NSD [the National Security Division within the FBI] confirm that they have no records related to wiretaps as described by the March 4, 2017, tweets."[49] But if Trump was not "tapped," his future campaign chair Paul Manafort apparently had been surveilled, for reasons most likely arising from Manafort's work for the pro-Russian regime in Ukraine overthrown in 2014. That surveillance may have swept up conversations with candidate Trump.

How were allies to interpret all this? A president caught in surveillance because he had accepted pro bono campaign services from the same operative who had previously served Putin's many in Kyiv? Something had obviously gone terribly wrong inside the American national security apparatus. That apparatus abruptly seemed largely powerless to protect itself, much less friends and allies. What choice did those allies and friends have except to make their own new arrangements for a world in which the United States could no longer be trusted? In which the president of the United States seemed at best a destructive incompetent; at worst, an outright Russian intelligence asset?

The wrongness sank deeper than national strategy, deeper than military affairs, deeper than staff and secrets. The wrongness seemed to have darkened and distorted the very idea of America to the rest of the world.

Early in 1990, in the joyous months after the collapse of the communist regimes of central Europe, Czechoslovakia's president, Václav Havel, addressed a joint session of Congress. To explain the past and future of his own country, the great writer interwove a long meditation on what the United States had meant to Europe and the world.

> Wasn't it the best minds of your country, people you could call intellectuals, who wrote your famous Declaration of Independence, your bill of human rights, and your Constitution and who, above all, took upon themselves practical responsibility for putting them into practice? . . . Those great documents . . . inspire us all; they inspire us despite the fact that they are over 200 years old. They inspire us to be citizens.[50]

Which democratic ally would address the United States Congress in such terms in the Trump era? The government of the United States seems to have made common cause with the planet's thugs, crooks, and dictators against its own ideals—and in fact to have imported the spirit of thuggery, crookedness, and dictatorship into the very core of the American state, into the most solemn symbolic oval center of its law and liberty. The man inside that oval center did not act alone. He held his power with the connivance of others. They executed his orders and empowered his whims for crass and cowardly reasons of their own: partisanship, ambition, greed for gain, eagerness for attention, ideological zeal, careerist conformity, or—in the worst cases—malicious glee in the wreck of things they could never have built themselves. They claim the symbols of the republic as they subvert its institutions. They pin the flag to their lapels before commencing the day's work of lying, obstructing, and corrupting. They speak for America to a world that remembers a different and better America. But that memory is already fading into a question of whether it was not perhaps always an illusion, whether this new regime of deceit and brutishness will not only form the future—but whether it also retrospectively discredits the American past.

CHAPTER 9

———

AUTOIMMUNE DISORDER

f the national security apparatus could not constrain President Trump, neither would it go down without a struggle. Trump had the power of the presidency; his bureaucratic opponents, the weapon of the leak. No administration ever has been so perforated by leaks as Donald Trump's. As the joke went, it fell to Donald Trump to deliver on Barack Obama's promise of "the most transparent administration ever."

Those leaks thwarted many of the worst impulses of the new Trump administration. Leaks swiftly removed from office Trump's profoundly compromised first choice for national security adviser, Michael Flynn. Leaks alerted the world that President Trump had blabbed a crucial military secret to the Russian foreign minister. Leaks deterred the Trump administration from lifting sanctions on Russia as soon as it entered office, as Michael Isikoff reported for *Yahoo News* in June 2017:

In the early weeks of the Trump administration, former Obama administration officials and State Department staff-

171

ers fought an intense, behind-the-scenes battle to head off efforts by incoming officials to normalize relations with Russia, according to multiple sources familiar with the events.

Unknown to the public at the time, top Trump administration officials, almost as soon as they took office, tasked State Department staffers with developing proposals for the lifting of economic sanctions, the return of diplomatic compounds and other steps to relieve tensions with Moscow.

These efforts to relax or remove punitive measures imposed by President Obama in retaliation for Russia's intervention in Ukraine and meddling in the 2016 election alarmed some State Department officials, who immediately began lobbying congressional leaders to quickly pass legislation to block the move, the sources said.[1]

Yet the same leaks that thwarted Trump's pro-Putin agenda also exacted a heavy price. Those leaks revealed US surveillance capabilities in a way that compromised national security. For example, Greg Miller, Adam Entous, and Ellen Nakashima broke the news in the February 9, 2017, *Washington Post* that Flynn had lied when he denied speaking to Russian ambassador Sergey Kislyak about sanctions relief.

Nine current and former officials, who were in senior positions at multiple agencies at the time of the calls, spoke on the condition of anonymity to discuss intelligence matters.

All of those officials said Flynn's references to the election-related sanctions were explicit. Two of those officials went further, saying that Flynn urged Russia not to overreact to the penalties being imposed by President Barack Obama,

making clear that the two sides would be in position to review the matter after Trump was sworn in as president.

"Kislyak was left with the impression that the sanctions
would be revisited at a later time," said a former official.[2]

Kislyak, being no novice and no fool, would have conducted
his conversation with Flynn by some modality he regarded as safe
from American surveillance. In order to expose Flynn's lie, the nine
officials who talked to the *Post* also revealed to the Russians that
the United States had cracked a link that Russian intelligence op-
eratives had regarded as secure.

It had to be assumed that the Russian embassy would immediately alter its communications methods, denying the United States
future information flows, at least for some period of time. To protect the United States from a compromised national security adviser, nine senior intelligence officials agreed to burn an important
American national secret.

Such trade-offs would occur again and again.

As noted in the previous chapter, Trump blurted an important secret to Russian foreign minister Sergey Lavrov in the Oval
Office on May 10, 2017. Trump's boastful blabber mouthery was
bad for many reasons, but on its own, the blurt may have done
only limited harm. The secret purportedly exposed an Israeli penetration of ISIS communications. The Russians might have shared
that information with their clients inside Syria and their partners
in Iran. But would any of those actors—Russia, Iran, or the Assad
regime—have shared the information with ISIS? Perhaps ISIS in
turn has penetrated the Assad regime. Still, all those risks were more
roundabout than what happened next: the possible divulgence of
the substance of the secret to the news media by disgusted national

security professionals. (I've used hedged language here because it is not impossible that the secondary round of leaks consisted of deliberate *disinformation* from national security professionals, frantically trying to minimize the harm of the president's mistake.)

Even if the round-two leaks were disinformation, however, the revelation, as legitimately public spirited as it was, inflicted yet another harm. A president—any president—would normally expect his staff to protect the confidentiality of his deliberations, including the inevitable mistakes that any human being will make: the goofs, gaffes, grievances, lapses of memory, political incorrectnesses, and remarks-best-not-repeated-outside-this-room that have echoed off the walls of government ever since those walls were erected.

Donald Trump says more things that should not be said than any president in American history. But also more than any president in history, he works in an office he cannot trust and knows he cannot trust. Donald Trump may not be a proper president, or a competent president, or a patriotic president, or even a legitimate president in any larger ethical sense of the word "legitimate." But he is the lawful president, charged with public functions. In order to stop him from betraying his office and the country, the professionals around him have also effectively prevented him from fulfilling his office and serving his country, supposing he were ever minded to do that. He must do his job, however he conceives that job, within a narrow ambit of relatives and cronies, selected mostly for their negative qualities: their lack of knowledge, their lack of experience, their lack of independence, their lack of integrity. The dysfunction inside the White House is Trump's fault, but it is not only Trump's problem.

The executive office of the president has until now almost always been staffed by committed people who take their jobs highly seriously. There are few slackers at a White House. The smallest jobs must be done with the greatest care; a future election can turn on whether the president has offended a local notable by mispronouncing her husband's name.

The Trump White House is a mess of careless slobs. At the highest levels, one sees mutual sabotage, easily decoded "on background" name-calling, false filings of disclosure documents, and institutionalized lying about readily ascertainable facts. The failure of leadership at the top contaminates the whole enterprise. Even the most routine work product of the Trump White House is strewn with errors of spelling, fact, and protocol, sometimes of quite serious consequence. Daniel Dale of the *Toronto Star* compiled a list of some thirty such goofs. The funniest was perhaps a July 12, 2017, release attacking the accuracy of the Congressional Budget Office that misspelled the word "inaccurately" as "innacurately." The most serious was a July 8 reference to China's Xi Jinping as "president of the Republic of China"—the Republic of China being the official name of Taiwan, of course. Along the way, the Trump White House misspelled not only the names of many of its own newly appointed officials, but also that of the prime minister of Great Britain.[3] In a prime-time television address in August 2017 about his decision to escalate the US commitment to Afghanistan, President Trump described that country's prime minister as its president. More bafflingly, on October 1, 2017, the official spokesperson for the Department of State assured the world via Twitter that North Korea would never attain the "nuclear capability" it had in fact attained in 2006.[4]

At best, the dysfunction of the Trump team has actively advanced the public interest, by unintentionally thwarting the Trump administration's more sinister instincts. But at worst, the casual incompetence has risked authentic harm. During the visit of Japanese prime minister Shinzo Abe to the United States in February

2017, Trump received word of a North Korean missile test while dining on the patio at his Mar-a-Lago club. Rather than withdraw into the secure communications area established for a president wherever he may go, Trump read a report on the situation on the spot, illuminating his reading by the light of aides' cell phones—a shocking security breach. Because mobile phones can so easily be hacked and converted into spy cameras, it's not permitted even to bring them into a secure facility, much less to point them at a sensitive document. Not only did Trump ignore that rule, so did the half dozen aides who crowded around him in the photographs snapped by other diners and posted on Facebook.[5] By the time of the May meeting with Lavrov, these egregious departures from basic operational security had been curbed, to the public benefit.

If Trump were not so locked into a tiny circle by his distrust of outsiders, his handling of health care reform might also have amounted to less of a fiasco. Trump started as something like a moderate on the health care issue. He has praised the universal systems of Canada and the United Kingdom, promised broader coverage, and defended Medicaid against criticism from the congressional party. It's easily imaginable that a more professional policy process inside the White House would have enabled him to triangulate against both congressional Democrats and Republicans, arriving at a position broadly acceptable to much of public opinion. Given Trump's extreme ignorance of health care issues, however, such a plan would require bringing aboard some authentic nonpartisan experts who could draft a policy consistent with Trump's own surprisingly generous instincts on the issue. But by the time the health care debate was reaching its peak, FBI director Comey had been fired, a special counsel, Robert Mueller, had been appointed, and the Trump White House had immured itself for siege. Welcoming somebody with no special loyalty to Trump into the council of such an embattled president: impossible and unthinkable. This enabled the do-or-die House Republicans under Speaker Ryan to hornswoggle a president with no particular commitment to their ideology into subscribing to the most crushingly unpopular item on their agenda.

The pattern would repeat itself on tax reform. Trump allowed congressional Republicans to write a tax plan that delivered little or nothing to his own constituencies within the party. Trump relied heavily for advice on a treasury secretary so politically tone-deaf that he had sought a government plane to transport him around Europe on a three-week honeymoon. A more modest revision of the notorious inefficiency of the corporate income tax might well have gained bipartisan support: John Kerry had endorsed corporate-tax reform in 2004. Instead, Trump committed himself to yet another shove-it-through plan that left him hostage to any three nervous Republican senators.

I am not suggesting here that Trump was a victim of anything or anyone other than himself. There were sound reasons for professionals of all kinds to keep a far distance from the Trump White House. Some forty people were indicted as a result of the Watergate scandal. Among those sentenced to prison: the attorney general of the United States, the White House counsel, and President Nixon's two most senior White House aides. A dozen men were convicted or pleaded guilty to a range of charges after the Iran-Contra affair. White Houses can be dangerous places under leadership that does not respect the law. Official lying is usually unethical, but not always illegal—until suddenly the official is called before a congressional committee or federal investigation. Then he or she must choose either to confess the lie or repeat it under oath. The terms of service in the Trump White House were not only dishonorable and humiliating, but also dangerous. People with sense and people with options preferred to stay away.

Trump's abuse of the power of the presidency invited reciprocal abuses by members of other branches of government.

When President Trump banned travelers from certain Muslim-majority nations from entering the United States, he was exercising a lawful power of his office. It's well-established law that the president has power to bar "any class of aliens" both as immigrants and as nonimmigrants and to impose on their ordinary comings and goings "any restrictions he may deem appropriate."[6]

Some argued that Trump violated the Constitution by imposing a restriction that disadvantaged adherents of one religion from traveling to the United States. But the Constitution applies only to Americans. The Supreme Court ruled as recently as 2015 that the president could deny a visa to an alien for no stated reason at all! Aliens have no due process rights against the United States, and no First Amendment rights against the United States.[7]

Yet the courts have shredded Trump's travel ban anyway. In the words of the first of a series of federal judges to rule against the Trump administration: the courts could not overlook "significant and unrebutted evidence of religious animus driving the promulgation of the Executive Order and its related predecessor."[8]

To amend an old saying: Bad presidents make bad law. Because President Trump behaved in what the courts regarded as a wrongful way, the courts responded in ways they would have regarded as wrongful only twelve months before. For it was not only one judge in Hawaii who stripped Trump of previous presidential powers; the travel ban litigation would snake its way through the Ninth Circuit to the Supreme Court, the Trump administration losing at almost every step of the way. (In July 2017, the Supreme Court would uphold the administration's rights to reduce the intake of previously accepted refugees.[9])

In the travel ban litigation, the courts asserted a new power to disregard long-established and long-accepted formal law if the president's personal words created a basis for mistrusting his motives. In response to the danger posed by Trump, other holders of American power are tempted to jettison their historic role too, and to use any tool at hand, no matter how doubtfully legitimate, to stop him. In order to save the constitutional system, its defenders are at risk of corroding it.

Nowhere is that risk more acute than in the realm of civilian-military relations—and from two directions.

The first directional risk is the movement of the military into government. Barack Obama appointed one former general, Eric Shinseki, to his cabinet, to lead the Department of Veterans Affairs, and another, David Petraeus, to head the Central Intelligence Agency. George W. Bush appointed some as well, including Colin Powell as secretary of state. Bill Clinton appointed a general, Barry McCaffrey, as director of the office of drug control policy, and an admiral, William J. Crowe, as his first ambassador to the United Kingdom. Retired and active generals have more than once held the job of national security adviser: Brent Scowcroft under George H. W. Bush; Colin Powell under Ronald Reagan.

Never before, however, had a president concentrated anything near so much power in former military hands as Donald Trump did. The National Security Act of 1947 expressly forbids active or recently retired generals from serving as the secretary of defense. The ban was waived only once before, in September 1950, to permit George C. Marshall to reorganize the US armed forces, which were demoralized after their humiliating retreat down the Korean Peninsula. No such emergency existed in 2017, but Trump asked for and got a second waiver to appoint James Mattis as secretary of defense.

Trump appointed the retired general John Kelly as Homeland Security secretary and his ally, the retired general Michael Flynn, as national security adviser. When Flynn was forced to resign, Trump offered the post to a retired admiral, Bob Harward. Harward declined because Trump would not allow him to remove Steve Bannon and Jared Kushner from the NSC principals' committee. Trump next turned to General H. R. McMaster, who as an active-duty officer could not refuse. Another general, Keith Kellogg, was awkwardly inserted alongside the "No, I won't go" K. T. McFarland as a second deputy national security adviser. John Kelly would replace Reince Priebus as White House chief of staff on July 28, 2017. President Trump even appointed a former general to head the federal bureau of prisons.[10]

These are all honorable and capable men. The United States is lucky to have their service. But it's unprecedented and troubling to concentrate so many former military people into any administration. In this administration, the concentration sounds even louder warnings. The nongenerals in high office in the Trump administration were a worryingly weak group. Chris Ruddy, the CEO of *Newsmax*, emerged from a February 2017 visit with the president to disparage Chief of Staff Priebus to the *Washington Post*:

> I think on paper Reince looked good as the chief of staff—and Donald trusted him—but it's pretty clear the guy is in way over his head. He's not knowledgeable of how federal agencies work, how the communications operations work.[11]

Trump's standing secretary of state, Rex Tillerson, was weakened by a troubling Russia history of his own. In July 2017, the US Treasury Department issued a stinging assessment of Tillerson's former employer: "Exxon Mobil demonstrated reckless disregard for U.S. sanctions requirements. Exxon Mobil caused significant harm to the Ukraine-related sanctions program."[12] In light of the severity of those words, the comparatively light fine of $2 million raised yet more questions about Tillerson's role inside government and out. Even without that backstory, Tillerson would have been diminished by President Trump's evident disregard for him and his own systematic deconstruction of the department he headed. As late as midsummer 2017, the Trump administration had not submitted nominations for the assistant secretaryships of Eurasian and East Asian affairs; for Near Eastern or African affairs; for chief of protocol, for chief counselor, or for its top counterterrorism and nonproliferation jobs.[13] Despite crises in Spain and South Korea, the United States had no ambassador in either country as of October 1, 2017. There was not even a State–White House liaison— which may explain how nobody noticed that "Republic of China" mistake.[14]

In a government so weak and mismanaged, the competence of its former military personnel exerted even more gravity than otherwise. Which might have been a mercy—who wouldn't prefer that the United States be led by James Mattis than Donald Trump?—but for this fact: Military men, like people trained to any demanding specialty, acquire certain habits of mind, certain ways of looking at the world. Within a well-functioning administration, this perspective is enriching; within an administration like Donald Trump's, it can be supremely dangerous.

High among those dangers is impatience with law. Military people are selected, trained, and promoted to get results. There are no wrong ways to win a battle, after all. Procedures and protocols are all very well in their way, but to the military mind they never can be, and never should be, ends in themselves. Nobody should want to change that outlook! But that outlook, good in its place, must always be balanced in a republic of laws by the lawyer's insistence on the supremacy of legality. The most wrenching post-Watergate scandal—Iran-Contra—was the work of three military men who refused to heed this insistence: John Poindexter, Bud McFarlane, and Oliver North. Unlike the Watergate burglars, these men aimed only at the public good as they understood it. To the extent that the trammels of the law impeded them, they sliced through them as so much irritating and unnecessary red tape. Under a president who despises law even more than the most impatient general, a general's instincts become even more dangerous to him, to the government, and to the nation.

Vice President Pence enjoined the 2017 graduating class at the US Naval Academy to "follow the chain of command without exception. Submit yourselves, as the saying goes, to the authorities that have been placed above you. Trust your superiors, trust your orders, and you'll serve and lead well."[15] But that is not the American way. American officers are bound to obey only *lawful* orders. The unthinking obedience recommended by the vice president is the mentality of authoritarian states, not rule-of-law societies. Ten years after the ratification of the Constitution, the US Supreme Court rejected forever the "I was just following orders" defense. Instructions from a superior officer "cannot change the nature of the transaction, or legalize an act which without those instructions would have been a plain trespass."[16]

Most American officers do understand and will comply with that principle—which leads to the second directional risk to civilian-military relations under President Trump: the risk that the military will quietly cut an unfit president out of the chain of command.

How much does the military now tell President Trump about what it is doing, and how exactly does it follow his orders, to the extent he issues orders? In crisis zones from Syria to North Korea, the military seems to be operating with unprecedented autonomy.

President Trump has delegated to his secretary of defense the authority to set troop levels in Afghanistan.[17] The April 2017 decision to drop America's most powerful nonnuclear bomb on an ISIS compound in eastern Afghanistan was taken by the theater commander, General John Nicholson, without approval even by the secretary of defense, according to a report by Dexter Filkins in the *New Yorker*.[18] As we have already observed, the president was for days on end wholly unaware not only of the location, but even of the direction of navigation of the *Carl Vinson* carrier group.

No paper record has ever been found, but some historians of the Watergate period believe that as Richard Nixon's personality dissolved, Secretary of Defense James Schlesinger ordered the Joint Chiefs of Staff to ignore any presidential directive unless also approved by him. Is anything like that happening now? How would we know? When would we know?

That "fire and fury" threat from Donald Trump—look at what happened next. Trump clearly intended it; he repeated it twice. Yet within hours, it had been disavowed by almost every other branch of the US government.

Josh Dawsey of *Politico* tweeted the next day:

"Fire and fury" from yesterday was not carefully vetted language from Trump, per several ppl with knowledge. "Don't read too much into it."[19]

Secretary of State Tillerson also pooh-poohed the president's words, saying, "Nothing that I have seen and nothing that I know of would indicate that the situation has dramatically changed in the last twenty-four hours. Americans should sleep well at night."[20]

The final and definitive word, however, was issued as a formal written statement by Defense Secretary Mattis two days after President Trump's outburst.

The United States and our allies have the demonstrated capabilities and unquestionable commitment to defend ourselves from an attack. Kim Jong Un should take heed of the United Nations Security Council's unified voice, and statements from governments the world over, who agree the DPRK poses a threat to global security and stability. The DPRK must choose to stop isolating itself and stand down its pursuit of nuclear weapons. The DPRK should cease any consideration of actions that would lead to the end of its regime and the destruction of its people.

President Trump was informed of the growing threat last December and on taking office his first orders to me emphasized the readiness of our ballistic missile defense and nuclear deterrent forces. While our State Department is making every effort to resolve this global threat through diplomatic means, it must be noted that the combined allied militaries now possess the most precise, rehearsed and robust defensive and offensive capabilities on Earth. The DPRK regime's actions will continue to be grossly overmatched by ours and would lose any arms race or conflict it initiates.[21]

The statement stressed that war would come only if North Korea *initiated* it.

These were saner words than those mouthed by the president. But what has happened to the United States when a president—even a reckless and foolish president—is overruled by his military, even a military led by a secretary as wise as James Mattis?

Mattis's own low personal regard for President Trump accidentally became public when video emerged of Mattis in a small-group conversation with military personnel in Jordan. After praising them, the defense secretary added, "You're a great example for our country right now. It's got some problems. You know it, and I know it. It's got problems that we don't have in the military. You just hold the line, my fine young soldiers, sailors, airmen, and marines. You just hold the line until our country gets back to understanding and respecting each other, and showing it—of being friendly to one another, of understanding what Americans owe to one another. . . . We've got two powers: the power of inspiration—and you'll get the inspiration back—and the power of intimidation, and that's you."[22]

Hotheads and janissaries seldom rise to the highest ranks of the US armed forces. Men like Mattis and Kelly and McMaster have demonstrated an appreciation of and a commitment to liberal democracy exceeding that of their civilian commander in chief. Yet the principle of civilian supremacy remains indispensable even when the civilian in question has revealed himself as unfit for office. His abuses of power are for the president's fellow civilians to check, correct, and punish through the civilian processes laid down by law. The habits of military disobedience (or non-obedience), however sympathetic their origin, can quickly mutate into a chronic hazard to the state and the Constitution.

As Donald Trump settled into office, an American armored brigade was deploying in Poland, part of a repositioning of NATO forces that based a British-led force in Estonia, a Canadian-led force in Latvia, and a German-led force in Lithuania. The American force's new home is the town of Zagan, only twenty-five miles east of the German border—about the most cautious possible move into Poland without altogether abandoning the idea. Still, there they are, facing a much bigger and more rapid Russian buildup to the north and east. A soldier or officer assigned to that duty—and their families back in the United States—must wonder about the integrity of the orders that could issue from a Russia-compromised president of the United States. If they should be called on to risk their lives to serve their country, will they wonder which country their Putin-infatuated commander in chief is ultimately serving?

It's a terrible question for a patriotic soldier, a terrible dilemma for those who bear intermediate commands between the fighting troops and that compromised president. Twice in the debates of the Philadelphia convention of 1787, a delegate raised the precedent of Charles II, the king of Great Britain from 1660 to 1685, and thus then the king of America too. Charles had accepted bribes from Louis XIV to sway British foreign policy. Could such temptation come the way of an American president? Charles Cotesworth Pinckney argued that it could: "His office is not to be permanent, but temporary; and he might receive a bribe which would enable him to live in greater splendor in another country than his own."[23] Against this risk, answered Gouverneur Morris, stood the remedy of impeachment. "No one would say that we ought to expose ourselves to the danger of seeing the first Magistrate in foreign pay without being able to guard [against] it by displacing him."[24]

Yet in important ways, President Trump already is being displaced—first by his own disavowal of ordinary responsibility, then by the countermeasures being put in place against him by the national security agencies. Perhaps everything will return to normal when and if Donald Trump departs the scene. But perhaps it will not.

In national security—as with ethics in government more generally—what is usually meant by the word "normal" is the norm that prevailed from Watergate to 9/11: national security operations closely monitored by both the executive branch and Congress. Yet there have been other "normal." From Pearl Harbor until the scandals of the mid-1970s, the president often knew little—and Congress often knew nothing—about what the national security agencies were doing. Since 9/11, some of those old habits have revived, and in the Trump years they may became fully animated. National security professionals do not always trust the competence, commitment, and integrity of their political counterparts, and in the first year of the Trump presidency, those professionals have been given abundant reasons for that distrust. Will they post-Trump revert to their pre-Trump—really pre-9/11—form? What if the next president also looks like an outlier from the point of view of the Department of Defense, the CIA, and the NSA? Will the national security agencies respect a future president of the radical Left any more than they respect a President Trump? It is not only the ethno-nationalist Right that rejects the civic patriotic values the national security agencies uphold. Bureaucracies always yearn to escape political control, and the national security agencies are the most powerful, autonomous, and well-funded bureaucracies within the American state. Trump has given them powerful and righteous motives to emancipate themselves. Will they ever again fully resume the subordination that may feel by the 2020s like a relic from a bygone era?

CHAPTER 10

RESENTMENTS

N ext only to the rise of Donald Trump, the most surprising political story of 2016 was the fall of Roger Ailes. The creator and presiding eminence behind Fox News, Ailes exerted more personal and immediate influence than any media mogul since perhaps William Randolph Hearst.

And while doing so, Ailes engaged in flagrant sexual abuse of uncounted women in his power, employees and would-be employees. After the fact, Fox's publicists sadly explained, "Nobody knew." Meaning, nobody knew except all the women. *They* knew.

They knew too about Fox News's dominant on-air personality, Bill O'Reilly, who would cost the network millions in sexual-harassment settlements before ultimately being severed. They knew about the offscreen "lesser Rogers," who had learned from the master to treat their female employees as targets and opportunities.

That of course was Donald Trump's philosophy as well. Trump's partnership with Ailes was often contentious, but partnership it was—one that intensified in the final months of the 2016 election.

On NBC's *Meet the Press* after the Republican convention—and the termination of Roger Ailes by Fox News—Chuck Todd asked, "Finally, Roger Ailes. Is he helping you? Is he advising you?" Trump answered:

> Well, I don't want to comment. But he's been a friend of mine for a long time, and I can tell you that some of the women that are complaining, I know how much he's helped them. And even recently, and when they write books that are fairly recently released, and they say wonderful things about him.
>
> And now all of a sudden they're saying these horrible things about him. It's very sad. Because he's a very good person. I've always found him to be just a very, very good person. And by the way, a very, very talented person. Look what he's done. So I feel very badly. But a lot of people are thinking he's going to run my campaign.[1]

It never quite formally happened that way. Yet Trump and Ailes remained in close communication throughout the campaign. The two men shared a deep understanding of the imperatives of television—and an even more intimate connection to the resentments of the white American male.

Back in March 2016, on the night he won the Mississippi and Michigan primaries, Trump had celebrated with a triumphal press conference. The stage was decorated with Trump-branded products; somebody even found a Trump label to affix to a package of steaks, in homage to that defunct Trump brand. Sopan Deb of CBS News pressed Trump about the harsh language he had used in an ad. Trump erupted at him:

Oh, you're so politically correct. You're so beautiful. Oh. He's so—oh, I know. You've never heard a little bad, a little off language. I know, you're so perfect. Aren't you perfect? Aren't you just a perfect young man? Give me—hey, give me a break. You know what, it's stuff like that, that people in this country are tired of.[2]

Again and again through his campaign, Trump would denounce "political correctness."

At the Republican debate in Cleveland on August 6, 2015:

I think the big problem this country has is being politically correct. I've been challenged by so many people and I don't, frankly, have time for total political correctness. And to be honest with you, this country doesn't have time, either.[3]

Speaking in Portsmouth, New Hampshire, on December 10, 2015:

We can't worry about being politically correct. We just can't afford any more to be so politically correct. There's nobody in this country—if I wanted to be—that could be more politically correct than me. Nobody. I have a high education, went to an Ivy League school, I know everything, it's perfect. I could be so good. . . . But there's nobody. And I will say this: we're going to get down to brass tacks.[4]

Trump blamed "political correctness" for the atrocity at Orlando's Pulse nightclub in June 2016, the deadliest mass shooting in American history until the Las Vegas massacre of September 2017.

The current politically correct response cripples our ability to talk and think and act clearly. We're not acting clearly. We're not talking clearly. We've got problems. If we don't get tough, and if we don't get smart and fast, we're not going to have a country anymore. There will be nothing, absolutely nothing left.

We cannot talk around issues anymore. We have to address these issues head-on. I called for a ban after San Bernardino. And was met with great scorn and anger. Many are saying that I was right to do so, and although the pause is temporary, we must find out what is going on. We have to do it. It will be lifted, this ban, when and as a nation we're in a position to properly and perfectly screen these people pouring into our country. They're pouring in and we don't know what we're doing.[5]

In Des Moines, Iowa, at the third rally of his post-election "thank you" victory tour, Trump offered these thoughts about his recent appearance on the cover of *Time* magazine as its Person of the Year.

I was lucky enough to receive the *Time* Person of the Year. They used to call it "Man of the Year," but they can't do that anymore, so they call it "person." They want to be politically correct. That's OK.[6]

Trump used the phrase "politically correct" to mean many different things, from ordinary good manners to equal protection under the law. But other people heard other things, even a promise of liberation. The comedian D. L. Hughley—himself under fire for an untimely joke about the death of Debbie Reynolds—suggested in

January 2017 that "PC culture" "probably is why" Donald Trump got elected. "People are tired of being told what to think and say."[7] The *Washington Post* invited readers who had voted for Donald Trump to explain why they had done so. The paper received 1,600 responses—and PC culture was mentioned impressively often.

"I am a gay millennial woman and I voted for Donald Trump because I oppose the political correctness movement, which has become a fascist ideology of silence and ignorance," wrote a twenty-one-year-old from Gilbert, Arizona. "He was an outsider. He spoke truth about political correctness," wrote a twenty-eight-year-old woman from Sacramento, California. "I was afraid to speak my mind because of the possibility it might hurt my reputation socially and professionally," wrote a twenty-two-year-old woman from Manchester, New Hampshire.[8]

One of Trump's conservative critics during the campaign published a beguilingly candid message on election eve. "Donald Trump is a boorish buffoon with dangerously fascist instincts and on Tuesday I will vote for him, sadly, but without a qualm."[9] Why? Over the next few months, this writer—Andrew Klavan of PJ Media—would return again and again to the justification of his decision:

> A few dopey intellectuals and their absurd little notions can have outsized power: the power of the echo chamber, the power of fashionable acceptance, the power of creating the atmosphere within the Beltway Bubble. And while Republicans frequently strut and fret about their opposition to leftist malarkey, they just as frequently acquiesce to it in the event. . . . Trump [is] deaf to the echo chamber, indifferent to media acceptance, immune to the atmosphere. In fact, some of the very things that make Trump unappealing to

gentle folk like me—his belligerence, his recklessness, his bullish and even bullying insistence on his own vision—are also what sometimes lift him above the Leftist Crazy.[10]

A lot of people in America felt bullied and humiliated. Not all of them were old white men either. Some were young white men.

"There is nothing you can do to erase the problem of your own existence." That line comes from a play pungently titled *Straight White Men*. Probably not one Trump voter in a hundred thousand ever heard of the play's existence.[11] But they heard its message loud and clear, replicated and repeated across the vast cultural mindscape of the United States, and they did not like it. "How does it feel to be a problem?" W. E. B. DuBois had mused at the beginning of the twentieth century. The short answer: bad.

For all the talk of how millennials elected Barack Obama, Mitt Romney beat Obama in 2012 by seven points among whites under the age of thirty. Among white *men* under age thirty, Romney beat Obama by a hearty thirteen points.[12]

Young white men do not watch Fox News. Young people do not watch much traditional TV, period.[13] But the Fox News *message* of resentment, displacement, and humiliation—that did resonate, not through cable, but through newer online and social media.

A George Washington University research paper tracked a 600 percent increase in the followership of American white nationalist accounts on Twitter between 2012 and 2016, the followers of these accounts overtaking those of pro-ISIS accounts as the leading radical users of the platform.[14]

"When we talk about online radicalization we always talk about Muslims. But the radicalization of white men online is at astronomical levels," tweeted the sharp social observer Siyanda Mohutsiwa the morning after the 2016 election. "That's why I never got one strategy of Clinton's campaign: highlighting Trump's sexism." She continued: "Trump supporters love him BECAUSE of his sexism. Internet groups radicalized their sexual frustration into bigotry. These online groups found young white men at their most vulnerable & convinced them liberals were colluding to destroy white Western manhood."[15]

The observation about sexual frustration was astute. Millennials were having less sex than their elders. The percentage of people in their twenties neither married nor cohabiting rose from 52 percent in 2004 to 64 percent in 2014.[16] Pew reported in 2016 that for the first time since the nineteenth century, more people under thirty lived with a parent than with a partner.[17] Despite the agitations and anxieties of their disapproving elders, millennials are not doing much "hooking up": in the 2015 and 2016 General Social Surveys sponsored by the federal government, the percentage of people under age twenty-five with *zero* sexual contacts since turning eighteen had spiked to levels not seen since before the sexual revolution of the 1960s.[18]

Sociologists and sex researchers vied to offer explanations in the op-eds of America, blaming smartphones and body image and online dating apps. It's probably wisest to start with the basics: the dwindling rate of steady employment among young men since the Great Recession. In 2014, only 71 percent of men aged eighteen to thirty-four were employed, compared with 84 percent in 1960.[19]

What happens to young men out of work and disconnected from women?

Noncollege young men out of work reported spending an average of 3.4 hours per week playing video games before the recession. Their counterparts half a decade later played *more than twice as much:* an average of 8.6 hours per week.[20] In 2016, 19 percent of Americans under the age of thirty regularly smoked marijuana—

twice as many as before the recession—and young men were twice as likely to smoke as young women.[21]

Tallying the online consumption of pornography by Americans is more difficult, but here is a proxy: What would become the world's largest porn site, Pornhub, launched in 2007. It reported one million daily visits in November 2007, five million in July 2008, ten million at the nadir of the recession in April 2009, twenty-five million in February 2012, and fifty million by February 2015.[22] Americans led the world in per capita usage of the site: 191 page views per US resident, as compared with 165 page views per resident of the runner-up, Canada. (Pornhub reports the poignant fact that the single most frequently used word in the comments on its videos is the word "love"—the one thing that nobody will ever find there.)

Shrewd entrepreneurs and politicians deftly capitalized on the accumulating resentments they perceived around them. The Breitbart provocateur and hustler Milo Yiannopoulos would punctuate his campus talks with imagined thanks from his audience. He imagined them saying,

> Thank you for standing up for me, and for boys who have no voice. . . .
>
> Thank you for speaking up against power. Because feminism is the power now, in many ways. Hillary Clinton is running for president on the back of racism against whites and sexism against men, touting the mythical gender gap we all know so well.[23]

And, indeed, Hillary Clinton's candidacy repelled whites and men unlike any candidacy before it, very much including the candidacy of Barack Obama. Peter Beinart measured the rejection in the *Atlantic*:

The percentage of Americans who hold a "strongly unfavorable" view of [Clinton] substantially exceeds the percentage for any other Democratic nominee since 1980, when pollsters began asking the question. Antipathy to her among white men is even more unprecedented. According to the Public Religion Research Institute, 52 percent of white men hold a "very unfavorable" view of Clinton. That's a whopping 20 points higher than the percentage who viewed Barack Obama very unfavorably in 2012, 32 points higher than the percentage who viewed Obama very unfavorably in 2008, and 28 points higher than the percentage who viewed John Kerry very unfavorably in 2004.[24]

Male resistance to Hillary Clinton animated not only the Trump campaign, but also the Bernie Sanders campaign. Sanders outperformed Clinton among white men in every one of the twenty Democratic primaries for which exit polling exists.[25] The margins were always large, sometimes huge. On average, white male Democrats backed Sanders by 26.4 points more than white women did.[26]

Clinton had stayed married; Trump was twice divorced. Clinton was a lifelong Methodist; Trump could not correctly name the books of the Bible. Yet no group adhered more loyally to Trump against Clinton than evangelical Christians. The conservative columnist Ross Douthat marveled:

In a different campaign or era, it would have been a race-altering moment; in this one, it was barely a scandal. There was Melania Trump, the potential first lady of the United States, posing stark naked in '90s-era photos published by the *New York Post*—and then in the next day's edition, canoodling lipstick-lesbian style in bed. Yet the press yawned, her husband's latest outrage overshadowed it, and it only stayed a story because the date of the photos raised questions about the future Mrs. Trump's immigration status.

This election was supposed to be a referendum on Hillary Clinton, long a polarizing figure because she seemed to embody the cultural transformations of the 1960s—the liberal, feminist, working-mother spouse of the first boomer president.

But in the year of Donald Trump, the religious conservatives who fought many of those transformations find themselves reduced to a hapless rump. The best have retreated to rebuild; the worst have abased themselves before a sybaritic, irreligious presidential nominee.[27]

In the summer of 2016, an alumnus of the website I'd run in the first Obama term sat me down to explain what I was missing in Donald Trump. *He's the first postreligious conservative of my lifetime. The first who doesn't hate gays, doesn't care if women have abortions—the first who talks about things that matter now.* What was "alt" about the alt-right was precisely this stripping away of religiosity, to reveal a politics of resentment and domination ungrounded in any traditional moral claim.

Say this for Trump: In all the vast arsenal of his faults, one was missing. There is no hypocrisy about Donald Trump. A parable he loved to repeat culminated in the zinger: "You knew I was a snake when you took me in"—and if his audiences missed the obvious application of the line to the man who pronounced it, that was hardly his fault. No Trump supporter could fairly complain that he or she had not been amply warned.

It did not matter, for a reason brilliantly analyzed by Dale Beran in an essay for *Quartz* about the unexpected influence of the provocative 4chan message board from which so much of the alt-right slouched into existence:

> Since these men, like Trump, wear their insecurities on their sleeve, they fling insults in wild rabid bursts at everyone else.
>
> Trump the loser, the outsider, the hot mess, the pathetic joke, embodies this duality. Trump represents both the alpha and the beta. He is a successful person who, as the left often notes, is also the exact opposite—a grotesque loser, sensitive and prideful about his outsider status, ready at the drop of a hat to go on the attack, self-obsessed, selfish, abrogating, unquestioning of his own mansplaining and spreading, so insecure he must brag about assaulting women. . . .
>
> But, what the left doesn't realize is that this is not a problem for Trump's younger supporters—rather, it's the reason why they support him.
>
> Trump supporters voted for the con-man, the labyrinth with no center, because the labyrinth with no center is how they feel, how they feel the world works around them. A labyrinth with no center is a perfect description of their mother's basement with a terminal to an endless array of escapist fantasy worlds.
>
> Trump's bizarre, inconstant, incompetent, embarrassing, ridiculous behavior—what the left (naturally) perceives as his weaknesses—are to his supporters his strengths. . . .
>
> Trump is loserdom embraced. Trump is the loser who has won.[28]

Trump drew support from crackpots, extremists, racists, and neo-Nazis. On election night 2016, one of them was caught on video throwing a Hitler-style salute into the air and shouting "Hail Trump! Hail our people! Hail victory!"[29]

But there are simply not enough such crackpots in America to elect a president, no matter how lucky the break in the Electoral College. What boosted Trump was not the self-conscious white nationalism of the media-savvy Sieg Heiler, but the pervading unease of whites devoid of any ideology at all.

Many people doing well enough in material terms still felt displaced in an unfamiliar and even hostile landscape. Shortly after Obama's first inauguration, the *Daily Show* on Comedy Central featured a mock focus group with white schoolchildren, hosted by the show's "senior black correspondent," Larry Wilmore. Wilmore interviewed the children about the risks to their "once proud race" from a demographic future as a minority group. One little girl answered, "We're not upset in any way, shape or form." Wilmore replied, "You will be."[30]

Wilmore was right. A 2013 survey for the Rockefeller Foundation asked Americans to estimate the consequences for the United States of rising ethnic diversity. Half of those surveyed predicted that rising diversity would lead to more crime. A majority predicted intensified competition for jobs. More than 60 percent feared that government services would fall short.[31]

Trump offered this one promise above all others to the disaffected young men who followed him: a world that had been turned upside down by forces beyond their control, he would turn rightside up again. "You're going to hear it once," he told protesters at Virginia's Radford University, "all lives matter."[32] Trump was not speaking there to some racist fringe. He was speaking to those who just wanted things restored to normal, as they understood normal. He promised to restore cultural power to those who believed themselves the rightful bearers of that power.

"You can say again Merry Christmas because Donald Trump is now the president. You can say it again. It's OK to say!" enthused

Trump's former campaign manager Corey Lewandowski to Fox's Sean Hannity on December 6, 2016. "It's not a pejorative word anymore!"[33]

That had been Trump's promise, literally dozens of times: "We'll all be saying Merry Christmas again!"[34] Yet the Christmas Donald Trump celebrated was not exactly a celebration of peace on earth and goodwill to men. At 4:46 a.m. on Christmas morning, 2016, Trump tweeted his holiday greeting: a photograph of himself standing in front of a decorated Christmas tree, his fist raised in a gesture of militancy and dominance.[35]

The phrase "white privilege" transitioned from the academy into common speech in the Obama years—at exactly the moment that millions of white Americans were experiencing the worst social trauma since the Great Depression. For the first time in American history, life expectancy was actually declining, and most steeply among non-Hispanic whites. Non-Hispanic white males, 31 percent of the population, accounted for 70 percent of the suicides in the United States in 2014.[36] Of the 33,091 Americans who died in 2015 of opioid overdoses, 27,056 were non-Hispanic whites.[37] In the late 1990s, the risk that a non-college-educated white person would die in his or her early fifties was 30 percent lower than for a comparable black person. By 2015, the non-college white person's risk was 30 percent *higher* than his or her non-college black counterpart.[38] Behind these "deaths of despair," as they came to be known, lay an unfolding economic malaise. Working-class white men suffered a 9 percent income decline between 1996 and 2014.[39] Marriage, church attendance, civic participation, all plummeted.[40] Compared with any other ethnic group—and to whites with college educations—noncollege whites expressed most pessimism about their personal prospects in the decade ahead, and the prospects for their children after them.[41] Elite America did not care, because it mostly did not notice. Between November 8, 2015, and November 8, 2016, the word "transgender" appeared in the *New York Times* 1,169 times. The word "opioid"—only 284.[42]

Rush Limbaugh offered a pungent description of what Trump had to offer. He was speaking two weeks before Trump entered the presidential race, and about an entirely different subject: Bruce Jenner's self-transformation into Caitlyn. Yet Limbaugh's words applied much more broadly than that.

> Folks, one of the motivations, one of the reasons—purposes, if you will—of defining a new normal is also defining the new weirdoes. . . .
>
> Who do you think the new weirdoes are? I don't think there is any doubt that this is a studied attempt. At least from those that are doing all of this with a political agenda attached, the objective here—and it's not new. It's been happening for quite a while right in front of our eyes. It is to portray conservatives/Christians/Republicans as the real weirdoes. "They're the real oddballs! They are the ones! They're the ones that are not cool. I mean, they're antiques. They're from a long-gone era that has long ago been bypassed. They're just relics, and they've got to be just phased out."[43]

Salena Zito, writing in the *Atlantic* in September 2016, postulated that Trump's supporters take him seriously but not literally.[44] The phrase would become one of the most famous of the Trump era, and also an all-purpose excuse. The Fox News personality Jeanine Pirro complained in May 2017 that President Trump "cannot speak—or his staff cannot speak—without someone going through it with a fine-toothed comb."[45] The pro-Trump blogger Gavin McInnes had expressed a similar complaint in March 2017.

On a tour of Israel with the Canadian website *Rebel Media*, he uploaded a video titled "Ten Things I Hate about Jews." He was—of course—just kidding. "It's frustrating that everyone takes everything you say 1000 per cent literally."[46]

Two weeks before Zito's formulation appeared, the *Claremont Review of Books* published one of the most important essays of the 2016 cycle, an impassioned plea to fellow conservatives to take Trump deadly seriously.

> 2016 is the Flight 93 election: charge the cockpit or you die. You may die anyway. You—or the leader of your party—may make it into the cockpit and not know how to fly or land the plane. There are no guarantees.
>
> Except one: if you don't try, death is certain. To compound the metaphor: a Hillary Clinton presidency is Russian Roulette with a semi-auto. With Trump, at least you can spin the cylinder and take your chances.[47]

Nor was this life-and-death alternative intended as a figure of speech. In the author's telling, not only Clinton but all of Trump's Republican rivals and recent predecessors epitomized

> a party, a society, a country, a people, a civilization that wants to die. Trump, alone among candidates for high office in this or in the last seven (at least) cycles, has stood up to say: I want to live. I want my party to live. I want my country to live. I want my people to live.[48]

The "Flight 93" essay captured attention across the political spectrum. Limbaugh read the whole essay aloud on his radio program; it was debated across print and television. No writer more forcefully articulated the apocalyptic despair of conservatives in the Obama era—or their disenchantment with the compromises and concessions that sustain constitutional government.

> Only in a corrupt republic, in corrupt times, could a Trump rise. It is therefore puzzling that those most horrified by Trump are the least willing to consider the possibility that the republic is dying.[49]

The author of the "Flight 93" essay had used a pseudonym, Publius Decius Mus, a hero from Livy's annals who intentionally sacrificed his own life to win a battle for the Romans. The true identity was soon revealed as an alumnus of the George W. Bush administration and a colleague of mine from the 2008 Rudy Giuliani presidential campaign, Michael Anton. Anton's contributions would shortly be recognized with a communications job on Trump's National Security Council. It was a strange assignment for a man haunted by visions of civil war and impending dictatorship. Yet such visions haunted more dreams than Anton's. The seditious revolution that this latter-day Publius dreaded beckoned to more than one lost boy as a last best hope.

CHAPTER 11

BELIEVERS

Election 2016 looked on paper like the most sweeping Republican victory since the Jazz Age. Yet there was a hollowness to the Trump Republicans' seeming ascendancy over the federal government and in so many of the states. The Republicans of the 1920s had drawn their strength from the country's most economically and culturally dynamic places. In 1924, Calvin Coolidge won almost 56 percent of the vote in cosmopolitan New York State, 65 percent in mighty industrial Pennsylvania, 75 percent in Michigan, the hub of the new automotive economy.

Not so in 2016. Where technologies were invented and where styles were set, where diseases cured and innovations launched, where songs were composed and patents registered—there the GOP was weakest. Donald Trump won vast swathes of the nation's landmass. Hillary Clinton won the counties that produced 64 percent of the nation's wealth. Even in Trump states, Clinton won the knowledge centers, places like the Research Triangle of North Carolina.

The Trump presidency only accelerated the divorce of political power from cultural power. Business leaders quit Trump's advisory boards lest his racist outbursts sully their brands. Companies like Facebook and Microsoft denounced his immigration policies. Popular singers refused invitations to his White House; great athletes boycotted his events. By the summer of 2017, Trump's approval among those under thirty had dipped to 20 percent.[1]

And this was before Trump's corruption and collusion scandals begin to bite.

Whatever Trump's personal fate, his Republican Party seems headed for electoral trouble—or worse. Yet it will require much more than Republican congressional defeats in 2018 to halt Trumpocracy. Indeed, such defeats may well perversely strengthen President Trump. Congressional defeats will weaken alternative power centers within the Republican party. If they lose the House or the Senate or many governorships—or some combination of those defeats—then Republicans may feel all the more compelled to defend their president. The party faithful may interpret any internal criticism of Trump as a treasonable surrender to Nancy Pelosi and Chuck Schumer. As the next presidential race nears, it will become ever more imperative to rally around Trump. The more isolated Trump becomes within the American political system as a whole, the more he will dominate whatever remains of the conservative portion of that system. He will devour his party from within.

Maybe you do not much care about the future of the Republican Party. You should. Conservatives will always be with us. If conservatives become convinced that they cannot win democratically, they will not abandon conservatism. They will reject democracy. The stability of American society depends on conservatives' ability to find a way forward from the Trump dead end, toward a conservatism that can not only win elections but also govern responsibly, a conservatism that is culturally modern, economically inclusive, and environmentally responsible, that upholds markets at home and US leadership internationally.

In the most immediate sense, that means accepting that the Affordable Care Act is here to stay, and to work to reform it so that it costs less and protects middle-class families more. That means slowing the pace of immigration so that the existing population of the country does not feel it is being displaced and replaced. Economists will argue that a country with a slow-growing population needs more immigrants to sustain the growth of its labor force. But a population is a citizenry as well as a labor force, and when it grows slowly, it can less easily assimilate newcomers. Immigration is to natural population increase as wine is to food: a good complement, a bad substitute.

A more responsible conservatism would recognize that reducing marginal taxes at the top—while in principle a desirable goal—cannot be a paramount priority at a time of wide and accelerating income inequality. Conservative ideology on taxes has left tax credits as almost the only policy tool, notwithstanding that they are typically inefficient ways to get things done. The mortgage interest deduction does not make middle-income housing more affordable, as most economic research has shown. Tax subsidies for college tuition incentivize above-inflation fee increases. Per-child tax credits are a very roundabout way of assisting families with their childcare needs. Instead of indirectly subsidizing things that cost too much already, from health care to college education, the party less dependent on the votes of government workers should dedicate itself to bringing those costs down.

A post-Trump GOP will need to get serious again about honesty in government, after Donald Trump's immolation of ethical standards. It should fiercely uphold US democracy and sovereignty against the sinister clandestine influences, foreign and domestic, that held so much sway over the Trump presidency. Those people implicated in Trump's wrongdoing—and especially in his connections with the Russian government—need to be lustrated from political roles, quite separate from whatever legal jeopardy they may face.

Many Republicans and many conservatives have played honorable individual parts against Trump. But they formed an embattled and ultimately unpopular minority. Many of them—perhaps even most of them—ultimately succumbed to the imperatives of party, pocketbook, or peer group. Trump has contaminated thousands of careers and millions of minds. He has ripped the conscience out of half of the political spectrum and left a moral void where American conservatism used to be.

> Every critic, every detractor, will have to bow down to President Trump. It's everyone who's ever doubted Donald, who ever disagreed, who ever challenged him. It is the ultimate revenge to become the most powerful man in the universe.[2]

Those words were spoken by Trump's protégé Omarosa Manigault, but they could well have come from the man himself. Trump expressed his vision of political leadership in an April 2016 interview with Bob Woodward and Bob Costa of the *Washington Post*:

> The coalition building for me will be when I win. Vince Lombardi, I saw this. He was not a big man. And I was sitting in a place with some very, very tough football players. Big, strong football players. He came in—these are tough cookies—he came in, years ago—and I'll never forget it, I was a young man. He came in, screaming, into this place.

And screaming at one of these guys who was three times bigger than him, literally. And very physical, grabbing him by the shirt. Now this guy could've whisked him away and thrown him out the window in two seconds. This guy— the player—was shaking. A friend of mine. There were four players, and Vince Lombardi walked in. He was angry. And he grabbed—I was a young guy—he grabbed him by the shirt, screaming at him, and the guy was literally. . . . And I said, wow. And I realized the only way Vince Lombardi got away with that was because he won.[3]

I was not there, obviously, but I strongly doubt this story is true. Lombardi described his method of leadership as exactly the opposite of the Trump method:

It is essential to understand that battles are primarily won in the hearts of men. Men respond to leadership in a most remarkable way and once you have won his heart, he will follow you anywhere.[4]

The battle for men's hearts is one that Trump never won, because he never fought it. There is only one sure and safe way to defeat internal opponents, and that is by making them your friends. This is how Barack Obama did it and Ronald Reagan and every governor or mayor who united a formerly divided party. This is what Trump could never do—and that his supporters never understood that a party leader must do.

"All this garbage from you Never Trumper jerks out there," Sean Hannity erupted in a pre-election radio broadcast. "I've had it. By the way, that's more unfinished business. November 9th, I'll have a lot to say about all of you."[5]

November 9 should have dawned a happy day for Sean Hannity. And yet he never did seem happy ever again. On Fox News, "Never Trumpers" came to play a role like that of Trotskyist wreckers in Stalin's Soviet Union: simultaneously utterly irrelevant, doomed to defeat, and also all-powerful, the reason the shops have no potatoes.

Thus Newt Gingrich and Hannity agreed on the night of November 9 that "the little, whiney, sniveling negative cowards who were 'Never Trumpers' are beneath our paying attention to them. Let them drift off into the ashbin of history while we go ahead and work with Donald Trump and with the House and Senate Republicans to create a dramatically new future."[6]

Off the Never Trumpers did drift—but not to the ashbin of history. They drifted to those places where we send guilty knowledge. And no matter how loudly they thumped their chests, Trump's supporters could never still the sound of moral reproach.

Speaking on Fox News in August 2016, Bill Bennett, a former education secretary under President Reagan (and the author, incidentally, of the mega-bestseller *The Book of Virtues*), denounced "some of my friends—or maybe former friends—who suffer from a terrible case of moral superiority and put their own vanity and taste above the interest of the country."[7] That same day, Trump's future communications adviser Anthony Scaramucci complained on Twitter, "Never Trump putting their vanity and taste over the interest of the country with false moral superiority."[8] The columnist William McGurn fumed in the *Wall Street Journal* in October 2016 against "the cheap moralizing of Never Trump."[9] David Limbaugh, who had been an ardent opponent of Trump's in the primaries, but turned his coat after Trump won, complained in a column in July 2017 of the "snobbish condemnation on social media"[10] from anti-Trump conservatives.

But it was not snobbery that drove the condemnation of Trump. It was conscience.

In 2004, an Illinois state senator named Barack Obama delivered an eloquent appeal to national unity at the Democratic convention in Boston:

> There's not a liberal America and a conservative America— there's the United States of America. There's not a black America and white America and Latino America and Asian America; there's the United States of America. The pundits like to slice and dice our country into red states and blue states; red states for Republicans, blue states for Democrats. But I've got news for them, too. We worship an awesome God in the blue states, and we don't like federal agents poking around our libraries in the red states. We coach Little League in the blue states and have gay friends in the red states. There are patriots who opposed the war in Iraq and patriots who supported it. We are one people, all of us pledging allegiance to the stars and stripes, all of us defending the United States of America.[11]

Those words propelled Obama to a national career that would culminate in the presidency. In 2008, he would win the most decisive mandate of any Democrat since Lyndon Johnson. Four years later, he became the first Democrat since Franklin Roosevelt to win a majority of the popular vote in two consecutive presidential elections. Along the way, he would win votes from many people who would cast ballots for Donald Trump in 2016. He left those voters—as he leaves history—with a troubling question: Was he right or wrong in 2004? Are we still "one people" even if we no longer speak one language? Or share one religion, or any religion at all? Even if we no longer can agree on national heroes and villains? Or on the meaning of such basic concepts as free speech, equality under the law, and the right to bear arms? Even if some of those who live among us do so without legal right—even as they receive a panoply of legal benefits? Even if some of us seem to be lavished with all the benefits of a new, more global economic order, while others bear all the costs?

"The divide is not between the left and right anymore, but between patriots and globalists," declared Marine Le Pen, announcing her candidacy for the president of France in February 2017.[12] Those words sat ill in the mouth of a candidate funded by secret Russian money, but they contained at least this much truth: the old ideological compass did not provide a very accurate guide to the new political map.[13]

Trump polled better among workers earning between $50,000 and $99,999 than with those earning over $100,000, a freakish outcome for a Republican.[14] He posted the best showing among union households by any Republican since 1984.[15] He performed surprisingly well among Latino and black men, boosting his share in those two demographics above the level of Mitt Romney's in 2012.[16]

Meanwhile, Hillary Clinton—excoriated by the right-wing media as a radical and a socialist—scored exceptionally well among the richest Americans, winning almost exactly half the votes of those who earn more than $250,000 per year. She did extraordinarily badly among white women without a college degree, losing that group to Donald Trump by the staggering margin of 27 points.[17] How could this be? In the fall of 2016, *New York* magazine interviewed six women who had decided not to cast a vote in the Clinton-Trump election. One, identified as a thirty-year-old teacher, had this to say:

I do not believe that feminism can "trickle down"—that having more women on corporate boards will make life better for working-class women. If your primary concern is creating gender parity within the upper class, it's rational to support Hillary Clinton. If you are a working woman, things aren't so clear.[18]

Throughout most of their lives, members of the postwar baby boom generation (those born between 1945 and 1960) held views considerably more liberal than those of the generation before them (born between 1930 and 1945). As late as the year 2000, only 35 percent of baby boomers described themselves as "conservative."[19]

Then struck the financial crisis, followed by the presidency of Barack Obama. The proportion of baby boomers who called themselves "angry with government" surged from 15 percent before 2008 to 26 percent the next year. By 2011, 42 percent of baby boomers were labeling themselves "conservative," the same percentage as the next generation up.[20]

It's important to understand what right-leaning baby boomers mean by the word "conservative." On social issues such as gay rights and the role of women, boomers, like all Americans, continued to evolve in liberal directions in the Obama years.[21] Nor did aging boomers adopt a more pro-business outlook. On the contrary, boomers in the 2010s expressed much *more* suspicion of business than the same demographic cohort did in the 1990s, when they were younger and otherwise more liberal.[22] Boomer conservatives exhibited little enthusiasm for the "on your own" ideology of the mainstream GOP. In fact, 64 percent of boomers complained in a 2011 poll that the government didn't do enough to help older people, a much higher proportion than in any other age group, including their elders.[23]

Boomers adamantly rejected any cuts to entitlement programs— and by *larger* margins than their elders of the 1930–1945 cohort.[24] If necessary to protect those programs, a majority of boomers would breach the ultimate conservative taboo: they would accept tax increases on high earners.[25] Paul Ryan conservatives they were not.

Here's what those right-leaning boomers *did* mean by "conservatism." If read a list of fiscally liberal statements like, "It is the responsibility of government to take care of people who cannot take care of themselves," boomers became increasingly likely to deliver a stern no over the twenty years between the 1990s and the 2010s. In fact, by 2010, they had become the age cohort *most* likely to answer no, more so than either their elders or juniors.[26] They were the cohort most likely to attribute individual economic troubles to those individuals' own personal failings, rather than to ill fortune, racism, or any other systemic cause.

It would be easy to caricature these views as the politics of "I've got mine." But look again at the contrasting generational experiences: People born between 1930 and 1945 entered the workforce just in time to ride the longest boom in middle-class living standards from beginning to end. They bought their first houses when housing was cheap and sold their empty nests in the real estate bubble of the 2000s. The youngest of them had qualified for Medicare before the Republicans took control of Congress in 2010, and all of them were exempted from the cost cutting projected by Paul Ryan. The boomers had faced more competition for everything, from jobs to housing, and now faced an ominous retirement environment. If they acted like shipwreck survivors in an already overcrowded lifeboat . . . well, the boat really was jammed awfully tight.

"Seventy-five percent of Americans nearing retirement age in 2010 had less than $30,000 in their retirement accounts," reported

Teresa Ghilarducci of the *New York Times*.[27] They would need their federal retirement benefits much more than they had anticipated back when they were younger and more liberal. The slogan "Keep the Government's Hands Off My Medicare" was easily mocked, but it actually stated a perfectly plausible position: Who else but the government *could* lay hands on your Medicare? Among Americans aged fifty to sixty-four, agreement with the sentiment "government has become too involved in health care" rose sixteen points between 2009 and 2013. (Among Americans over sixty-five, by contrast, agreement with that sentiment rose only eight points over the same period.)[28] These Americans were not ignorantly denying that the government paid for Medicare. They were indignantly objecting lest government pay for anything else. As when they had resisted the draft in the 1960s, so now when they refused changes to Medicare, the politics of the baby boom generation were the politics of generational self-defense.

In a close and careful 2011 study of the politics of the Tea Party, three Harvard scholars, Vanessa Williamson, Theda Skocpol, and John Coggin, remarked, "Tea Partiers judge entitlement programs not in terms of abstract free-market orthodoxy, but according to the *perceived deservingness of recipients*."[29] Tea Partiers differentiated between those who worked (or who *had* worked) and those who sought something for nothing—in other words, between people as they imagined themselves and the people they imagined competing against them.

The Tea Party was often described as a libertarian movement, opposed to big spending and big deficits. And certainly those were themes often sounded by Republican candidates in the 2010 primaries and elections. But that's not what Tea Party voters and rally attenders cared about. Here's a piece of oratory from the TV star made by the Tea Party movement, Glenn Beck, then on Fox News:

Do you watch the direction that America is being taken in and feel powerless to stop it? Do you believe that your voice isn't loud enough to be heard above the noise anymore? Do you read the headlines everyday and feel an empty pit in your stomach . . . as if you're completely alone? If so, then you've fallen for the Wizard of Oz lie. While the voices you hear in the distance may sound intimidating, as if they surround us from all sides—the reality is very different. Once you pull the curtain away you realize that there are only a few people pressing the buttons, and their voices are weak. The truth is that they don't surround us at all. We surround them.[30]

We versus them. Not state versus society. Certainly not revenues versus expenditures. *We versus them.*

In a multiethnic society, economic redistribution inescapably implies ethnic redistribution. I wrote those words after the 2012 election, and they apply even more forcefully after 2016.[31] Of the US residents who lacked health insurance prior to the 2008 financial crisis, 27 percent were foreign born.[32] As the Obama administration squeezed Medicare to fund the Affordable Care Act, it's not surprising that many white boomers perceived Obamacare as a transfer of health care resources from "us" to "them"—by a president who identified with "them" and not with "us."

The social scientist Robert Putnam observed with dismay in 2007 that "new evidence from the US suggests that in ethnically diverse neighbourhoods residents of all races tend to 'hunker down.' Trust (even of one's own race) is lower, altruism and community cooperation rarer, friends fewer."[33] Projects of social and economic reform crash into the reality that human beings most willingly cooperate when they feel common identity. In a society undergoing rapid demographic change, loyalties narrow.

Republican politicians since the 1980s had spoken a language of "hope" and "opportunity." They repeated the performance in 2015. "We will lift our sights again, make opportunity common again, get events in the world moving our way again," declared Jeb Bush in his presidential announcement address.[34] "I want to talk to you this morning about reigniting the promise of America," said Ted Cruz in his, and Marco Rubio likewise hailed "our nation's identity as a land of opportunity."[35]

"Believe in America!" "A new American century!" *What are they talking about?* wondered voters battered and bruised by the previous American century. Donald Trump, the oldest candidate on the Republican stage, was also the first to discern that the political language of the 1980s had lost its power. The most common age for white Americans in 2015 was fifty-five.[36] These older white voters were more eager to protect what they had than to hustle for more. They wanted less change, not more. They cared about security, not opportunity. Protection of the status quo was what candidate Trump offered.

Donald Trump created in effect a three-party system in the United States, by building a new Trump party in between the Democratic and Republican parties. In the decisive state of Pennsylvania, for example, Trump and the successful Republican candidate for US Senate, Pat Toomey, won almost exactly equal numbers of votes: 2.97 million for Trump; 2.95 million for Toomey. But Trump and Toomey won their votes in very different places. In Pennsylvania's four richest counties—Chester, Montgomery, Bucks, and Delaware—Toomey received altogether 177,000 more votes than Trump. In all the rest of the state, Toomey ran well behind Trump.

One poll found that nearly half of all white working-class voters agreed with the statement, "Things have changed so much that I often feel like a stranger in my own country."[37] As America has become more diverse, tribalism has intensified. The Left's hopes for a social democratic politics founded on class without regard to race look only slightly less moribund than the think-tank conservatism of low taxes and open borders.

Perhaps the very darkness of the Trump experience can summon the nation to its senses and jolt Americans to a new politics of commonality, a new politics in which the Trump experience is remembered as the end of something bad, and not the beginning of something worse. Trump appealed to what was mean and cruel and shameful. The power of that appeal should never be underestimated. But once its power fades, even those who have succumbed will feel regret.

Those who have expressed regret will need some kind of exit from Trumpocracy, some reintegration into a politics again founded on decency. The best justice is reconciliation, urged Desmond Tutu as he chaired South Africa's inquiry into its past. That was also the teaching of America's greatest president too in the country's most searing agony of trial. If Lincoln could say it then, we can in this so much less harrowing passage surely repeat:

> Human nature will not change. In any future great national trial, compared with the men of this, we shall have as weak, and as strong; as silly and as wise; as bad and good. Let us, therefore, study the incidents of this, as philosophy to learn wisdom from, and none of them as wrongs to be revenged.[38]

CHAPTER 12

─────────

HOPE

n the spring of 2017, I received an email from a reader of the *Atlantic*. It read, in relevant part:

I have made a point to make a concrete (if small) act of civic engagement every weekday. These acts have included contacting my school board regarding digital media literacy, calling my national and state legislators about important issues, and embarking on a program of self-education. I have read about the history, politics, and the philosophical ideals of our republic. To date I have read (albeit at a slow pace) Paine's *Common Sense*, Slack's *Liberty's First Crisis*, and I am in the middle of reading John Stuart Mill's essay "On Liberty." I would have taken none of those actions prior to this last election.

These are dark days for the United States, yet they are pierced by shafts of light. A new spirit of citizen responsibility is waking in the land. Americans are turning off cable networks that lie to them to consume instead more and better news.[1] Instead of theatrical street protests, concerned citizens have turned to productive political action: phone calls to congressional offices, registration to vote.

Most of this book has dealt with the harm done by the presidency of Donald Trump and by those who enabled it. Yet good can come of bad. From raging fires rise young forests. From former errors can be gained new wisdom. What can we gain from Trump? What unexpected gifts may yet be seized from this bad moment in American politics?

The first gift to gain from the Trump moment is the gift of wider vision.

Cynically yes, but effectively too, Donald Trump seized more accurately than any candidate in 2016 on issues neglected by more conventional politicians: the ravages of drug addiction, the costs of immigration, the cultural and economic decline of the industrial working class.

As America evolves toward a more unequal, more plutocratic society, its politicians—and certainly its federal politicians—inhabit the world of a remote upper class. Even when they start poor, as Bill Clinton did, they do not stay that way.

Despite his flamboyant claims to wealth, Donald Trump succeeded in speaking *to* and *for* huge sections of the American electorate that other politicians spoke only *about*. He identified forgotten and angry parts of America. His hurts, his grievances, his resentments, enabled him to channel theirs. It was fraud, but it was not all fraud.

The dangers posed by Trump exposed the dangers posed by his supporters. Working-class America has not seemed dangerous for a long time. But back when it did seem dangerous, that danger persuaded the privileged—or enough of them—that concessions must be made.

We urge control and supervision by the nation as an antidote
to the movement for state socialism. Those who advocate total lack of regulation, those who advocate lawlessness in the
business world, themselves give the strongest impulse to what
I believe would be the deadening movement toward unadul-
terated state socialism.[2]

So urged Theodore Roosevelt more than a century ago. His
urgings would not become realities, however, until the Depression
and the Cold War forced reforms to avert the menace of communism at home and overseas. It was in very large part fear of communism that induced businesses to provide pensions and health
care benefits to employees . . . that inspired the federal government
to invest in great public universities . . . and that compelled the
United States to uproot racial segregation. President John F. Kennedy argued that case explicitly in a televised address in 1963: "Today, we are committed to a worldwide struggle to promote and
protect the rights of all who wish to be free. And when Americans
are sent to Vietnam or West Berlin, we do not ask for whites only."[3]

Fears of revolutionary socialism have faded. For more than
a quarter century, we have lived in a world where economic and
cultural elites have felt secure from challenge as seldom before.
Unsurprisingly, those elites have over that same time become far
less inclined to share their prosperity with the rest of their society. "Power concedes nothing without a demand. It never did and
never will," as Frederick Douglass famously said. Along with all his
boasting and bullying, his crassness and cruelty, his ignorance and
his indolence, his tantrums and his treasons, Donald Trump also
carried with him the text of a demand that—this time—could not
be shrugged off by society's leaders and owners.

A second gift from Trump's inadvertent hand is the rediscovery of the preciousness of truth. "Post-truth is pre-fascism," wrote Yale historian Timothy Snyder in a viral Facebook post just days after Donald Trump won a majority in the Electoral College, "and to abandon facts is to abandon freedom."[4] Profound words, and true. But it was not only Donald Trump who had left truth behind, who scorned the very concept of truth. Trump entered a culture prepared for him; he filled a cavity excavated by the work of thousands of toiling academics and intellectuals. An example of their handiwork:

> The idea that there is a single truth–"the Truth"–is a construct of the Euro-West that is deeply rooted in the Enlightenment, which was a movement that also described Black and Brown people as both subhuman and impervious to pain. This construction is a myth and white supremacy, imperialism, colonization, capitalism, and the United States of America are all of its progeny. The idea that the truth is an entity for which we must search, in matters that endanger our abilities to exist in open spaces, is an attempt to silence oppressed peoples.[5]

That is an extract from an open letter drafted by students at Pomona College to justify the use of force and threat of violence to prevent a campus talk by a scholar they disliked. The most radical thing about that statement was precisely how conventional its contents were.

When the phrase "post-truth" began to circulate in the 1980s, it originated as something close to a compliment. The idea that things were "true" or "false" was outmoded, even reactionary! Michel Foucault and other advanced thinkers had shown that liberation would follow only once we accepted that "truth" served merely as a euphemism for self-serving ideologies devised by holders of power.[6] All we can know for certain, insisted this glamorous new system of thought, are "narratives": yours, mine—and no way of judging between them, except on the basis of race/class/gender.

But if there is no truth, there can be no lying. And suddenly Americans are appreciating that "lying" is a concept very badly needed by democratic politics. Americans are discovering that it's important also to distinguish between the normal tools of the politician's trade—evasion, equivocation, the timely change of subject—and the inversion of reality that is routinely heard from Donald Trump.

A leader who lies constantly can distort a nation's perception of reality. "You are annihilated, exhausted, you can't control yourself or remember what you said two minutes before. You feel that all is lost," as one man who had been subject to Mao Zedong's "reeducation" campaign in China put it to the psychiatrist Robert Lifton. "You accept anything he says."[7]

Trump's incessant lying has indeed warped the minds of his core supporters. As noted earlier, more than half of Republicans have accepted Trump's false claim to have won the popular vote;[8] only 9 percent of Republicans acknowledge that Russia tried to influence the 2016 election.[9]

Yet 60 percent of Americans—and the number is steadily rising—reject Trump's lies about his connections to Russia.[10] Even as Trump marches his ever-dwindling band of supporters toward ever more threadbare untruths, a growing majority of Americans crave truth, seek truth, and vindicate truth. They cherish truth as something real in itself, *not* a construct of power, *not* a "narrative" that varies according to the hyphens in one's personal identity. "In a room where people unanimously maintain a conspiracy of silence, one word of truth sounds like a pistol shot." So said the great Polish poet Czeslaw Milosz in his 1980 Nobel Prize lecture.[11] Long before Trump and his deceitful crew appeared on the scene, a conspiracy against the ideal of truth had gained the upper hand among those entrusted with the education of the young and the sustaining of high culture. If revulsion against Trump's lies should at last discredit and overthrow that conspiracy, what a fine second gift that would be.

A nation that teaches its children to abhor bullying discovered it had installed the noisiest bully in the country in the highest office in the land. Trump surrounded himself with a staff cringing and obsequious to him—and overbearing toward everybody else. As the country got to know this gang, Americans unwrapped a third gift of Trump: a renewal of their disgust for those who join power to cruelty.

On the morning of July 26, 2017, President Trump awoke to uncongenial news. The FBI had raided the Virginia home of Trump's former campaign manager, Paul Manafort. Trump reacted to this indignity as bullies typically do: by lashing out at someone more vulnerable. At 8:56 a.m., the president tweeted this attention-grabbing message: "After consultation with my Generals and military experts, please be advised that the United States Government will not accept or allow . . ." He paused there for eight minutes, leaving the world to wonder what might follow such a dramatic opening. At 9:04, he posted part two: ". . . Transgender individuals to serve in any capacity in the U.S. Military. Our military must be focused on decisive and overwhelming . . ." etc.

Americans quickly learned that, as usual, the president was speaking impulsively. There had been no consultation; in fact, the military was taken completely by surprise. The last-minute Obama policy opening the military to transgender soldiers had been postponed by the incoming administration in January; there was no particular reason to take any action at all on July 26. One aide suggested the motive was political. "This forces Democrats in Rust Belt states like Ohio, Michigan, and Wisconsin to take complete ownership of this issue," the aide said to Jonathan Swan of *Axios*. But that was transparently an after-the-fact rationalization rather than an actual motive. The move was not cleared in advance with Republican members in Congress, a number of whom quickly opposed it, so Democrats were *not* forced to "take complete ownership." The most plausible explanation of events was that Trump tweeted simply to enjoy the momentary pleasure of power over others, without any plan or even intention to translate his imperious words into policy.

But here's the gift: Americans almost instantly recognized Trump's cynical bullying for what it was—and overwhelmingly condemned it. A week after Trump's order, polls found that 68 percent of Americans supported open service by transgender military personnel; only 27 percent agreed with the president's ban.[12] What's remarkable about this turn is that Americans by large majorities *reject* the main claim that transgender people make about themselves, that they authentically belong to a sex different from that into which they were born at birth.[13] Once Donald Trump started tweeting, those prior positions ceased to matter. Whatever their other opinions, if any, about what it meant to call oneself transgender, a large majority of Americans agreed that it should not mean a kicking from a holder of power to salve his hurt ego.

"Americans hate a bully." We tell ourselves this, but in 2015 and 2016 we had reason to doubt the self-assurance. For eighteen months on the campaign trail, Trump modeled behaviors that would seem in any other context about as repugnant as could be—and yet despite it all he was ushered to the most honored place in American society. From that place, however, he has jolted

Americans to recover their best character. Americans *do* hate a bully.

In the early shock of the Trump presidency, some bookish people circulated a vision of the future published by the philosopher Richard Rorty in 1998.

> At that point, something will crack. The nonsuburban electorate will decide that the system has failed and start looking around for a strongman to vote for—someone willing to assure them that, once he is elected, the smug bureaucrats, tricky lawyers, overpaid bond salesmen, and postmodernist professors will no longer be calling the shots. . . .
>
> One thing that is very likely to happen is that the gains made in the past 40 years by black and brown Americans, and by homosexuals, will be wiped out. Jocular contempt for women will come back into fashion.[14]

Chilling! Only . . . this is precisely what did not happen. Gains were not wiped out. Contempt did not return to fashion. To the contrary, it's remarkable how the ascendancy of Trump coincided with the wreck of the careers of America's most notorious and flagrant abusers of women: Roger Ailes, Bill O'Reilly, Harvey Weinstein, and their lesser emulators.

"The president's primary problem as a leader," Peggy Noonan stingingly remarked,

> is not that he is impetuous, brash or naive. It's not that he is inexperienced, crude, an outsider. It is that he is weak and sniveling. It is that he undermines himself almost daily by ignoring traditional norms and forms of American masculinity. He's not strong and self-controlled, not cool and

tough, not low-key and determined; he's whiny, weepy and self-pitying. He throws himself, sobbing, on the body politic. He's a drama queen.[15]

Trump reminded Americans of the old schoolyard lesson: the bully is a coward. Another gift.

Trump has recalled Americans of the Left to an appreciation of the vital role of national security agencies. It seems an eon ago that Edward Snowden was hailed as a hero. The outcome of the 2016 election reminded Americans of the Left that in this age of asymmetric warfare, national security threats often take covert and clandestine forms, and so therefore must national defense. The integrity of American voting systems is an even more vital part of the nation's indispensable national infrastructure than power grids or gas pipelines. Since 9/11, the nation has spent tens of billions to harden those—while leaving exposed to subversion and corruption the master system that governs them all.

One hears as well justified self-criticism from veterans of the Obama team. "I feel like we sort of choked," the *Washington Post* quoted a former senior official involved in the Obama administration's deliberations on Russia. "It is the hardest thing about my entire time in government to defend."[16] The Obama administration can cite explanations, including the resistance of the Republican congressional leadership, and the even more aggressive defiance of Republican state party leaders. Like many of us, they underestimated Trump's political chances. Why risk a political convulsion to protect the country against a sure loser? But there are no "sure losers" in presidential politics, only probable losers—and the improbable sometimes happens.

In 2012, President Obama and many Democrats mocked Mitt Romney for sounding a prescient alarm about Russian aggression under Vladimir Putin. "The 1980s are now calling to ask for their foreign policy back," Obama chided in the presidential candidates' foreign policy debate. But Romney was right and Obama wrong, as many in Obama's own party now concede.[17] Left-of-center Americans have now also awoken to the havoc Vladimir Putin is wreaking on the international system and the danger he poses to their country and its democratic institutions. A harder, tougher, and less illusioned American Left: a strange gift from Donald Trump, but real.

Gifts have arrived too for the political Right. The Republican Party had dead-ended itself in the Obama years, which is precisely why it lay vulnerable to a manifest charlatan like Donald Trump. Many—perhaps most—conservatives will follow Trump down the MAGA path to whichever doom it leads. But the principled and creative have resisted—and after many years of frozen orthodoxy, now at last an opportunity for reform and renewal may open.

For conservatives, recovery from Trump will not be a fast or easy process. The Trump experience will likely bequeath a severely damaged Republican Party. At the Cleveland convention in June 2016, I struck up a conversation with a delegate wearing a queasy expression on his face. He ran a trade association in a purple state, had been a Romney supporter in 2012, had voted anybody-but-Trump in his state's primary in 2016.

"So what will you do now?"

"I suppose I'll have to vote for him: he's the nominee."

"And your wife?"

"Oh no, she won't."

"Your kids?"

"They've re-registered as Democrats."

Trump has repelled a generation of young people from conservatism and Republicanism. He has imprinted upon his party his own prejudices, corruption, and ignorance. Republican candidates will pay a price for that legacy for years and decades ahead. But if nothing else, there is no denying now the outdatedness of the dogmas that gripped the Republican Party over the past decade. The old ways have conclusively failed, been repudiated even by their own previous supporters. New answers must be devised, and may finally gain a hearing. Some fantasize that the two-party system is to blame for the ills of US politics, that the answer is for moderates and independents to join together for a sensible politics of the center. Trump demonstrated that the independents are not moderates, and that the center is not always so sensible. What's most needed is not to insert moderation in some no-man's-land *between* the parties, but to restore moderation *to* the parties, and especially to the self-radicalized Republican Party. It may seem a long shot, but, to borrow a line from the movie *Argo,* "this is the best bad plan we have."

Sullied as it is by Trump, the Republican Party will outlast him. It must be redeemed and repurposed. If and as conservatives accept that reality, they can again offer useful public service, after the bitter waste that was Trumpocracy.

Trump has given gifts to the world outside the United States as well.

Donald Trump entered electoral politics in 2015 as just one among the many authoritarian populists bidding for power in the aftermath of the global economic crisis. There seemed to be fellow Trumps on the march everywhere across the Western developed world. That march has not halted. Marine Le Pen lost the French presidency in 2017, but with double the share of the vote received by her father in 2002. The German center held, but the parties of the extremes are rising as social democracy fades. From England to Austria to Catalonia, nationalism and statism are rising. Yet Trump has at least checked the forward momentum of Europe's nationalist authoritarians. His behaviors have brought enough discredit upon his style of politics to buy time for conservative liberals and liberal conservatives to regroup, rethink, renew, and revive.

"Have you ever considered that the purpose of your life may be to serve as a warning to others?" That sardonic message appears on a poster satirizing the inspirational messages offered by coaches and guidance counselors. The Trump administration may exist to fulfill just such a destiny: to remind other peoples in other countries that while constitutional government may sometimes look like an endless and pointless squabble, the promises of superior results from supposed strongmen are always self-serving lies. The American president who most despised European democracy may end by perversely and unintentionally preserving and enhancing it. You're welcome.

But of all the gifts of Trump, the best is that which heads this chapter: the surge in civic spirit that has moved Americans since the ominous night of November 8, 2016. It is as if millions of people awoke the next morning to the realization, "I must become a better citizen."

I've quoted many surveys and polls in this book, but here is the one that alarmed me the most when it was published and alarms me the most still. It is a cross-national study conducted by Roberto Foa and Yascha Mounk, and published in the *Journal of Democracy* in July 2016.

Citizens in a number of supposedly consolidated democracies in North America and Western Europe have not only grown more critical of their political leaders. Rather, they have also become more cynical about the value of democracy as a political system, less hopeful that anything they do might influence public policy, and more willing to express support for authoritarian alternatives. The crisis of democratic legitimacy extends across a much wider set of indicators than previously appreciated.

How much importance do citizens of developed countries ascribe to living in a democracy? Among older generations, the devotion to democracy is about as fervent and widespread as one might expect: In the United States, for example, people born during the interwar period consider democratic governance an almost sacred value. When asked to rate on a scale of 1 to 10 how "essential" it is for them "to live in a democracy," 72 percent of those born before World War II check "10," the highest value. So do 55 percent of the same cohort in the Netherlands. But . . . the millennial generation (those born since 1980) has grown much more indifferent. Only one in three Dutch millennials accords maximal importance to living in a democracy; in the United States, that number is slightly lower, around 30 percent.[18]

The new disenchantment with democracy is most often expressed by the more affluent. About one-third of Americans in the top three income deciles said it would be "good" or "very good" to be governed by a "strong leader" who "doesn't have to bother with elections." The younger the age cohort, Foa and Mounk observe, the wider this "democracy gap" between the more and less affluent.

It should be stressed that the democratic fade-out is not exclusively a right-of-center phenomenon. A 2015 Pew survey of attitudes toward free speech found that Democrats were twice as likely as Republicans to agree that the government should have the power to suppress speech offensive to minority groups: 35 percent to 18 percent.[19] These repressive attitudes also prevailed most strongly among the young: 40 percent of millennials would empower the state to suppress speech offensive to minority groups, as opposed to 25 percent of the middle aged, and only 12 percent of those born before World War II.

Belief in democracy waxes and wanes. Alexander Keyssar's history of American voting rights quotes an unsigned contribution to the *Atlantic Monthly* in 1879:

> Thirty or forty years ago it was considered the rankest heresy to doubt that a government based on universal suffrage was the wisest and best that could be devised. . . . Such is not now the case. Expressions of doubt and distrust in regard to universal suffrage are heard constantly in conversation, and in all parts of the country.[20]

Such doubts would shadow Americans for half a century, until the rise of totalitarianism in the 1930s confronted them with the real-world alternative to democracy: not the patrician elitism of the superior magazines, but the violent brutalities of fascism, communism, and Nazism. The Americans who absorbed that lesson, often in blood and suffering and grief, held it fast through their lives.

But Nazism is now only an epithet and communism not even that. Liberal democracy imposes limits and requires compromises. To people raised in wealthy societies, accustomed to having their wishes not only exactly met but delivered to their door, liberal democracy must seem grudging and unsatisfactory. You don't get exactly what you want! You often must settle for something you dislike, in order to avert something you would dislike more.

It seems unromantic—until you encounter the alternative. "Unhappy is the land that breeds no heroes," remarks a character in Bertolt Brecht's *Galileo*. "No," replies the title character. "Unhappy is the land that needs heroes." If you seek revolution, go seek it in business, in technology, in the arts. The steadiness and predictability of well-functioning liberal democracy enables innovation in every other area of life.

The candidate who won the most support from young voters in 2016, Bernie Sanders, noisily promised to upend that status quo:

> With your support and the support of millions of people throughout this country, we begin a political revolution to transform our country economically, politically, socially, and environmentally.[21]

Sanders promised a politics of ever-accelerating change, of boundless goals, a politics that offered answers to the existential questions. In a constitutional democracy, these questions should fall to each of us to resolve individually, outside of politics, not collectively and by means of politics. People who have never suffered the tyranny and terror of utopian politics may hearken to radical and revolutionary slogans. We see them in black masks, professing to be "antifascist" even as they emulate the street violence of Blackshirts and Brownshirts against the targets of their own totalitarian ideology. The Trump presidency may administer a much-needed booster shot to enhance the anti-authoritarian immunities of a younger generation apparently lacking in them.

Democratic Party gains in 2018 would surely do something to check President Trump. Merely partisan fluctuations will not, however, suffice to restore American institutions or halt the drift away from rule-of-law democracy. To achieve those ends, we must aspire to a deeper citizenship and wider loyalties. A few days before the 2016 election, I posted an essay at the *Atlantic* to explain my intention to do something I once never could have imagined: cast a ballot for Hillary Clinton for president. Except I was not voting for her. I was voting for the American system. I was voting for the rules, the norms, the Constitution that I expected her to respect even as she implemented policies with which I disagreed—unlike Donald Trump, who would subvert those standards even in those cases where he did things I might approve. I wrote then:

> I will vote for the candidate who rejects my preferences and offends my opinions. (In fact, I already have voted for her.) Previous generations accepted infinitely heavier sacrifices and more dangerous duties to defend democracy. I'll miss the tax cut I'd get from united Republican government. But there will be other elections, other chances to vote for what I regard as more sensible policies. My party will recover to counter her agenda in Congress, moderate her nominations to the courts, and defeat her bid for re-election in 2020. I look forward to supporting Republican recovery and renewal.
>
> This November, however, I am voting not to advance my wish-list on taxes, entitlements, regulation, and judicial appointments. I am voting to defend Americans' profoundest shared commitment: a commitment to norms and rules that today protect my rights under a president I don't favor, and that will tomorrow do the same service for you.[22]

And now over to you, reader. I have written much about the corruption the candidacy and presidency of Donald Trump have wrought on Americans as a people. Resistance begins by refusing to let him corrupt you personally. At the 2017 Politicon conference in Pasadena, California, I was accosted by an attendee who objected to my comments in a panel discussion. My interlocutor said something like, *We can't stop Donald Trump by going soft. If we want to stop him, we have to imitate him.* I answered, "But if you imitate him, you won't stop him. You'll only replace him."

As President Trump is cruel, vengeful, egoistic, ignorant, lazy, avaricious, and treacherous, so we must be kind, forgiving, responsible, informed, hardworking, generous, and patriotic. As Trump's enablers are careless, cynical, shortsighted, morally obtuse, and rancorous, so Trump's opponents must be thoughtful, idealistic, wise, morally sensitive, and conciliatory. "They go low, we go high," a wise woman said.

Those citizens who fantasize about defying tyranny from within fortified compounds have never understood how liberty is actually threatened in a modern bureaucratic state: not by diktat and violence, but by the slow, demoralizing process of corruption and deceit. And the way that liberty must be defended is not with amateur firearms, but with an unwearying insistence on the honesty, integrity, and professionalism of American institutions and those who lead them. We are living through the most dangerous challenge to the free government of the United States that anyone alive has encountered. What happens next is up to you. Don't be afraid. This moment of danger can also be your finest hour as a citizen and an American.

ACKNOWLEDGMENTS

The first word must go to my brilliant and generous-spirited colleagues at the *Atlantic*, and especially to Yoni Appelbaum, David Bradley, Jeffrey Goldberg, Don Peck, and Scott Stossell. It was in the *Atlantic*'s pages and on its site that the ideas developed here were first advanced—and by the rigorous editing of Yoni and Don that those ideas were challenged and sharpened. Parts of this book have previously appeared in the *Atlantic*, and in those cases, they are reproduced here with permission.

I offer my deep gratitude to those who read and commented on earlier versions of this book, especially Senator Linda Frum and Noah Kristula-Green. Thanks to my volunteer proofreaders, Tom Dolan and Yvonne Worthington. I am grateful especially to Windsor Mann, who meticulously fact-checked, corrected, and brought order to my footnotes.

Thanks to my editor at HarperCollins, Eric Nelson, and to my agent at WME, Jay Mandel. They dragged this book into being when I nervously wondered whether—given the pace of events of 2015–2017—it might not be wiser to comment on events via Twitter and Snapchat rather than irreversible print. Thanks, too, to Eric Meyers and the superb production team at HarperCollins.

ACKNOWLEDGMENTS

As with so many of its fellows, this book of mine was very largely written on the shores of Lake Ontario, on land formerly belonging to my in-laws Peter and Yvonne Worthington, now passed to my wife, Danielle, and me. Almost every day in our little village of Wellington and the nearby towns of Hillier, Bloomfield, or Picton, somebody offered a word of interest and encouragement in my work. These casual encounters brightened many days when I was depressed by the grim topics dealt with here. I extend a very personal thank-you to my neighbors and friends of Prince Edward County, Ontario.

Not only I, but everyone who cares about American democracy, owe a vast moral debt to my colleagues across the vast array of titles and platforms we call the American media. No single person could possibly plumb the foulnesses of the Trump presidency. I have gratefully relied on the discoveries and analyses of others. I have done my best to give credit not only in footnotes but in the text of this book to the people who have made of the Trump years—if nothing else—a golden age of courageous and honest reporting.

Ever and always, closest and dearest, my wife, Danielle Crittenden Frum, brought to these pages her keen editorial eye, her clear memory for detail, her biting sense of absurdity, and her noble heart that detests a bully and hates a lie. This is the ninth book through which she has helped me. All are finer and wiser for her guidance—as is their author.

NOTES

INTRODUCTION

1. Charles de Montesquieu, *Montesquieu: The Spirit of the Laws*, trans. and ed. Anne M. Cohler, Basia C. Miller, and Harold S. Stone (Cambridge, UK: Cambridge University Press, 1989), 71.
2. Michelle Ye Hee Lee, "Donald Trump and Iraq: Not Loud, Not Strong, and No Headlines," *Washington Post*, February 25, 2016, https://www .washingtonpost.com/news/fact-checker/wp/2016/02/25/timeline-of-trumps -comments-on-iraq-invasion-not-loud-not-strong-and-no-headlines/.
3. Eric Trump, foreword to Newt Gingrich, *Understanding Trump* (New York: Hatchette Book Group, 2017), xii; Adam Kelsey and Ali Rogin, "Steve Bannon Says Media 'Always Wrong' about Trump, President 'Maniacally Focused' on Agenda," *ABC News*, February 23, 2017, http://abcnews.go.com /Politics/steve-bannon-media-wrong-trump/story?id=45691100.
4. James Neugass, quoted in *The Edinburgh Companion to Twentieth-Century Literatures in English*, ed. Brian McHale and Randall Stevenson (Edinburgh, UK: Edinburgh University Press, 2006), 87.

CHAPTER 1: PRE-EXISTING CONDITIONS

1. "Transcript of the President's Speech, Conceding His Defeat by Clinton," *New York Times*, November 4, 1992, B5, http://www.nytimes .com/1992/11/04/us/1992-elections-disappointment-transcript-president-s -speech-conceding-his-defeat.html.
2. "Transcript of President Barack Obama with Univision," *LATimes.com*, October 25, 2010, http://latimesblogs.latimes.com/washington/2010/10 /transcript-of-president-barack-obama-with-univision.html.

3. Barack Obama, "Remarks by the President on Comprehensive Immigration Reform in El Paso, Texas," May 10, 2011, https://obamawhitehouse .archives.gov/the-press-office/2011/05/10/remarks-president-comprehensive -immigration-reform-el-paso-texas.

4. Barack Obama, "Remarks by the President in an 'Open for Questions' Roundtable," September 28, 2011, https://obamawhitehouse.archives.gov /the-press-office/2011/09/28/remarks-president-open-questions-roundtable.

5. Tom Cohen, "Obama administration to stop deporting some young illegal immigrants," *CNN.com*, June 16, 2012, http://www.cnn.com/2012/06/15 /politics/immigration/index.html.

6. "2014 Executive Actions on Immigration," U.S. Citizenship and Immigration Services, last modified April 15, 2015, https://www.uscis.gov /immigrationaction. The 2014 order also further relaxed standards of eligibility for the 2012 order.

7. Ariane de Vogue and Tal Kopan, "Deadlocked Supreme Court Deals Big Blow to Obama Immigration Plan," *CNN.com*, June 23, 2016, http://www .cnn.com/2016/06/23/politics/immigration-supreme-court/index.html.

8. That latter argument—that to qualify as a "natural-born citizen" under Article II of the Constitution an American must be born of American parents—originated, curiously, in a learned 1916 pamphlet arguing that the Republican presidential nominee Charles Evans Hughes was disqualified because of his father's British birth. The author, Breckenridge Long, would rise high in the Democratic Party, culminating his career as Franklin Delano Roosevelt's immigration commissioner, notorious for his indifferent response to the desperate Jewish emigration from Nazi Germany and Austria. See United States Holocaust Memorial Museum, "Breckinridge Long," *Holocaust Encyclopedia*, https://www.ushmm.org/wlc/en/article .php?ModuleId=10008298. The 1916 pamphlet can be read at https://www .scribd.com/doc/68922032/Natural-Born-Citizen-Within-Meaning-of -Constitution-by-Breckenridge-Long-Democrat-1916.

9. Josh Clinton and Carrie Roush, "Poll: Persistent Partisan Divide Over 'Birther' Question," *NBC News*, August 10, 2016, http://www.nbcnews.com/politics/2016 -election/poll-persistent-partisan-divide-over-birther-question-n627446.

10. *Meet the Press*, NBC, February 13, 2011, http://www.nbcnews.com /id/41536793/ns/meet_the_press-transcripts/t/meet-press-transcript-feb/.

11. It should be noted that the "I take him at his word" formula was originally coined by Hillary Clinton back in 2008. In an interview with Steve Kroft on CBS's *60 Minutes*, she added a new twist: asked whether Obama was a Muslim, she replied, "There's nothing to base that on"—and then added lethally, "as far as I know." *60 Minutes*, CBS, March 2, 2008, https://www .cbsnews.com/news/all-eyes-on-ohio-29-02-2008/4/.

12. Aliyah Shahid, "Donald Trump Takes Lead in Gop Primary Poll, Beats Romney, Huckabee, Palin, Gingrich, Bachmann, Paul," New York *Daily News*, April 15, 2011, http://www.nydailynews.com/news/politics/donald -trump-takes-lead-gop-primary-poll-beats-romney-huckabee-palin-gingrich -bachmann-paul-article-1.112460.

13. Dan Balz and Robert Costa, "Gov. Scott Walker: 'I Don't Know' Whether Obama Is a Christian," *Washington Post*, February 21, 2015, https://www .washingtonpost.com/politics/walker-says-he-is-unaware-whether-obama-is-a -christian/2015/02/21/6fde0bd0-ba17-11e4-bc30-a4e75503948a_story.html.

14. Bruce Ackerman, "The Court Packs Itself," *American Prospect*, December 3, 2001, http://prospect.org/article/court-packs-itself.

15. Elaina Plott, "Eric Cantor: 'If You've Got That Anger Working for You, You're Gonna Let It Be,'" *Washingtonian*, July 26, 2017, https://www .washingtonian.com/2017/07/26/eric-cantor-republicans-obamacare-donald -trump/.

16. John McCain, Senate floor statement, July 25, 2017, https://www.mccain .senate.gov/public/index.cfm/2017/7/mccain-on-senate-floor-today.

17. "Direction of Country," *RealClearPolitics*, accessed September 11, 2017, https://www.realclearpolitics.com/epolls/other/direction_of_country-902 .html.

18. Tom Perkins, letter to the editor, *Wall Street Journal*, January 24, 2014, https://www.wsj.com/articles/progressive-kristallnacht-coming-1390600169.

19. Nathan Vardi, "Inside the Obama Stock Market's 235% Return," *Forbes*, January 17, 2017, https://www.forbes.com/sites/nathanvardi/2017/01/17 /inside-the-obama-stock-markets-235-rise/.

20. "Man Carries Assault Rifle to Obama Protest—and It's Legal," *CNN.com*, August 17, 2009, http://www.cnn.com/2009/POLITICS/08/17/obama .protest.rifle/.

21. Manny Fernandez, Richard Pérez-Peña, and Jonah Engel Bromwich, "Five Officers Killed as Payback, Chief Says," *New York Times*, July 9, 2016, A1, https://www.nytimes.com/2016/07/09/us/dallas-police-shooting.html.

22. Thomas E. Mann and Norman J. Ornstein, *It's Even Worse Than It Looks: How the American Constitutional System Collided with the New Politics of Extremism* (New York: Basic Books, 2012).

CHAPTER 2: ENABLERS

1. Hugh Hewitt, Twitter, August 17, 2017, 8:34 p.m., https://twitter.com /hughhewitt/status/898387559230742528.

2. Hugh Hewitt, Twitter, August 17, 2017, 8:36 p.m., https://twitter.com /hughhewitt/status/898388112274997248; Hewitt, August 17, 2017, 8:39 p.m., https://twitter.com/hughhewitt/status/898388940347932672; Hewitt,

August 17, 2017, 8:40 p.m., https://twitter.com/hughhewitt/status /898389181885431813.

3. Dan Balz, "After Charlottesville, Republicans Remain Stymied over What to Do about Trump," *Washington Post*, August 19, 2017, https://www .washingtonpost.com/politics/after-charlottesville-republicans-remain -stymied-over-what-to-do-about-trump/2017/08/19/774bddd4-81d4-11e7 -ab27-1a21a8e006ab_story.html.

4. David A. Fahrenthold, "Trump Recorded Having Extremely Lewd Conversation about Women in 2005," *Washington Post*, October 8, 2016, https://www.washingtonpost.com/politics/trump-recorded-having-extremely -lewd-conversation-about-women-in-2005/2016/10/07/3b9ce776-8cb4-11e6 -bf8a-3d26847eeed4_story.html.

5. Alex Isenstadt, "RNC Halts Victory Project Work for Trump," *Politico*, October 8, 2016, http://www.politico.com/story/2016/10/rnc-halts-all -victory-project-work-for-trump-229363.

6. Matt Fuller, "Paul Ryan Responds to Donald Trump's Misogyny," *Huffington Post*, October 7, 2016, http://www.huffingtonpost.com/entry/paul-ryan -donald-trump-misogyny-silence_us_57f81f60e4b068ecb5de8a5c.

7. A recording of the call would become public only in March 2017, but its gist was widely reported almost immediately afterward. See Matthew Boyle, "Exclusive—Audio Emerges of When Paul Ryan Abandoned Donald Trump: 'I Am Not Going to Defend Donald Trump—Not Now, Not in the Future,'" *Breitbart*, March 13, 2017, http://www.breitbart.com/big-government /2017/03/13/exclusive-audio-emerges-of-when-paul-ryan-abandoned-donald -trump-i-am-not-going-to-defend-donald-trump-not-now-not-in-the-future/.

8. Travis Andersen, "Ayotte and Other Republicans Criticize Trump's Lewd Remarks," *Boston Globe*, October 8, 2016, https://www.bostonglobe.com /metro/2016/10/07/ayotte-and-other-republicans-criticize-trump-lewd -remarks/XbLfZbuEzBMdVlX4coAtMP/story.html.

9. "McConnell: Trump Must Apologize for 'Repugnant' Comments," *Politico*, October 7, 2016, http://www.politico.com/story/2016/10/mcconnell-trump -must-apologize-for-repugnant-comments-229332.

10. David Weigel, "Sen. Mike Lee Urges Trump to Quit, as Utah Republicans Abandon Their Party's Nominee," *Washington Post*, October 8, 2016, https:// www.washingtonpost.com/news/post-politics/wp/2016/10/08/sen-mike-lee -urges-trump-to-quit-as-utah-republicans-flee-from-their-presidential-nominee/.

11. Reena Flores, "Republicans Who Have Called on Donald Trump to Quit 2016 Race," *CBS News*, October 8, 2016, https://www.cbsnews.com/news /republicans-who-have-called-on-donald-trump-to-quit-2016-race/.

12. John Thune, Twitter, October 8, 2016, 9:51 a.m., https://twitter.com /SenJohnThune/status/784798261781598208.

13. Cristiano Lima, "'I'm Out': Rep. Chaffetz Withdraws His Endorsement of Trump," *Politico*, October 8, 2016, http://www.politico.com/story/2016/10/rep-chaffetz-withdraws-his-endorsement-of-trump-229335.

14. Donald J. Trump, Twitter, October 7, 2016, 9:19 p.m., https://twitter.com/realDonaldTrump/status/784609194234306560.

15. WikiLeaks, Twitter, October 7, 2016, 1:32 p.m., https://twitter.com/wikileaks/status/784491543868665856.

16. Roger Stone, Twitter, October 1, 2016, 9:52 p.m., https://twitter.com/RogerJStoneJr/status/782443074874138624.

17. "WikiLeaks' Julian Assange Dashes Hopes of #NeverHillary Alt-Right with Boring 2-Hour Informercial," *Week*, October 4, 2016, http://theweek.com/speedreads/652833/wikileaks-julian-assange-dashes-hopes-neverhillary-altright-boring-2hour-informercial.

18. Ken Meyer, "Alex Jones Rips 'Hillary Butt-Plug' Julian Assange After Disappointing WikiLeaks Announcement," *Mediaite*, October 4, 2016, https://www.mediaite.com/online/alex-jones-rips-hillary-butt-plug-julian-assange-after-disappointing-wikileaks-announcement/.

19. Chris Kahn, "Clinton Leads Trump by 5 Points in Presidential Race: Reuters/Ipsos Poll," Reuters, October 7, 2016, http://www.reuters.com/article/us-usa-election-poll-idUSKCN1272F1.

20. "HRC Paid Speeches," *WikiLeaks*, https://wikileaks.org/podesta-emails/emailid/927.

21. Ibid.

22. Third presidential debate, University of Nevada–Las Vegas, Paradise, NV, October 19, 2016. See "Final 2016 Presidential Debate (Full) | The New York Times," YouTube video, 1:33:01, posted by "The New York Times," October 19, 2016, https://www.youtube.com/watch?v=Z_pEb1bDN-w.

23. Scott Clement and Emily Guskin, "Post-ABC Tracking Poll Finds Race Tied, as Trump Opens Up an 8-Point Edge on Honesty," *Washington Post*, November 2, 2016, https://www.washingtonpost.com/news/the-fix/wp/2016/11/02/tracking-poll-finds-race-tied-as-trump-opens-up-an-8-point-edge-on-honesty/.

24. Mark Hensch, "Trump: 'I Love WikiLeaks,'" *Hill*, October 10, 2016, http://thehill.com/blogs/ballot-box/presidential-races/300327-trump-i-love-wikileaks.

25. "Presidential Candidate Donald Trump Rally in Fletcher, North Carolina," C-SPAN video, 43:18, https://www.c-span.org/video/?417259-1/donald-trump-campaigns-fletcher-north-carolina; Judd Legum, "Trump mentioned Wikileaks 164 times in last month of election, now claims it didn't impact one voter," *ThinkProgress*, January 8, 2017, https://thinkprogress.org/trump-mentioned-wikileaks-164-times-in-last-month-of-election-now-claims-it-didnt-impact-one-40aa62ea5002.

26. "Re: Conservative Catholicism," *WikiLeaks*, https://wikileaks.org/podesta
-emails/emailid/4364.

27. "Re: opening for a Catholic Spring? just musing . . . ," *WikiLeaks*, https://
wikileaks.org/podesta-emails/emailid/6293.

28. "U.S. Catholics Open to Non-Traditional Families," *Pew Research Center*,
September 2, 2015, http://www.pewforum.org/2015/09/02/u-s-catholics
-open-to-non-traditional-families/.

29. Sarah Pulliam Bailey, "WikiLeaks Emails Appear to Show Clinton
Spokeswoman Joking about Catholics and Evangelicals," *Washington Post*,
October 12, 2016, https://www.washingtonpost.com/news/acts-of-faith
/wp/2016/10/12/wikileaks-emails-show-clinton-spokeswoman-joking-about
-catholics-and-evangelicals/.

30. Cooper Allen, "Pence at Liberty University Calls on Christians to Forgive
Trump," *USA Today*, October 12, 2016, https://www.usatoday.com/story
/news/politics/onpolitics/2016/10/12/mike-pence-liberty-trump-forgive
/91948768/.

31. Jennifer Jacobs, Twitter, October 12, 2016, 10:30 a.m., https://twitter.com
/JenniferJJacobs/status/786257660324622336.

32. Charles J. Chaput, "About Those Unthinking, Backwards Catholics," *First
Things*, October 13, 2016, https://www.firstthings.com/blogs/firstthoughts
/2016/10/about-those-unthinking-backwards-catholics.

33. Eric Fehrnstrom, "Clinton's Revolution against the Catholic Church," *Boston
Globe*, October 20, 2016, https://www.bostonglobe.com/opinion
/2016/10/20/clinton-revolution-against-catholic-church/GrFpxMOU
pKtGUCqPK95B6J/story.html.

34. Julie Asher, "WikiLeaks Hack Exposes Clinton Staff's Past Catholic
Conversations," *National Catholic Reporter*, October 13, 2016, https://www
.ncronline.org/news/politics/wikileaks-hack-exposes-clinton-staffs-past
-catholic-conversations.

35. Marc A. Thiessen, "Hillary Clinton Is a Threat to Religious Liberty,"
Washington Post, October 13, 2016, https://www.washingtonpost.com
/opinions/hillary-clinton-is-a-threat-to-religious-liberty/2016/10/13
/878cdc36-9150-11e6-a6a3-d50061aa9fae_story.html.

36. Nick Gass, "Trump Rips Pope Francis for Visiting Mexican Border," *Politico*,
February 11, 2016, http://www.politico.com/story/2016/02/donald-trump
-pope-francis-mexican-border-219154.

37. Daniel Burke, "Pope Suggests Trump 'Is Not Christian,'" *CNN.com*,
February 18, 2016, http://www.cnn.com/2016/02/18/politics/pope-francis
-trump-christian-wall/.

38. Donald Trump, Facebook, February 18, 2016, 9:23 a.m., https://www
.facebook.com/DonaldTrump/posts/10156658168535725.

39.   Craig Silverman and Jeremy Singer-Vine, "The True Story Behind the Biggest Fake News Hit of the Election," *BuzzFeed News*, December 16, 2016, https://www.buzzfeed.com/craigsilverman/the-strangest-fake-news-empire.

40.   Alan Abramowitz and Steven Webster, "All Politics Is National: The Rise of Negative Partisanship and the Nationalization of U.S. House and Senate Elections in the 21st Century" (paper prepared for presentation at the Annual Meeting of the Midwest Political Science Association, Chicago, IL, April 16–19, 2015), http://stevenwwebster.com/research/all_politics_is_national.pdf.

41.   Niraj Chokshi, "The 100-plus Times Donald Trump Assured Us That America Is a Laughingstock," *Washington Post*, January 27, 2016, https://www.washingtonpost.com/news/the-fix/wp/2016/01/27/the-100-plus-times-donald-trump-has-assured-us-the-united-states-is-a-laughingstock/.

42.   Richard Johnson, "DC Private Schools Giving Kellyanne Conway the Brush-Off," *New York Post*, December 28, 2016, http://pagesix.com/2016/12/28/dc-private-schools-giving-kellyanne-conway-the-brush-off/.

43.   David Sanders, "Principled Losers," *Radix Journal*, May 23, 2016. Archived at http://archive.is/YcsgQ#selection-591.0-599.524.

44.   Peter Augustine Lawler, "Trump Today," *National Review Online*, August 7, 2016, http://www.nationalreview.com/postmodern-conservative/438751/entering-new-american-disorder.

45.   Harvey C. Mansfield, "Why Donald Trump Is No Gentleman," *Wall Street Journal*, July 30, 2016, A13, http://www.wsj.com/articles/why-donald-trump-is-no-gentleman-1469831003.

46.   Donald J. Trump, Twitter, June 29, 2017, 8:52 a.m., https://twitter.com/realdonaldtrump/status/880408582310776832.

47.   Donald J. Trump, Twitter, June 29, 2017, 8:58 a.m., https://twitter.com/realdonaldtrump/status/880410114456465411.

48.   Christian Holub, "White House Defends Trump Tweets: He 'Fights Fire with Fire,'" *EW.com*, June 29, 2017, http://ew.com/tv/2017/06/29/donald-trump-white-house-mika-brzezinski/.

49.   *Rush Limbaugh Show*, June 13, 2017, https://www.rushlimbaugh.com/daily/2017/06/13/a-deep-dive-into-shakespeare-in-the-park-madness/.

50.   Alexander Hamilton, *Federalist*, No. 68, March 14, 1788, in *The Federalist* (Washington, DC: Regnery, 1998), 509.

CHAPTER 3: APPEASERS

1.   Michael Barbaro, "Jeb Bush's Image Gives G.O.P. Something to Think About Before 2016," *New York Times*, May 25, 2014, A19, https://www.nytimes.com/2014/05/25/us/politics/jeb-bush-gives-party-something-to-think-about.html.

2.   Ibid.

3.   "Greatest Century | Jeb Bush," YouTube video, 1:04, posted by "Jeb Bush," June 15, 2015, https://www.youtube.com/watch?v=Vet1HHyYtZQr.

4.   Only 3 percent of the donations to Jeb Bush's presidential fund arrived in increments of $200 or less. More than one-quarter of the $103 million collected by Jeb Bush's super PAC arrived in gifts of $1 million or more.

5.   Alexandra Jaffe, "CNN/ORC Poll: Bush Surges to 2016 GOP Frontrunner," *CNN.com*, December 28, 2014, http://www.cnn.com/2014/12/28/politics /bush-leads-gop-field-poll/index.html.

6.   Donald Trump, presidential campaign announcement, New York, NY, June 16, 2015. See "Donald Trump Presidential Campaign Announcement Full Speech (C-SPAN)," YouTube video, 47:08, posted by "C-SPAN," June 16, 2015, https://www.youtube.com/watch?v=apjNfkysjbM.

7.   Ryan Struyk, "Ben Carson Falls from Frontrunner Status in a New National Poll," *ABC News*, December 2, 2015, http://abcnews.go.com/Politics/ben -carson-falls-frontrunner-status-national-poll/story?id=35521989.

8.   Charles Krauthammer, "The Way Forward," *Washington Post*, November 9, 2012, A29.

9.   Benjamin Hart, "Sean Hannity Flips on Immigration Reform, Now Supports Pathway to Citizenship," *Huffington Post*, November 8, 2012, http://www .huffingtonpost.com/2012/11/08/sean-hannity-immigration-pathway-to -citizenship_n_2096255.html.

10. Rupert Murdoch, Twitter, November 7, 2012, 4:55 p.m., https://twitter.com /rupertmurdoch/status/266343060265377794.

11. Alicia Mundy, "Sheldon Adelson: 'I'm Basically a Social Liberal,'" *Washington Wire* (blog), *Wall Street Journal*, December 5, 2012, https://blogs.wsj.com /washwire/2012/12/05/sheldon-adelson-im-basically-a-social-liberal/.

12. Chris Cillizza, "Three Sentences on Immigration That Will Haunt Republicans in 2016," *Washington Post*, July 1, 2014, https://www .washingtonpost.com/news/the-fix/wp/2014/07/01/three-sentences-on -immigration-that-will-haunt-republicans-in-2016/, citing Republican National Committee, "Growth and Opportunity Project," https://assets .documentcloud.org/documents/623664/republican-national-committees -growth-and.pdf.

13. Donald Trump, presidential campaign announcement, New York, June 16, 2015. See "Donald Trump Presidential Campaign Announcement Full Speech (C-SPAN)," YouTube video, 47:08, posted by "C-SPAN," June 16, 2015, https://www.youtube.com/watch?v=apjNfkysjbM.

14. Ronald Brownstein, "How Obama Won: Marrying Old and New Democratic Coalitions," *Atlantic*, November 7, 2012, https://www.theatlantic.com /politics/archive/2012/11/how-obama-won-marrying-old-and-new

-democratic-coalitions/264884/. Brownstein did not explicitly include the latter three groups in the coalition, but any definition of the "ascendant" in 2010s America must include them.

15. David Brady and Douglas Rivers, "Decoding Trump's Supporters," *Defining Ideas*, September 15, 2015, http://www.hoover.org/research/decoding-trumps -supporters.

16. Ibid.

17. Ibid.

18. "Trump Supporters Think Obama Is a Muslim Born in Another Country," *Public Policy Polling*, September 1, 2015, http://www.publicpolicypolling .com/main/2015/08/trump-supporters-think-obama-is-a-muslim-born-in -another-country.html.

19. Ibid.

20. Donald Trump, presidential campaign announcement, New York, NY, June 16, 2015. See "Donald Trump Presidential Campaign Announcement Full Speech (C-SPAN)," YouTube video, 47:08, posted by "C-SPAN," June 16, 2015, https://www.youtube.com/watch?v=apjNfkysjbM.

21. Republican primary debate, Cleveland, OH, televised by Fox News Network, August 6, 2015. See "First Republican Primary Debate—Main Stage— August 6 2015 on Fox News," YouTube video, 1:55:17, posted by "2016 US Presidential Debates," April 15, 2016, https://www.youtube.com /watch?v=2rU4W3yfd58.

22. Robert Costa, Philip Rucker, and Dan Balz, "Donald Trump Plots His Second Act," *Washington Post*, October 7, 2015, https://www.washingtonpost .com/politics/donald-trump-plots-his-second-act/2015/10/06/305790c2 -6c68-11e5-9bfe-e59f5e244f92_story.html.

23. Javier de Diego, "Despite Having D.C.'s Toughest Job, RNC Chair Priebus Doesn't Want Pity," *CNN.com*, April 20, 2016, http://www.cnn.com/2016 /04/20/politics/reince-priebus-republican-national-committee/index.html.

24. Drew Griffin, Marshall Cohen, and Scott Zamost, "Trump Paid $12.5 Million to His Own Businesses during Race," *CNN.com*, December 16, 2016, http://money.cnn.com/2016/12/16/news/companies/donald-trump -campaign-fec/index.html.

25. Christine Wang, "Trump Says Billionaire, Former Critic Paul Singer Visited White House," *CNBC.com*, February 16, 2017, http://www.cnbc.com/2017 /02/16/trump-says-billionaire-former-critic-paul-singer-visited-white-house .html.

26. Nicholas Fandos, "Corporations Open Spigot to Bankroll Inauguration," *New York Times*, January 16, 2017, A12, http://www.nytimes.com/2017/01/15 /us/politics/trump-inauguration-donations-corporations.html; Fredreka Schouten, "What's Happened to Trump's Leftover Inaugural Money? Six

Months Later, We Don't Know," *USA Today*, July 20, 2017, modified July 22, 2017, https://www.usatoday.com/story/news/politics/2017/07/20/what -happened-president-trumps-leftover-inaugural-money-six-months-later-we -dont-know/493397001/.

27. David Wright, Tal Kopan, and Julia Manchester, "Cruz Unloads with Epic Takedown of 'Pathological Liar,' 'Narcissist' Donald Trump," *CNN.com*, May 3, 2016, http://www.cnn.com/2016/05/03/politics/donald-trump-rafael-cruz -indiana/index.html.

28. Ted Cruz, Facebook, September 23, 2016, 12:24 p.m., https://www.facebook .com/tedcruzpage/posts/10154476728267464.

29. Will Jordan, Twitter, October 19, 2016, 10:24 a.m., https://twitter.com /williamjordann/status/788792988503769088.

30. Joshua Green and Sasha Issenberg, "Inside the Trump Bunker, with Days to Go," *Bloomberg Businessweek*, October 27, 2016, https://www.bloomberg.com /news/articles/2016-10-27/inside-the-trump-bunker-with-12-days-to-go.

31. *Mark Levin Show*, April 5, 2016. See Josh Feldman, "Mark Levin Rips #NeverTrump 'Buffoons': You Would 'Passively' Help Hillary Win?," *Mediaite*, April 6, 2016, https://www.mediaite.com/online/mark-levin-rips -nevertrump-buffoons-you-would-passively-help-hillary-win/.

32. *CNN Tonight*, CNN, August 7, 2015.

33. Sam Reisman, "Fox News Responds to Trump's Latest 'Twitter Poll' with First-Rate Trolling," *Mediaite*, January 26, 2016, http://www.mediaite.com /online/fox-news-responds-to-trumps-latest-twitter-poll-with-first-rate -trolling/.

34. Sam Reisman, "Trump Attacks Megyn Kelly Again: Nobody Knew Her Before the Debate," *Mediaite*, January 25, 2016, http://www.mediaite.com /online/trump-attacks-megyn-kelly-again-nobody-knew-her-before-the -debate/.

35. Sam Reisman, "Fox Responds to Trump's Latest Attack on Megyn Kelly: Trump Is Showing a Lot of Fear," *Mediaite*, January 25, 2016, https://www .mediaite.com/online/fox-responds-to-trumps-latest-attack-on-megyn-kelly -trump-is-showing-a-lot-of-fear/.

36. David A. Fahrenthold, "Trump Announced His Gifts to Veterans. Here's What We Learned," *Washington Post*, May 30, 2016, https://www .washingtonpost.com/news/post-politics/wp/2016/05/30/tomorrow-trump -will-give-more-details-about-his-donations-to-vets-heres-what-we-still-dont -know/.

37. *The Kelly File*, Fox News Network, October 25, 2016.

38. Chris Spargo, "Megyn Kelly Says Trump Aide Dan Scavino Is Responsible for Inciting Violent Threats against Her—and That She and Her Kids Have Needed Armed Guards to Protect Them for 16 Months," *Daily Mail*,

December 8, 2016, http://www.dailymail.co.uk/news/article-4014680
/Megyn-Kelly-says-Trump-aide-Dan-Scavino-responsible-inciting-violent
-threats-against-kids-needed-armed-guards-protect-16-months.html.

39. Dan Gunderman, "Sean Hannity Brings up Seth Rich Again, Alludes to
DNC Emails and Suspicious Murder," New York *Daily News*, June 23, 2017,
http://www.nydailynews.com/news/politics/sean-hannity-brings-seth-rich
-alludes-dnc-emails-article-1.3272124.

40. *Fox News Sunday*, Fox News Network, June 25, 2017.

41. Kellyanne Conway, interview by Chuck Todd, *Meet the Press*, NBC, January
22, 2017, https://www.nbcnews.com/meet-the-press/video/conway-press
-secretary-gave-alternative-facts-860142147643.

42. Chris Ariens, "MSNBC Wins Its First Week Ever in Prime Time," *Ad Week*,
May 22, 2017, http://www.adweek.com/tvnewser/for-1st-time-in-17-years
-fox-news-was-3rd-in-prime-time-demo/329902.

43. David E. Bernstein, *Lawless: The Obama Administration's Unprecedented
Assault on the Constitution and the Rule of Law* (New York: Encounter, 2015).

44. Kurt Schlichter, Twitter, August 25, 2017, 6:43 p.m., https://twitter.com
/KurtSchlichter/status/901258810966200320.

CHAPTER 4: PLUNDER

1. Transparency International, "Corruption Perceptions Index 2016," January
25, 2017, https://www.transparency.org/news/feature/corruption
_perceptions_index_2016.

2. Peter Applebome, "Gingrich Gives Up $4 Million Advance on His Book Deal,"
New York Times, December 31, 1994, A01, http://www.nytimes.com/1994
/12/31/us/gingrich-gives-up-4-million-advance-on-his-book-deal.html.

3. Brian Montopoli, "Daschle Withdraws HHS Nomination," *CBS News*,
February 3, 2009, https://www.cbsnews.com/news/daschle-withdraws-hhs
-nomination/.

4. Carol D. Leonning, Tom Hamburger, Rosalind S. Helderman, "Trump's
Business Sought Deal on a Moscow Trump Tower during Campaign,"
Washington Post, https://www.washingtonpost.com/video/politics
/trumps-business-sought-deal-on-a-moscow-trump-tower-during
-campaign/2017/08/27/595964f6-8ba0-11e7-9c53-6a169beb0953_video
.html.

5. Dan Merica, "Trump on Pace to Surpass 8 Years of Obama's Travel Spending
in 1 Year," *CNN.com*, April 11, 2017, http://www.cnn.com/2017/04/10
/politics/donald-trump-obama-travel-costs/index.html.

6. Nicholas Fandos, "Budget Deal Allots $120 Million More for First Family's
Security," *New York Times*, May 2, 2017, A18, https://www.nytimes.com
/2017/05/01/us/politics/secret-service-trump-protection.html.

7. Kevin Johnson, "Exclusive: Secret Service Depletes Funds to Pay Agents Because of Trump's Frequent Travel, Large Family," *USA Today*, August 21, 2017, https://www.usatoday.com/story/news/politics/2017/08/21/secret-service-cant-pay-agents-because-trumps-frequent-travel-large-family/529075001/.

8. Laura Strickler, Analisa Novak, and Julianna Goldman, "Trump Kids' Ski Vacation Incurs over $300,000 in Security Costs," *CBS News*, September 29, 2017, https://www.cbsnews.com/news/trump-kids-ski-vacation-incurs-over-300000-in-security-costs/.

9. "Exclusive: Like Mother Like Daughter! Tiffany Trump and Marla Maples Flaunt Their Enviable Figures in Bikinis as They Soak up the Italian Sunshine aboard a Luxury Yacht," *Daily Mail*, July 16, 2017, http://www.dailymail.co.uk/news/article-4701466/Tiffany-Trump-Marla-Maples-aboard-luxury-yacht.html.

10. Jonathan O'Connell, "Trump D.C. Hotel Turns $2 Million Profit in Four Months," *Washington Post*, August 10, 2017, https://www.washingtonpost.com/politics/trump-dc-hotel-turns-2-million-profit-in-four-months/2017/08/10/23bd97f0-7e02-11e7-9d08-b79f191668ed_story.html.

11. "Schedule B for ALL Line #'s—Candidate & Committee Viewer," Committee: REBUILDING AMERICA NOW, Federal Election Commission, accessed September 28, 2017, http://docquery.fec.gov/cgi-bin/forms/C00618876/1177312/sb/ALL.

12. Alexandra Berzon, "Trump Hotel in Washington Saw Strong Profit in First Four Months of 2017," *Wall Street Journal*, August 11, 2017, https://www.wsj.com/articles/trump-hotel-in-washington-saw-strong-profit-in-first-four-months-of-2017-1502424589.

13. Matea Gold and Anu Narayanswamy, "Republican Committees Have Paid Nearly $1.3 Million to Trump-Owned Entities This Year," *Washington Post*, August 21, 2017, https://www.washingtonpost.com/news/post-politics/wp/2017/08/21/republican-committees-have-spent-nearly-1-3-million-at-trump-owned-properties-this-year/.

14. Robert Frank, "Mar-a-Lago Membership Fee Doubles to $200,000," *CNBC.com*, January 25, 2017, https://www.cnbc.com/2017/01/25/mar-a-lago-membership-fee-doubles-to-200000.html.

15. Ashley Feinberg, "Trump's 2020 Campaign Has Already Paid Out $600K—to Trump," *Wired*, July 20, 2017, https://www.wired.com/story/trump-2020-campaign-money/.

16. Paul Sonne, "U.S. Military's Space in Trump Tower Costs $130,000 a Month," *Wall Street Journal*, July 19, 2017, https://www.wsj.com/articles/u-s-militarys-space-in-trump-tower-costs-130-000-a-month-1500428508.

17. Steve Eder and Jennifer Medina, "Settlement Is Approved in Trump University Suit," *New York Times*, April 1, 2017, A16, https://www.nytimes.com/2017/03/31/us/trump-university-settlement.html.

18. This account is based on the superb reporting of *Bloomberg News*. See Caleb Melby and David Kocieniewski, "Inside the Troubled Kushner Tower: Empty Offices and Mounting Debt," *Bloomberg News*, March 22, 2017, https://www.bloomberg.com/news/articles/2017-03-22/kushners-troubled-tower-debt-empty-offices-and-rising-fees.

19. Susanne Craig, Jo Becker, and Jesse Drucker, "A Second Empire by Trump's Side," *New York Times*, January 8, 2017, A01, https://www.nytimes.com/2017/01/07/us/politics/jared-kushner-trump-business.html.

20. Emily Rauhala and William Wan, "In a Beijing Ballroom, Kushner Family Pushes $500,000 'Investor Visa' to Wealthy Chinese," *Washington Post*, May 6, 2017, https://www.washingtonpost.com/world/in-a-beijing-ballroom-kushner-family-flogs-500000-investor-visa-to-wealthy-chinese/2017/05/06/cf711e53-eb49-4f9a-8dea-3cd836fcf287_story.html.

21. Ned Parker and Jonathan Landay, "Exclusive: Trump Son-in-Law Had Undisclosed Contacts with Russian Envoy—Sources," Reuters, May 26, 2017, http://www.reuters.com/article/us-usa-trump-fbi-kushner-exclusive idUSKBN18N018.

22. A helpful summary (with links) of the Spanish-language reporting on the conversations between Trump and Macri can be found here: https://thinkprogress.org/there-is-a-lot-more-to-the-trump-argentina-story-e4a5026a959c.

23. Kailash Babar, "Donald Trump Meets Indian Partners, Hails PM Modi's Work," *Economic Times* (Mumbai), November 17, 2016, http://economictimes.indiatimes.com/news/politics-and-nation/donald-trump-meets-indian-partners-hails-pm-modis-work/articleshow/55465060.cms.

24. Tara John, "Ivanka Trump Had Business at Stake When She Met Japan's Prime Minister," *Fortune*, December 5, 2016, http://fortune.com/2016/12/05/ivanka-trump-donald-trump-japan-shinzo-abe/.

25. Rachel Abrams, "Trump Brand Scuttles Deal Over Firm's Official Links," *New York Times*, June 13, 2017, B3, https://www.nytimes.com/2017/06/12/business/ivanka-trump-brand-japanese-business-deal.html.

26. Jana Winter and Elias Groll, "Here's the Memo That Blew Up the NSC," *Foreign Policy*, August 10, 2017, http://foreignpolicy.com/2017/08/10/heres-the-memo-that-blew-up-the-nsc/.

27. Michael Sullivan, "Who's the New Philippine Envoy? The Man Building Trump Tower Manila," *NPR*, November 22, 2016, http://www.npr.org/sections/parallels/2016/11/22/502895797/whos-the-new-philippine-envoy-the-man-building-trump-tower-manila.

28. "Transcript of Call between President Trump and Philippine President Duterte," *Washington Post*, http://apps.washingtonpost.com/g/documents/politics /transcript-of-call-between-president-trump-and-philippine-president-duterte /2446/.

29. Steve Eder and Ben Protess, "Snarl of Foreign Ties Arises in Trump Hotel Deal," *New York Times*, March 23, 2017, A1, https://www.nytimes.com/2017 /03/22/business/trump-organization-scion-hotel-deal.html.

30. Erika Kinetz, "China Grants Preliminary Approval to 38 New Trump Trademarks," Associated Press, March 9, 2017, https://apnews.com /8f54b14808a2459f9efcb0089f41f056/china-grants-preliminary-approval -38-new-trump-trademarks.

31. Michael Kruse, "Donald Trump Says He 'Called' the '08 Crash. Here's What Really Happened," *Politico*, October 7, 2016, http://www.politico.com /magazine/story/2016/10/donald-trump-says-he-called-the-08-crash-heres -what-really-happened-214327.

32. Adam Davidson, "Donald Trump's Worst Deal," *New Yorker*, March 13, 2017, http://www.newyorker.com/magazine/2017/03/13/donald-trumps-worst-deal.

33. Nathan Layne, Ned Parker, Svetlana Reiter, Stephen Grey, and Ryan McNeill, "Russian Elite Invested Nearly $100 Million in Trump Buildings," Reuters, March 17, 2017, http://www.reuters.com/investigates/special-report /usa-trump-property/.

34. Nick Penzenstadler, Steve Reilly, and John Kelly, "Most Trump Real Estate Now Sold to Secretive Buyers," *USA Today*, June 13, 2017, https://www .usatoday.com/story/news/2017/06/13/trump-property-buyers-make-clear -shift-secretive-llcs/102399558/.

35. Jean Eaglesham and Lisa Schwartz, "Startup That Got a Seat at White House Roundtable Is Part-Owned by Kushner Family," *Wall Street Journal*, July 15, 2017, https://www.wsj.com/articles/startup-that-got-a-seat-at-white-house -roundtable-is-part-owned-by-kushner-family-1500045800.

36. Jared Kushner, Public Financial Disclosure Report (OGE Form 278e), https://assets.documentcloud.org/documents/3534020/Jared-Kushner -Financial-Disclosure.pdf.

37. Jennifer Calfas, "Eric Trump Says He'll Give the President Quarterly Updates on Business Empire," *Fortune*, March 24, 2017, http://fortune.com/2017/03 /24/eric-trump-president-business-organization/.

38. Susanne Craig, "Trump's Empire: A Maze of Debts and Opaque Ties," *New York Times*, August 21, 2016, A1, https://www.nytimes.com/2016/08/21/us /politics/donald-trump-debt.html; Robert Costa, "Trump Family Members Met with GOP Leaders to Discuss Strategy," *Washington Post*, May 27, 2017, https://www.washingtonpost.com/news/post-politics/wp/2017/05/27/trump -family-members-met-with-gop-leaders-to-discuss-strategy/.

39. Dave Burke and Erica Tempesta, "'I Miss Her in New York!' Eric Trump shares photo of himself and sister Ivanka at the White House, as she posts a sweet snap of her eldest son at the Smithsonian museum," *Daily Mail*, March 10, 2017, http://www.dailymail.co.uk/news/article-4300780/Eric-Trump -poses-sister-Ivanka-White-House.html.

40. Associated Press, "President Trump's Daughter-in-Law Lara Has a New Job Helping the Trump Campaign," *Fortune*, March 29, 2017, http://fortune.com /2017/03/29/donald-trump-campaign-lara/.

41. Drew Harwell and Tom Hamburger, "Despite Promise, Trump's Business Offers Little Information about Foreign Profits," *Washington Post*, May 24, 2017, https://www.washingtonpost.com/business/economy/despite-promise -trumps-business-offers-little-information-about-foreign-profits/2017/05/24 /e4667da4-4091-11e7-9869-bac8b446820a_story.html.

42. Michael M. Grynbaum, "Trump Attacks News Media, Which Then Battle Among Themselves," *New York Times*, January 12, 2017, A19, http://www .nytimes.com/2017/01/11/business/media/donald-trump-buzzfeed-cnn.html.

43. Kellyanne Conway, interview by George Stephanopoulos, *This Week*, ABC, January 22, 2017.

44. Susanne Craig, "Trump's Empire: A Maze of Debts and Opaque Ties," *New York Times*, August 21, 2016, A01, https://www.nytimes.com/2016/08/21 /us/politics/donald-trump-debt.html.

45. Ibid.

46. Timothy O'Brien, interview by Kelly McEvers, *All Things Considered*, NPR, January 13, 2017, http://www.npr.org/2017/01/13/509722763/timothy -obrien-trump-could-divest-or-sell-assets-to-avoid-conflicts-of-interest; Theodoric Meyer and Matthew Nussbaum, "Trump reports assets of at least $1.4 billion in financial disclosure," *Politico*, June 16, 2017, http://www .politico.com/story/2017/06/16/us-ethics-office-releases-trumps-financial -disclosure-239649.

47. Sam Bloch, Jeremy Olds, Christian Erin-Madsen, and Renata Mosci, "Jared Kushner and Ivanka Trump Failed to Disclose Their Multimillion-Dollar Art Collection," *Artnet.com*, May 25, 2017, https://news.artnet.com/art-world /jared-kushner-ivanka-trump-art-970010; "Jared Kushner Didn't Disclose Startup Stake," *WSJ What's News* (podcast), 7:16, *Wall Street Journal*, May 2, 2017, http://www.wsj.com/podcasts/jared-kushner-didnt-disclose-startup -stake/42D3337E-5265-4C09-BCD5-FE756294FE69.html.

48. Charles Sumner, "Republicanism vs. Grantism," Speech in the US Senate, May 31, 1872, in Charles Sumner, *Charles Sumner: His Complete Works*, vol. 20, ed. George Frisbie Hoar (Boston: Lee and Shepard, 1900; Project Gutenberg, 2016), 145, http://www.gutenberg.org/files/51025/51025-h /51025-h.htm#REPUBLICANISM_VS_GRANTISM.

49. Hui Chen, "Mission Matters," LinkedIn, June 25, 2017, https://www.linkedin
.com/pulse/mission-matters-hui-chen.

50. Adam Edelman, "Trump Has Offered up 1 Replacement Nearly 3 Months
after Firing 46 Remaining Obama-Era U.S. Attorneys," New York *Daily
News*, June 4, 2017, http://www.nydailynews.com/news/politics/trump-1
-replacement-3-months-firing-46-u-s-attorneys-article-1.3217910.

51. Laura Jarrett, "President Has Rare Meeting with US Attorney Nominee,"
CNN.com, July 20, 2017, http://www.cnn.com/2017/07/20/politics/donald
-trump-jessie-liu-dc-us-attorney/index.html.

52. Donald J. Trump, Twitter, July 24, 2017, 5:49 a.m., https://twitter.com
/realdonaldtrump/status/889467610332528641.

53. Tim O'Brien, Twitter, July 27, 2017, 12:55 a.m., https://twitter.com/TimOBrien
/status/890435464007741442/photo/1.

54. "'It's Not on Me, You Know, They're Looking at a Lot of Things,'" *New York
Times*, July 20, 2017, A12, https://www.nytimes.com/2017/07/19/us/politics
/trump-interview-transcript.html.

55. "From George Washington to Samuel Vaughan, 21 March 1789," *Founders Online*,
National Archives, last modified June 29, 2017, http://founders.archives.gov
/documents/Washington/05-01-02-0325. Original source: *The Papers of George
Washington*, Presidential Series, vol. 1, *24 September 1788–31 March 1789*, ed.
Dorothy Twohig (Charlottesville, VA: University Press of Virginia, 1987), 424–30.

56. Tal Shalev and Lahav Harkov, "Kafe Knesset for May 25," *Jewish Insider*, May
25, 2017, http://jewishinsider.com/11762/kafe-knesset-for-may-25/.

57. "Ivanka Trump Takes Donald Trump Seat at G20 Leaders' Table," *BBC.com*,
July 8, 2017, http://www.bbc.com/news/world-40541611.

58. Eugene Scott, Evan Perez, and Pamela Brown, "DOJ: Hiring Kushner Does
Not Violate Anti-Nepotism Law," *CNN.com*, January 21, 2017, http://www
.cnn.com/2017/01/21/politics/jared-kushner-white-house-job-justice
-department-ruling/index.html.

59. "Thomas Jefferson to John Garland Jefferson, 25 January 1810," *Founders
Online*, National Archives, last modified June 29, 2017, http://founders
.archives.gov/documents/Jefferson/03-02-02-0145. Original source: *The
Papers of Thomas Jefferson*, Retirement Series, vol. 2, *16 November 1809 to
11 August 1810*, ed. J. Jefferson Looney (Princeton, NJ: Princeton University
Press, 2005), 183–184.

CHAPTER 5: BETRAYALS

1. Glenn Thrush, Twitter, May 24, 2017, 1:29 p.m., https://twitter.com
/glennthrush/status/867477564956323840.

2. Maggie Haberman, Twitter, May 24, 2017, 12:51 p.m., https://twitter.com
/maggienyt/status/867468019882115072.

3.   Carrie Dann, "Trump's Physician Says His Health Is 'Astonishingly Excellent,'" *NBC News*, December 14, 2015, http://www.nbcnews.com /politics/2016-election/trumps-physician-says-his-health-astonishingly -excellent-n479786.

4.   Clemence Michallon, "'Thank You, Baby': Donald Trump Pays Tribute to Kellyanne Conway for Going on CNN to 'Destroy' His Critics When 'My Men Are Petrified to Go On,'" *Daily Mail*, January 19, 2017, http://www .dailymail.co.uk/news/article-4138948/Donald-Trump-pays-tribute -Kellyanne-Conway.html.

5.   Saba Hamedy, "Kellyanne Conway: Comey's Firing 'Has Nothing to Do with Russia,'" *CNN.com*, May 9, 2017, http://www.cnn.com/2017/05/09/politics /kellyanne-conway-anderson-cooper-comey-firing-cnntv/index.html.

6.   Donald Trump, interview by Lester Holt, *NBC Nightly News*, NBC, May 11, 2017, https://www.nbcnews.com/news/us-news/trump-reveals-he-asked -comey-whether-he-was-under-investigation-n757821.

7.   Donald J. Trump, Twitter, May 12, 2017, 4:59 a.m., https://twitter.com /realdonaldtrump/status/863000553265270786.

8.   Mike Pence, interview by John Dickerson, *Face the Nation*, CBS, January 15, 2017.

9.   Shawn Boburg and Aaron C. Davis, "Trump Attorney Jay Sekulow's Family Has Been Paid Millions from Charities They Control," *Washington Post*, June 27, 2017, https://www.washingtonpost.com/investigations/trump -attorney-jay-sekulows-family-has-been-paid-millions-from-charities-they -control/2017/06/27/6428d988-5852-11e7-ba90-f5875b7d1876_story.html.

10.   Condoleezza Rice, speech at the 2000 Republican National Convention, Philadelphia, PA, August 1, 2000, http://www.washingtonpost.com/wp-srv /onpolitics/elections/ricetext080100.htm.

11.   Michael Flynn, speech at the 2016 Republican National Convention, Cleveland, OH, July 18, 2016, http://transcripts.cnn.com/TRANSCRIPTS /1607/18/se.04.html.

12.   James V. Grimaldi, Dion Nissenbaum, and Margaret Coker, "Ex-CIA Director: Mike Flynn and Turkish Officials Discussed Removal of Erdogan Foe from U.S.," *Wall Street Journal*, March 24, 2017, https://www.wsj.com /articles/ex-cia-director-mike-flynn-and-turkish-officials-discussed-removal -of-erdogan-foe-from-u-s-1490380426.

13.   Andy Kroll, "Donald Trump's White House Counsel Has One Main Job— and He's Failing at It," *Mother Jones*, June 2, 2017, http://www.motherjones .com/politics/2017/06/mcgahn-trump-flynn-russia-white-house/.

14.   Tara Palmeri, "Trump's Aides Build Their Own Empires in the West Wing," *Politico*, July 6, 2017, http://www.politico.com/story/2017/07/06/trump -west-wing-staff-kushner-240244.

15. Jonathan Martin and Glenn Thrush, "Trump Steps in with Late Pitch to Wary Senate," *New York Times*, June 28, 2017, A01, https://www.nytimes .com/2017/06/27/us/health-care-bill-trump-pence.html.

16. Ibid.

17. Donald J. Trump, Twitter, September 30, 2017, 7:19 a.m., https://twitter .com/realdonaldtrump/status/914087234869047296?lang=en.

18. Donald J. Trump, Twitter, September 30, 2017, 7:26 a.m., https://twitter .com/realdonaldtrump/status/914089003745468417?lang=en.

19. Donald J. Trump, Twitter, October 1, 2017, 8:22 a.m., https://twitter.com /realdonaldtrump/status/914465475777695744?lang=en.

20. Donald J. Trump, Twitter, July 1, 2017, 3:41 p.m., https://twitter.com /realDonaldTrump/status/881281755017355264.

21. Donald Trump, speech in Phoenix, AZ, August 22, 2017. See "President Trump Ranted For 77 Minutes in Phoenix. Here's What He Said," *Time.com*, August 23, 2017, http://time.com/4912055/donald-trump-phoenix-arizona-transcript/.

22. Nancy Cook and Josh Dawsey, "'He Is Stubborn and Doesn't Realize How Bad This Is Getting,'" *Politico*, August 16, 2017, http://www.politico.com /story/2017/08/16/trump-charlottesville-temper-chaos-241721.

23. Rachelle Blinder and Celeste Katz, "WATCH: Donald Trump Security Guard Hits Protester in Face after Taking Banner," New York *Daily News*, September 4, 2015, http://www.nydailynews.com/news/national/trump -security-guard-hits-protester-face-video-article-1.2348516.

24. Kate Bennett, "Trump family hires familiar face as chief usher," *CNN.com*, June 23, 2017, http://www.cnn.com/2017/06/23/politics/trump-timothy -harleth-chief-usher/index.html.

25. Errol Louis, "Trump Hires the Wedding Planner—to Oversee NY Federal Housing Program?," *CNN.com*, June 16, 2017, http://www.cnn.com /2017/06/16/opinions/patton-urban-development-louis-opinion/index.html.

26. Shawn Boburg, "Trump Seeks Sharp Cuts to Housing Aid, except for Program That Brings Him Millions," *Washington Post*, June 20, 2017, https:// www.washingtonpost.com/investigations/trump-seeks-sharp-cuts-to -housing-aid-except-for-program-that-brings-him-millions/2017/06/20 /bf1fb2b8-5531-11e7-ba90-f5875b7d1876_story.html.

27. Annie Ropeik, "Hundreds of Carrier Factory Jobs to Move to Mexico," *NPR*, June 26, 2017, http://www.npr.org/2017/06/26/534365565/hundreds-of -carrier-factory-jobs-to-move-to-mexico.

28. Chris Cillizza, "Donald Trump's Cabinet Members, Ranked by Their Over-the-Top Praise of Trump," *CNN.com*, June 12, 2017, http://www.cnn.com /2017/06/12/politics/trump-cabinet-ranked/index.html.

29. John McCain, press release, February 20, 2017, https://www.mccain.senate .gov/public/index.cfm/2017/2/statement-by-sasc-chairman-john-mccain-on

-president-trump-s-selection-of-lt-gen-h-r-mcmaster-for-national-security
-advisor.

30. David A. Graham, "Donald Trump Jr.'s Reply to an Offer of Russian Government Attorney: 'I Love It,'" *Atlantic*, July 11, 2017, https://www.theatlantic.com/politics/archive/2017/07/from-russia-with-love/533235/.

31. "Newt Gingrich Is Not Sure He Would Help Estonia against a Russian Invasion," YouTube video, 0:43, from an appearance by Newt Gingrich at the 2016 Republican National Convention, posted by "consumer," July 22, 2016, https://www.youtube.com/watch?v=78JZCvBfuNI.

32. Susan B. Glasser, "Trump National Security Team Blindsided by NATO Speech," *Politico*, June 5, 2017, http://www.politico.com/magazine/story/2017/06/05/trump-nato-speech-national-security-team-215227.

33. Michael D. Shear and Mark Landler, "Trump Expected to Back NATO Mutual Aid Pledge," *New York Times*, May 25, 2017, A09, https://www.nytimes.com/2017/05/24/world/trump-nato.html.

34. Susan B. Glasser, "Trump National Security Team Blindsided by NATO Speech."

35. "McMaster Says 'of Course' Trump Supports NATO Article 5," Reuters, May 27, 2017, http://www.reuters.com/article/us-g7-summit-nato-idUSKBN 18N0LV.

36. Eliot A. Cohen, "To an Anxious Friend . . . ," *American Interest*, November 10, 2016, https://www.the-american-interest.com/2016/11/10/to-an-anxious-friend/.

37. Eliot A. Cohen, "Don't Join This Team," *Washington Post*, November 17, 2016, A17, https://www.washingtonpost.com/opinions/i-told-conservatives -to-work-for-trump-one-talk-with-his-team-changed-my-mind/2016/11/15 /f02e1fac-ab7c-11e6-977a-1030f822fc35_story.html.

38. "Sanders, Scaramucci Full White House Briefing," YouTube video, 49:07, from a White House press briefing on July 21, 2017, posted by "CNN," July 21, 2017, https://www.youtube.com/watch?v=JQadb9WbDR4.

39. "Press Briefing by White House Principal Deputy Press Secretary Sarah Sanders and Incoming White House Communications Director Anthony Scaramucci," White House, July 21, 2017, https://www.whitehouse.gov/the -press-office/2017/07/21/press-briefing-white-house-principal-deputy-press -secretary-sarah.

40. Axios, Twitter, March 24, 2017, 8:28 a.m., https://twitter.com/axios/status /845296198839881728.

41. David Frum, "Advice for Those Weighing Jobs in the Trump Administration," *Atlantic*, January 28, 2017, https://www.theatlantic.com/politics/archive/2017 /01/trump-administration-jobs/514805/.

42. Peter Thiel, speech at the National Press Club, Washington, DC, October 31, 2016, http://www.mercurynews.com/2016/10/31/peter-thiel-on-trump-and -the-crazy-condition-of-our-country/.

43. Donald Trump, speech in Fort Dodge, IA, November 12, 2015; Donald Trump, speech in Greenville, NC, September 6, 2016.

44. Donald J. Trump, Twitter, October 23, 2016, 4:40 p.m., https://twitter.com /realdonaldtrump/status/790337063489040384.

45. Donald J. Trump, Twitter, April 21, 2017, 3:32 a.m., https://twitter.com /realDonaldTrump/status/855368516920332289.

46. Martin Pengelly, "Donald Trump Berates London Mayor over Response to Terror Attacks," *Guardian*, June 4, 2017, https://www.theguardian.com/uk -news/2017/jun/04/trump-berates-london-mayor-sadiq-khan-terror-attacks.

47. Stephen J. Adler, Jeff Mason, and Steve Holland, "Exclusive: Trump Vows to Fix or Scrap South Korea Trade Deal, Wants Missile System Payment," Reuters, April 27, 2017, http://www.reuters.com/politics/article/us-usa-trump -southkorea-exclusive-idUSKBN17U09M.

48. Bryan Harris, Katrina Manson, and Robin Harding, "South Korea Suspends Deployment of US Missile Shield," *Financial Times*, June 8, 2017, https:// www.ft.com/content/19060384-4b34-11e7-919a-1e14ce4af89b.

49. "Iran Nuclear: Trump Extends Obama's 'Worst Deal Ever,'" *BBC.com*, May 17, 2017, http://www.bbc.com/news/world-us-canada-39950827.

50. Ron Nixon, "Homeland Security Will Start Building Border Wall Prototypes This Summer," *New York Times*, June 28, 2017, https://www.nytimes.com /2017/06/27/us/politics/homeland-security-will-start-building-border-wall -prototypes-this-summer.html.

51. Eli Stokols, "Jeb Bush: George W. Spent Too Much Money," *Politico*, May 21, 2015, http://www.politico.com/story/2015/05/jeb-bush-differences -economic-issues-george-w-bush-118179.

52. Grover Norquist, speech at the 2012 Conservative Political Action Conference, Washington, DC, February 11, 2012. See "Grover Norquist Remarks," C-SPAN video, 23:36, https://www.c-span.org/video/?304376-9 /grover-norquist-remarks.

53. Jennifer Steinhauer, "Ryan Now Faces Tea Party Forces He Helped Unleash," *New York Times*, March 3, 2016, A13, http://www.nytimes.com/2016/03/03 /us/politics/paul-ryan-faces-tea-party-forces-that-he-helped-unleash.html.

54. Philip Rucker, "Trump Refuses to Endorse Paul Ryan in GOP Primary: 'I'm Just Not Quite There Yet,'" *Washington Post*, August 2, 2016, https:// www.washingtonpost.com/politics/trump-refuses-to-endorse-paul-ryan-in -gop-primary-im-just-not-quite-there-yet/2016/08/02/1449f028-58e9-11e6 -831d-0324760ca856_story.html; Eric Bradner, "Paul Ryan: 'I'm just not ready' to back Donald Trump," *CNN.com*, May 5, 2016, http://www.cnn .com/2016/05/05/politics/paul-ryan-donald-trump-gop-nominee/index .html.

55. Jeffrey M. Jones, "Avg. Midterm Seat Loss 36 for Presidents Below 50% Approval," *Gallup News*, August 9, 2010, http://www.gallup.com/poll/141812 /avg-midterm-seat-loss-presidents-below-approval.aspx.

56. McKay Coppins, "The Prince of Oversight," *Atlantic*, March 31, 2017, https://www.theatlantic.com/politics/archive/2017/03/jason-chaffetz -oversight/521271/.

57. Anna Brand, "Pence: Trump Is a Businessman, Not a Career Politician," *NBC News*, October 4, 2016, http://www.nbcnews.com/card/pence-trump -businessman-not-career-politician-n659766.

58. Todd Beamon, "Mitch McConnell on Trump: 'He's Learning the Job,'" *Newsmax*, April 13, 2017, http://www.newsmax.com/Headline/McConnell -Trump/2017/04/13/id/784257/.

59. "Speaker Ryan: 'The President's New at This, He's New to Government.' (C-SPAN)," YouTube video, 1:13, from the House Speaker's weekly briefing on June 8, 2017, posted by "C-SPAN," June 8, 2017, https://www.youtube .com/watch?v=_8DmceX5tD4.

60. Face the Nation, Twitter, July 2, 2017, 7:54 a.m., https://twitter.com /FaceTheNation/status/881526435332194305/video/1.

61. Aaron Blake, "Trump Is Starting to Tear the GOP Apart," *Washington Post*, August 24, 2017, https://www.washingtonpost.com/news/the-fix/wp/2017 /08/24/trump-is-starting-to-tear-the-gop-apart/.

62. William D. Cohan, "Decades-Old Questions Over Trump's Wealth and Education," *New York Times*, September 29, 2015, http://www.nytimes .com/2015/09/29/business/dealbook/decades-old-questions-over-trumps -wealth-and-education.html.

63. Michael Kruse, "'He's a Performance Artist Pretending to Be a Great Manager,'" *Politico*, February 28, 2017, http://www.politico.com/magazine /story/2017/02/hes-a-performance-artist-pretending-to-be-a-great-manager -214836.

64. Tara Palmeri, "Need to Reach Trump? Call Rhona," *Politico*, March 26, 2017, http://www.politico.com/story/2017/03/rhona-graff-trump-conduit-236484.

65. Associated Press, "Trump's Use of Private Cellphone Raises Security Concerns," *CNBC.com*, May 30, 2017, https://www.cnbc.com/2017/05/30 /trump-to-world-leaders-call-me-maybe--on-my-cellphone.html.

66. Andrew Exum, "Cheapening a Sacred Space," *Atlantic*, January 23, 2017, https://www.theatlantic.com/politics/archive/2017/01/no-way-to-honor -sacrifice/514097/; Ashley Parker and David Nakamura, "In tweet storm, Trump decries 'illegal leaks' and asserts 'all agree' he has complete power to pardon," *Washington Post*, July 22, 2017, https://www.washingtonpost .com/news/post-politics/wp/2017/07/22/trump-denounces-illegal-leaks

-in-new-accounts-of-his-campaigns-contact-with-russia/; Jim Sciutto, Twitter, July 27, 2017, 10:58 a.m., https://twitter.com/jimsciutto/status/89063253 6673492993/photo/1.

67. Philip Rucker and Robert Costa, "Bannon Vows a Daily Fight for 'Deconstruction of the Administrative State,'" *Washington Post*, February 23, 2017, https://www.washingtonpost.com/politics/top-wh-strategist-vows-a -daily-fight-for-deconstruction-of-the-administrative-state/2017/02/23 /03f6b8da-f9ea-11e6-bf01-d47f8cf9b643_story.html.

CHAPTER 6: ENEMIES OF THE PEOPLE

1. Will Jordan, Twitter, July 26, 2017, 7:29 a.m., https://twitter.com/william jordann/status/890217480236519426/photo/1.

2. "Large Majorities See Checks and Balances, Right to Protest as Essential for Democracy," *Pew Research Center*, March 2, 2017, http://www.people-press .org/2017/03/02/large-majorities-see-checks-and-balances-right-to-protest-as -essential-for-democracy/.

3. Laura Santhanam, "New Poll: 70% of Americans Think Civility Has Gotten Worse since Trump Took Office," *The Rundown* (blog), *PBS*, July 3, 2017, http://www.pbs.org/newshour/rundown/new-poll-70-americans-think -civility-gotten-worse-since-trump-took-office/.

4. Donald Trump, speech at the 2017 Conservative Political Action Conference, National Harbor, MD, February 24, 2017, https://www.whitehouse.gov/the -press-office/2017/02/24/remarks-president-trump-conservative-political -action-conference.

5. Donald J. Trump, Twitter, January 8, 2017, 8:05 p.m., https://twitter.com /realdonaldtrump/status/818307689323368448.

6. "Executive Order: Border Security and Immigration Enforcement Improvements," White House, January 25, 2017, https://www.whitehouse .gov/the-press-office/2017/01/25/executive-order-border-security-and -immigration-enforcement-improvements.

7. Alana Abramson, "Mitch McConnell Doesn't Think Mexico Will Pay for President Trump's Border Wall," *Time*, March 9, 2017, http://time.com /4696656/mitch-mcconnell-president-trump-mexico-wall/.

8. Jeremy Burke, "Trump Floated a Solar-Paneled Border Wall with Mexico— Here's What It Would Look Like," *Business Insider*, June 22, 2017, http:// www.businessinsider.com/trump-solar-border-wall-mexico-images-2017-6.

9. Donald J. Trump, Twitter, January 18, 2017, 4:34 a.m., https://twitter.com /realdonaldtrump/status/821697182235496450; Twitter, January 18, 2017, 4:44 a.m., https://twitter.com/realdonaldtrump/status/821699672687448064.

10. Ylan Q. Mui and Steven Overly, "The Myth and Reality of Donald Trump's Job Claims," *Washington Post*, January 3, 2017, https://www.washingtonpost

.com/news/wonk/wp/2017/01/03/trump-reiterates-threat-of-a-border-tax-this
-time-general-motors-is-in-the-crosshairs/.

11. Todd Spangler, "Trump Officials Greet Ford's Plan to Import Chinese Cars,"
USA Today, June 20, 2017, https://www.usatoday.com/story/money/cars/2017
/06/20/trump-officials-greet-fords-plan-import-chinese-cars/103049064/.

12. Donald J. Trump, Twitter, February 26, 2017, 10:16 a.m., https://twitter
.com/realdonaldtrump/status/835916511944523777.

13. Donald J. Trump, Twitter, June 23, 2017, 5:43 p.m., https://twitter.com
/realdonaldtrump/status/878413313188802560.

14. Donald J. Trump, Twitter, March 18, 2017, 6:15 a.m., https://twitter.com
/realdonaldtrump/status/843088518339612673.

15. Michael Birnbaum and Rick Noack, "Following Trump's Trip, Merkel Says
Europe Can't Rely On 'Others.' She Means the U.S.," *Washington Post*, May
28, 2017, https://www.washingtonpost.com/world/following-trumps-trip
-merkel-says-europe-cant-rely-on-us-anymore/2017/05/28/4c6b92cc-43c1
-11e7-8de1-cec59a9bf4b1_story.html.

16. Donald J. Trump, Twitter, February 17, 2017, 1:48 p.m., https://twitter.com
/realdonaldtrump/status/832708293516632065.

17. David Jackson, "Trump Again Calls Media 'Enemy of the People,'" *USA
Today*, February 24, 2017, https://www.usatoday.com/story/news/politics
/2017/02/24/donald-trump-cpac-media-enemy-of-the-people/98347970/.

18. For the record, Trump is not wrong that Amazon's rise was greatly assisted
by online retailing's exemption from the duty to collect and remit state sales
taxes. That exemption has long been upheld as party dogma by congressional
Republicans, abetted by outside lobbying groups like Americans for Tax Reform.
By 2016, however, Amazon not only collected sales in all forty-five states that
have one, but had begun to advocate a federal Internet sales tax too. Amazon
does not collect sales taxes from third-party sellers who use its platform. It seems
unlikely that President Trump has any awareness of any of these details.

19. Michael M. Grynbaum, "A Network vs. the President," *New York Times*, July
6, 2017, B01, https://www.nytimes.com/2017/07/05/business/media/jeffrey
-zucker-cnn-trump.html.

20. Kellyanne Conway, interview by Chuck Todd, *Meet the Press*, NBC, January
22, 2017, https://www.nbcnews.com/meet-the-press/meet-press-01-22-17
-n710491.

21. Nic Dawes, "Maneuvering a New Reality for US Journalism," *Columbia
Journalism Review*, November 22, 2016, https://www.cjr.org/the_feature
/trump_journalism_press_freedom_global.php.

22. Peter Bull, "Theresa May Has a Very Special Technique for Avoiding
Questions," *The Conversation*, October 24, 2016, https://theconversation
.com/theresa-may-has-a-very-special-technique-for-avoiding-questions-67424.

23. "Never Said That | The Briefing," YouTube video, 1:42, posted by "The Briefing," September 28, 2016, https://www.youtube.com/watch?v=EHclppeLdi0.

24. Masha Gessen, "The Putin Paradigm," *NYR Daily, New York Review of Books*, December 13, 2016, http://www.nybooks.com/daily/2016/12/13/putin -paradigm-how-trump-will-rule/.

25. Kellyanne Conway, interview by Alisyn Camerota, *New Day*, CNN, September 13, 2016.

26. Lou Cannon, "When Spokesmen Lie," *Washington Post*, April 18, 1988, A2, https://www.washingtonpost.com/archive/politics/1988/04/18/when -spokesmen-lie/9dd79b06-2367-4ff2-9aba-07def9479016/.

27. Arthur Sylvester, "The Government Has the Right to Lie," *Saturday Evening Post*, November 18, 1967, 10.

28. Jake Tapper, Twitter, June 29, 2017, 6:20 p.m., https://twitter.com/jaketapper /status/880596947421278208/photo/1.

29. Gary Langer, "6 Months In, a Record Low for Trump, with Troubles from Russia to Health Care (POLL)," *ABC News*, July 16, 2017, http://abcnews .go.com/Politics/months-record-low-trump-troubles-russia-health-care/story ?id=48639490.

30. Ibid.

31. *Fox & Friends*, Fox News Network, June 23, 2017.

32. *Fox & Friends*, Fox News Network, June 8, 2017.

33. *Hannity*, Fox News Network, June 29, 2017, http://www.foxnews.com /transcript/2017/06/29/levin-good-to-know-where-liberals-finally-draw-line -sekulow-speaks-out-about-scandals-that-need-investigation.html.

34. Sean Hannity, Twitter, November 23, 2016, 12:37 p.m., https://twitter.com /seanhannity/status/801525154740314112.

35. Maggie Haberman and Glenn Thrush, "'I'm Right Here!' Spicer Says, Keeping Podium While Toiling to Find Successor," *New York Times*, June 21, 2017, A13, https://www.nytimes.com/2017/06/20/us/politics/im-right-here -sean-spicer-says-while-toiling-to-find-successor.html.

36. "White House Briefing Bar: Media Groups Condemn Exclusion," *BBC.com*, February 25, 2017, http://www.bbc.com/news/world-us-canada-39088770.

37. Donald Trump, speech in Phoenix, AZ, August 22, 2017. See "President Trump Ranted for 77 Minutes in Phoenix. Here's What He Said," *Time.com*, August 23, 2017, http://time.com/4912055/donald-trump-phoenix-arizona -transcript/.

38. Mark Landler and Maggie Haberman, "Trump Again Blames Media in U.S. Divide," *New York Times*, August 23, 2017, A01, https://www.nytimes.com /2017/08/22/us/politics/trump-rally-arizona.html.

39. Chris Bucher, "LISTEN: Police Scanner Audio from Ben Jacobs & Greg Gianforte Incident," *Heavy.com*, May 24, 2017, modified May 25, 2017,

http://heavy.com/news/2017/05/greg-gianforte-body-slam-ben-jacobs-audio
-police-scanner-assault-listen-montana-reporter.

40. *Fox News Specialists*, Fox News Network, May 25, 2017.
41. *Rush Limbaugh Show*, May 25, 2017, https://www.rushlimbaugh.com
/daily/2017/05/25/montana-special-election-your-host-joins-the
-condemnation-of-the-studly-manly-republican-who-beat-up-a-skinny
-millennial-reporter-and-is-running-against-a-radical-leftist-posing-as-a
-cowboy/.
42. Thomas Phippen, "Montana Politician Raised $116,000 AFTER He Choke-
Slammed a Reporter," *Daily Caller*, June 28, 2017, http://dailycaller.com
/2017/06/28/montana-politician-raised-116000-after-he-choke-slammed-a
-reporter/.
43. Greg Bluestein, "Georgia 6th: Montana Victor Calls for Help Defeating
'Liberals in Georgia,'" *AJC.com*, May 27, 2017, http://politics.blog.ajc.com
/2017/05/27/georgia-6th-montana-victor-calls-for-help-defeating-liberals-in
-georgia/.
44. Adrian Chen, "The Agency," *New York Times Magazine*, June 7, 2015, https://
www.nytimes.com/2015/06/07/magazine/the-agency.html.
45. Massimo Calabresi, "Inside Russia's Social Media War on America," *Time.
com*, May 18, 2017, http://time.com/4783932/inside-russia-social-media-war
-america/.
46. Nancy Gibbs, "A Note to Our Readers," *Time*, January 24, 2017, http://time
.com/4645541/donald-trump-white-house-oval-office/.
47. Lindsey Ellefson, "Chris Cuomo, Trump Aide Tangle over 'Travel Ban'
Tweets," *CNN.com*, June 5, 2017, http://www.cnn.com/2017/06/05/politics
/cuomo-and-gorka-spar-cnntv/index.html.
48. *Hannity*, Fox News Network, June 5, 2017.
49. Aaron Blake, "Sarah Huckabee Sanders Lambastes Fake News—and Then
Promotes a Journalist Accused of Deceptive Videos," *Washington Post*, June
27, 2017, https://www.washingtonpost.com/news/the-fix/wp/2017/06/27
/sarah-huckabee-sanders-lambastes-fake-news-while-promoting-journalist
-known-for-deceptive-videos/.
50. "Does Macron Wash His Hands after Shaking Hands with Workers?," *First
Draft News*, April 28, 2017, https://crosscheck.firstdraftnews.com/checked
-french/macron-wash-hands-shaking-hands-workers.
51. Dustin Volz, "U.S. Far-Right Activists, WikiLeaks, and Bots Help Amplify
Macron Leaks: Researchers," Reuters.com, May 6, 2017, http://www.reuters
.com/article/us-france-election-cyber/u-s-far-right-activists-wikileaks-and
-bots-help-amplify-macron-leaks-researchers-idUSKBN1820QO.
52. Jordan Pearson, "The Same Twitter Bots That Helped Trump Tried to
Sink Macron, Researcher Says," *Motherboard, Vice*, July 6, 2017, https://

motherboard.vice.com/en_us/article/9kwak5/the-same-twitter-bots-that
-helped-trump-tried-to-sink-macron-researcher-says.

53. Mike Cernovich, "Susan Rice Requested Unmasking of Incoming Trump
     Administration Officials," *Medium*, April 2, 2017, https://medium.com
     /@Cernovich/susan-rice-requested-unmasking-of-incoming-trump
     -administration-officials-30085b5cff16.

54. Jim Hoft, "Update=> Erdogan Holds 1,500 US Servicemen Hostage at
     Incirlik Over Attempted Coup," *Gateway Pundit*, July 17, 2016, http://www
     .thegatewaypundit.com/2016/07/update-erdogan-holds-1500-us-servicemen
     -hostage-incirlik-attempted-coup/; Michael M. Grynbaum, "A Pro-Trump
     Blog Gains White House Credentials," *New York Times*, February 14, 2017,
     A18, https://www.nytimes.com/2017/02/13/business/the-gateway-pundit
     -trump.html.

55. "Rex Tillerson and Wilbur Ross Do Sword Dance in Saudi Arabia," YouTube
     video, 8:46, posted by "LIVE SATELLITE NEWS," May 20, 2017, https://
     www.youtube.com/watch?v=li9dGCC2SdU.

56. Julie Pace and Jonathan Lemire, "Trump's Frustrations Are Boiling over after
     Comey Dismissal," Associated Press, May 13, 2017, https://www.apnews.com
     /f6b3c3ebe5164c188072f5787357360f.

57. *CNN Newsroom*, CNN, July 7, 2017. See "CNN's David Gergen on Trump
     Putin Meeting: 'This Was Presidential, This Was Big League Stuff,'"
     YouTube video, 0:51, posted by "GOP War Room," July 7, 2017, https://
     www.youtube.com/watch?v=jNpqjRTHskk.

58. "Van Jones: Trump Became President in That Moment," YouTube video,
     1:45, posted by "CNN," February 28, 2017, https://www.youtube.com/watch
     ?v=KPhsSqXHRAs.

59. Donald Trump, joint press event with Polish President Andrzej Duda,
     Warsaw, Poland, July 6, 2017, http://transcripts.cnn.com/TRANSCRIPTS
     /1707/06/es.02.html.

60. Polish Helsinki Foundation for Human Rights, "Polish Journalists Face
     Strict Work Limitations for Covering Parliament," Civil Liberties Union for
     Europe, January 31, 2017, https://www.liberties.eu/en/news/limitations-on
     -work-of-parliamentary-correspondents-poland.

61. Tom Kludt, "Other Presidents Boosted Free Press Abroad; Trump Bashes It,"
     CNN.com, July 6, 2017, http://money.cnn.com/2017/07/06/media/poland
     -speech-donald-trump-media-attack/index.html.

62. The phrase was generally reported as "Are these the ones who have insulted
     you?" but my *Atlantic* colleague Julia Ioffe, a native speaker of Russian,
     explained to me that this was not quite right. The phrase Putin used was
     more something that a parent would say to an upset child than something
     one man would say to another who had suffered a true affront.

63. Committee to Protect Journalists, "Journalists Detained in Wake of Turkey Referendum," April 21, 2017, https://cpj.org/2017/04/journalists-detained -in-wake-of-turkey-referendum.php.

64. Committee to Protect Journalists, "South African Reporters Attacked Covering Protests, Broadcaster Suspends Journalists," June 24, 2016, https:// cpj.org/2016/06/south-african-reporters-attacked-covering-protests.php.

65. "NDTV India Ordered off Air on Nov 9 over Coverage of Pathankot Attack," *Hindustan Times* (New Delhi), November 3, 2016, http://www .hindustantimes.com/india-news/ndtv-india-to-be-taken-off-air-for-a-day -over-pathankot-attack-coverage/story-ABLkwpoDHpmS4rdg5jSUCK.html.

CHAPTER 7: RIGGED SYSTEM

1. Jens Manuel Krogstad and Mark Hugo Lopez, "Black Voter Turnout Fell in 2016, Even as a Record Number of Americans Cast Ballots," *Fact Tank* (blog), *Pew Research Center*, May 12, 2016, http://www.pewresearch.org/fact -tank/2017/05/12/black-voter-turnout-fell-in-2016-even-as-a-record-number -of-americans-cast-ballots/. This paper is the source for all the numbers cited in the first three paragraphs of this chapter.

2. Jonathan Martin, "Young Blacks Voice Doubts About Clinton," *New York Times*, September 5, 2016, A1, https://www.nytimes.com/2016/09/05/us /politics/young-blacks-voice-skepticism-on-hillary-clinton-worrying -democrats.html.

3. "FAQ," VoteTexas.gov, accessed September 28, 2017, http://www.votetexas .gov/faq/#2071.

4. Zachary Roth, "Wisconsin Throws up Major Voter Registration Hurdle," *MSNBC.com*, March 25, 2016, http://www.msnbc.com/msnbc/wisconsin -throws-major-voter-registration-hurdle.

5. Laura Santhanam, "New Poll: 70% of Americans Think Civility Has Gotten Worse since Trump Took Office," *The Rundown* (blog), *PBS*, July 3, 2017, http://www.pbs.org/newshour/rundown/new-poll-70-americans-think -civility-gotten-worse-since-trump-took-office/.

6. Paul Ryan, "The Path to Prosperity," speech at the American Enterprise Institute, Washington, DC, April 5, 2011, http://www.aei.org/publication /the-path-to-prosperity/.

7. Donald J. Trump Jr., Twitter, October 3, 2012, 1:23 p.m., https://twitter .com/donaldjtrumpjr/status/253545899958087680.

8. Donald Trump, interview by David Brody, *The Brody File*, Christian Broadcasting Network, September 9, 2016, http://www1.cbn.com /thebrodyfile/archive/2016/09/09/brody-file-exclusive-donald-trump -says-this-will-be-the-last-election-that-the-republicans-have-a-chance-of -winning.

9.   Donald J. Trump, Twitter, November 27, 2016, 3:30 p.m., https://twitter.com/realdonaldtrump/status/802972944532209664.

10. Jesse T. Richman, Gulshan A. Chattha, and David C. Earnest, "Do Non-Citizens Vote in U.S. Elections?," *Electoral Studies* 36 (December 2014), 149–57, https://doi.org/10.1016/j.electstud.2014.09.001.

11. Cleve R. Wootson Jr., "Sen. Al Franken Claims That Donald Trump's New Ad on the Economy Is Anti-Semitic," *Washington Post*, November 6, 2016, https://www.washingtonpost.com/news/the-fix/wp/2016/11/06/sen-al-franken-claims-that-donald-trumps-new-ad-on-the-economy-is-anti-semitic/.

12. Anti-Defamation League, Twitter, November 6, 2016, 10:40 a.m., https://twitter.com/ADL_National/status/795289665809088512.

13. Erica R. Hendry, "A Trump Commission Requested Voter Data. Here's What Every State Is Saying," *The Rundown* (blog), *PBS*, June 30, 2017, http://www.pbs.org/newshour/rundown/trump-commission-requested-voter-data-heres-every-state-saying/.

14. Donald J. Trump, Twitter, July 1, 2017, 9:07 a.m., https://twitter.com/realdonaldtrump/status/881137079958241280.

15. Alexa Corse, "South Carolina May Prove a Microcosm of U.S. Election Hacking Efforts," *Wall Street Journal*, July 16, 2017, https://www.wsj.com/articles/south-carolina-may-prove-a-microcosm-of-u-s-election-hacking-efforts-1500202806.

16. Alana Abramson, "President Trump's Lawyer Made a Mistake in Describing James Comey's Testimony," *Time*, June 8, 2017, http://time.com/4811888/comey-testimony-marc-kasowitz-mistake/.

17. Russian assistance to congressional Republicans is an insufficiently appreciated aspect of interference in the 2016 election. See Eric Lipton and Scott Shane, "Russians Hacked Democrats Vying for House Seats," *New York Times*, December 15, 2016, A1, https://www.nytimes.com/2016/12/13/us/politics/house-democrats-hacking-dccc.html.

18. Jo Becker, Adam Goldman, and Matt Apuzzo, "Emails Disclose Trump Son's Glee at Russian Offer," *New York Times*, July 12, 2017, A1, https://www.nytimes.com/2017/07/11/us/politics/trump-russia-email-clinton.html.

19. Tom Hamburger, Carol D. Leonnig, and Rosalind S. Helderman, "Trump Campaign Emails Show Aide's Repeated Efforts to Set up Russia Meetings," *Washington Post*, August 14, 2017, https://www.washingtonpost.com/politics/trump-campaign-emails-show-aides-repeated-efforts-to-set-up-russia-meetings/2017/08/14/54d08da6-7dc2-11e7-83c7-5bd5460f0d7e_story.html.

20. Issie Lapowsky, "Did Trump's Data Team Help Russians? Facebook Might Have the Answer," *Wired*, July 14, 2017, https://www.wired.com/story/trump-russia-data-parscale-facebook/.

21. Adam Entous, Ellen Nakashima, and Greg Miller, "Secret CIA Assessment Says Russia Was Trying to Help Trump Win White House," *Washington Post*, December 9, 2016, https://www.washingtonpost.com/world/national -security/obama-orders-review-of-russian-hacking-during-presidential -campaign/2016/12/09/31d6b300-be2a-11e6-94ac-3d324840106c_story .html.

22. Ibid.

23. Domenico Montanaro and Arnie Seipel, "McConnell, Differing with Trump, Says He Has 'Highest Confidence' in Intel Agencies," *NPR*, December 12, 2016, http://www.npr.org/2016/12/12/505260062/mcconnell-differing-with -trump-says-he-has-highest-confidence-in-intel-agencies.

24. Rebecca Shabad, "Russia Sanctions Bill Stalls in House as Trump Prepares for First Putin Meeting," *CBS News*, July 6, 2017, http://www.cbsnews.com /news/russia-sanctions-bill-stalls-in-house-as-trump-prepares-for-first-putin -meeting/.

25. Josh Dawsey and Elana Schor, "Trump Clashed with Multiple GOP Senators over Russia," *Politico*, August 23, 2017, http://www.politico.com/story/2017 /08/23/trump-senate-yell-phone-calls-241950.

26. "'The Administration Then Chose to Defame Me,'" *New York Times*, June 9, 2017, A22, https://www.nytimes.com/2017/06/08/us/politics/senate-hearing -transcript.html.

27. David Frum, Twitter, May 25, 2017, 2:55 p.m., https://twitter.com/davidfrum /status/867861680591695873.

28. This quote and others were all helpfully compiled by Natasha Bertrand and Maxwell Tani of *Business Insider*. See Natasha Bertrand and Maxwell Tani, "'Collusion Is Not a Crime': Trump's Media Allies Have a Striking New Talking Point That Experts Say Is 'Flawed' and 'Absurd,'" *Business Insider*, June 27, 2017, http://www.businessinsider.com/collusion-russia-trump-crime-2017-6.

29. Ibid.

30. Bertrand and Tani, "'Collusion Is Not a Crime."

31. *Hannity*, Fox News Network, June 22, 2017, http://www.foxnews.com /transcript/2017/06/22/gingrich-calls-for-gop-to-focus-on-deep-tax-cuts -tom-price-health-care-bill-move-in-right-direction.html.

32. Ibid.

33. *Fox News Sunday*, Fox News Network, June 25, 2017.

34. Dennis Prager, Twitter, July 14, 2017, 1:55 p.m., https://twitter.com /dennisprager/status/885920697708564480.

35. Chuck Todd, Mark Murray, and Carrie Dann, "Putting the Trump-Russia Timeline into Perspective," *First Read* (newsletter), *NBC News*, July 10, 2017, http://www.nbcnews.com/politics/first-read/putting-trump-russia-timeline -perspective-n781236.

36. "Russian Election: Big Victory for Putin-Backed Party United Russia," *BBC .com*, September 19, 2016, http://www.bbc.com/news/world-europe-37403242.

37. David Wagner, "Sorry, Conservatives, De Tocqueville Did Not Call the 2012 Election," *Atlantic*, November 8, 2012, https://www.theatlantic.com/politics /archive/2012/11/sorry-conservatives-de-tocqueville-did-not-call-2012 -election/321393/.

38. Jeffrey Sullivan, "Armed Group Appears at Council to Oppose Statue's Removal," *Rivard Report*, August 16, 2017, https://therivardreport.com/armed -group-appears-at-council-to-oppose-statues-removal/.

39. Abraham Lincoln to James C. Conkling, August 26, 1863, in *The Language of Liberty: The Political Speeches and Writings of Abraham Lincoln*, ed. Joseph R. Fornieri (Washington, DC: Regnery, 2003), 669.

40. Ryan J. Reilly, "A Guy in a Trump Shirt Carried a Gun Outside of a Virginia Polling Place. Authorities Say That's Fine," *Huffington Post*, November 4, 2016, http://www.huffingtonpost.com/entry/trump-supporter-gun-voter -intimidation-virginia_us_581cf16ee4b0aac624846eb5.

41. Christopher Ingraham, "The Average Gun Owner Now Owns 8 Guns— Double What It Used to Be," *Washington Post*, October 21, 2015, https:// www.washingtonpost.com/news/wonk/wp/2015/10/21/the-average-gun -owner-now-owns-8-guns-double-what-it-used-to-be/.

42. Donald Trump, "Remarks by President Trump on Infrastructure," New York, NY, August 15, 2017, https://www.whitehouse.gov/the-press-office/2017/08 /15/remarks-president-trump-infrastructure.

43. Donald Trump, speech in Phoenix, AZ, August 22, 2017. See "President Trump Ranted for 77 Minutes in Phoenix. Here's What He Said," *Time.com*, August 23, 2017, http://time.com/4912055/donald-trump-phoenix-arizona -transcript/.

44. Ben Schreckinger, "Trump on Protester: 'I'd like to Punch Him in the Face,'" *Politico*, February 23, 2016, http://www.politico.com/story/2016/02/donald -trump-punch-protester-219655.

45. Donald Trump, speech in Brentwood, NY, July 28, 2017.

46. Ibid.

47. Asawin Suebsaeng, Twitter, July 28, 2017, 2:34 p.m., https://twitter.com /swin24/status/891003873296490497.

CHAPTER 8: AMERICA ALONE

1. H. R. McMaster and Gary D. Cohn, "America First Doesn't Mean America Alone," *Wall Street Journal*, May 30, 2017, https://www.wsj.com/articles/ america-first-doesnt-mean-america-alone-1496187426.

2. "Highlights of Reuters Interview with Trump," Reuters, April 27, 2017, http:// www.reuters.com/article/us-usa-trump-interview-highlights-idUSKBN17U0D4.

3. Jeff Zeleny, Dan Merica, and Kevin Liptak, "Trump's 'Fire and Fury' Remark Was Improvised but Familiar," *CNN.com*, August 9, 2017, http://www.cnn .com/2017/08/09/politics/trump-fire-fury-improvise-north-korea/index.html.

4. "Remarks by President Trump to the 72nd Session of the United Nations General Assembly," White House, September 19, 2017, https://www.white house.gov/the-press-office/2017/09/19/remarks-president-trump-72nd-session -united-nations-general-assembly.

5. Chun Han Wong, Jonathan Cheng, and Alastair Gale, "'Duped by Trump': U.S. Taunted Over Carl Vinson Aircraft Carrier Tale," *Wall Street Journal*, April 19, 2017, https://www.wsj.com/articles/false-narrative-on-u-s-aircraft -carrier-elicits-jeers-in-asia-1492577625.

6. "WSJ Trump Interview Excerpts: China, North Korea, Ex-Im Bank, Obamacare, Bannon, More," *Washington Wire* (blog), *Wall Street Journal*, April 12, 2017, https://blogs.wsj.com/washwire/2017/04/12/wsj-trump -interview-excerpts-china-north-korea-ex-im-bank-obamacare-bannon.

7. Richard Wike, Bruce Stokes, Jacob Poushter, and Janell Fetterolf, "U.S. Image Suffers as Publics Around World Question Trump's Leadership," *Pew Research Center*, June 26, 2017, http://www.pewglobal.org/2017/06/26/u-s -image-suffers-as-publics-around-world-question-trumps-leadership/.

8. Greg Miller, "Trump Urged Mexican President to End His Public Defiance on Border Wall, Transcript Reveals," *Washington Post*, August 3, 2017, https://www.washingtonpost.com/world/national-security/you-cannot-say -that-to-the-press-trump-urged-mexican-president-to-end-his-public-defiance -on-border-wall-transcript-reveals/2017/08/03/0c2c0a4e-7610-11e7-8f39 -eeb7d3a2d304_story.html.

9. Dorothy Manevich and Hanyu Chwe, "Globally, More People See U.S. Power and Influence as a Major Threat," *Fact Tank* (blog), *Pew Research Center*, August 1, 2017, http://www.pewresearch.org/fact-tank/2017/08/01 /u-s-power-and-influence-increasingly-seen-as-threat-in-other-countries/.

10. Ben Knight, "Merkel Congratulates Trump as Politicians Express Shock," *DW.com*, November 9, 2016, http://www.dw.com/en/merkel-congratulates -trump-as-politicians-express-shock/a-36318866.

11. Tracy Wilkinson and Brian Bennett, "After Trump Reluctantly Certifies Iran Is Obeying Nuclear Deal, He Slaps It with New Sanctions," *Los Angeles Times*, July 18, 2017, http://www.latimes.com/nation/la-fg-trump-iran -20170718-story.html.

12. Thomas Erdbrink, "Arab Rift with Qatar Is Welcome in Tehran," *New York Times*, July 5, 2017, A4, https://www.nytimes.com/2017/07/04/world /middleeast/for-iran-qatar-crisis-is-a-welcome-distraction.html.

13. Karen DeYoung and Ellen Nakashima, "UAE Orchestrated Hacking of Qatari Government Sites, Sparking Regional Upheaval, According to U.S.

Intelligence Officials," *Washington Post*, July 16, 2017, https://www
.washingtonpost.com/world/national-security/uae-hacked-qatari-government
-sites-sparking-regional-upheaval-according-to-us-intelligence-officials/2017
/07/16/00c46e54-698f-11e7-8eb5-cbccc2e7bfbf_story.html.

14. Marc Champion and Marek Strzelecki, "The Real Impact of Trump's Foreign
Trips Happens After He Leaves," *Bloomberg News*, July 18, 2017, https://
www.bloomberg.com/news/articles/2017-07-18/when-trump-goes-abroad
-radical-change-follows-in-his-footsteps.

15. Fredreka Schouten, "President Trump's Hotel Received $270,000 from Saudi
Arabia," *CNBC.com*, June 6, 2017, http://www.cnbc.com/2017/06/06
/president-trumps-dc-hotel-received-270000-from-saudi-arabia.html.

16. Donald Trump, speech in Warsaw, Poland, July 6, 2017, https://www.white
house.gov/the-press-office/2017/07/06/remarks-president-trump-people
-poland-july-6-2017.

17. Matthew Tostevin, "Trump Factor Weighs as Vietnam Intensifies Crackdown
on Dissidents," Reuters, August 2, 2017, http://www.reuters.com/article/us
-vietnam-arrests-idUSKBN1AI0LF.

18. Miles Parks and Tamara Keith, "Timeline of Trump and Russia in Mid-2016:
A Series of Coincidences or Something More?," *NPR*, July 17, 2017, http://
www.npr.org/2017/07/17/537323120/timeline-of-trump-and-russia-in-mid
-2016-a-series-of-coincidences-or-something-m.

19. George W. Bush, "President Bush, European Leaders Act to Fight Global
Terror," June 25, 2003, https://georgewbush-whitehouse.archives.gov/news
/releases/2003/06/20030625-12.html.

20. William J. Clinton, "Remarks to Future Leaders of Europe in Brussels,"
January 9, 1994. Online by Gerhard Peters and John T. Woolley, *The
American Presidency Project*, http://www.presidency.ucsb.edu/ws/?pid=49643.

21. "Transcript: Donald Trump on NATO, Turkey's Coup Attempt and the
World," *New York Times*, July 22, 2016, http://www.nytimes.com/2016/07
/22/us/politics/donald-trump-foreign-policy-interview.html.

22. Noah Barkin, "Exclusive: White House Delivered EU-skeptic Message before
Pence Visit—Sources," Reuters, February 21, 2017, http://www.reuters.com
/article/us-europe-trump-idUSKBN1601DS.

23. Max Ehrenfreund, "'We Are in a Trade War,' Trump's Commerce Secretary
Says after Stern German Warning," *Washington Post*, March 31, 2017, https://
www.washingtonpost.com/news/wonk/wp/2017/03/31/we-are-in-a-trade
-war-trumps-commerce-secretary-says-after-stern-german-warning/.

24. David Lawder, "Trump Adviser Navarro: U.S., Germany Should Discuss
Trade outside EU," Reuters, March 6, 2017, http://www.reuters.com/article
/us-usa-trump-trade-navarro-idUSKBN16D1KK.

25. "U.S.'s Tillerson praises Turkish 'courage' during coup attempt," Reuters, July 9, 2017, https://www.reuters.com/article/us-usa-turkey/u-s-s-tillerson-praises-turkish-courage-during-coup-attempt-idUSKBN19U0WE.

26. "Joint Press Conference with President Trump and German Chancellor Merkel," White House, March 17, 2017, https://www.whitehouse.gov/the-press-office/2017/03/17/joint-press-conference-president-trump-and-german-chancellor-merkel.

27. Ibid.

28. Donald J. Trump, Twitter, May 30, 2017, 3:40 a.m., https://twitter.com/realDonaldTrump/status/869503804307275776.

29. Eli Watkins, "While Campaigning, Merkel Says Europeans Can't 'Completely' Rely On US, Others," *CNN.com*, May 28, 2017, http://www.cnn.com/2017/05/28/politics/angela-merkel-donald-trump-g7/index.html.

30. Donald Trump, speech at the 2017 Conservative Political Action Conference, National Harbor, MD, February 24, 2017, https://www.whitehouse.gov/the-press-office/2017/02/24/remarks-president-trump-conservative-political-action-conference.

31. Greg Miller and Stephanie Kirchner, "Germany Orders CIA Station Chief to Leave over Spying Allegations," *Washington Post*, July 10, 2014, https://www.washingtonpost.com/world/europe/germany-expels-us-intelligence-station-chief-over-spying-allegations/2014/07/10/dc60b1f0-083c-11e4-8a6a-19355c7e870a_story.html.

32. Greg Miller and Greg Jaffe, "Trump Revealed Highly Classified Information to Russian Foreign Minister and Ambassador," *Washington Post*, May 15, 2017, https://www.washingtonpost.com/world/national-security/trump-revealed-highly-classified-information-to-russian-foreign-minister-and-ambassador/2017/05/15/530c172a-3960-11e7-9e48-c4f199710b69_story.html.

33. Lachlan Markay, Asawin Suebsaeng, and Noah Shachtman, "Trump Officials: 'He Looks More and More Like a Complete Moron,'" *Daily Beast*, May 19, 2017, http://www.thedailybeast.com/trump-officials-he-looks-more-and-more-like-a-complete-moron.

34. J. Lester Feder, "This Is How Steve Bannon Sees the Entire World," *BuzzFeed News*, November 15, 2016, https://www.buzzfeed.com/lesterfeder/this-is-how-steve-bannon-sees-the-entire-world.

35. Christopher Caldwell, speech at Hillsdale College National Leadership Seminar in Phoenix, AZ, February 15, 2017, https://imprimis.hillsdale.edu/how-to-think-about-vladimir-putin/.

36. Vivian Salama, "Trump's Embrace of Russia Making Top Advisers Wary," Associated Press, July 20, 2017, https://apnews.com/4b4b7e380f20

4b45a8c3055a5d45255e/Trump's-embrace-of-Russia-making-top-advisers
-wary.

37. Greg Jaffe and Adam Entous, "Trump Ends Covert CIA Program to Arm
Anti-Assad Rebels in Syria, a Move Sought by Moscow," *Washington Post*,
July 19, 2017, https://www.washingtonpost.com/world/national-security
/trump-ends-covert-cia-program-to-arm-anti-assad-rebels-in-syria-a-move
-sought-by-moscow/2017/07/19/b6821a62-6beb-11e7-96ab-5f38140b38cc
_story.html.

38. Elise Labott, Nicole Gaouette, and Richard Roth, "US Signals Openness to
Assad Staying Put," *CNN.com*, March 30, 2017, http://www.cnn.com
/2017/03/30/politics/tillerson-haley-syria-assad-turkey/index.html.

39. Alexander Bolton, "McConnell: Assad Must Go," *Hill*, April 7, 2017, http://
thehill.com/homenews/senate/327826-mcconnell-assad-must-go.

40. Ed Royce, "Chairman Royce: Assad Must Go," press release, April 4, 2017,
https://foreignaffairs.house.gov/press-release/chairman-royce-assad-must-go/.

41. Marco Rubio, "Rubio Statement on U.S. Airstrikes in Syria," press release,
April 6, 2017, https://www.rubio.senate.gov/public/index.cfm/press-releases
?ID=E4F4A2DA-C8C3-4492-BB72-3C49503F3838; Cory Gardner,
"Gardner Statement on US Strikes in Syria," press release, April 6, 2017,
https://www.gardner.senate.gov/newsroom/press-releases/gardner-statement
-on-us-strikes-in-syria; James Lankford, "Senator Lankford: Assad Must Go,"
press release, April 4, 2017, https://www.lankford.senate.gov/news/press
-releases/senator-lankford-assad-must-go; Bob Corker, "Corker Statement on
U.S. Missile Strikes in Syria," press release, April 6, 2017, https://www
.foreign.senate.gov/press/chair/release/corker-statement-on-us-missile-strikes
-in-syria.

42. John McCain, "McCain on the Need for Action in Syria," press release, April
6, 2017, https://www.mccain.senate.gov/public/index.cfm/2017/4/statement
-by-sasc-chairman-john-mccain-on-the-need-for-action-in-syria; Tom
Cotton, "Cotton Statement on Chemical Attack in Syria," press release, April
4, 2017, https://www.cotton.senate.gov/?p=press_release&id=651.

43. Paul Ryan, "Statement on Passage of Syria Sanctions," press release, May 17,
2017, https://www.speaker.gov/press-release/statement-passage-syria
-sanctions.

44. Mark Landler, "Rare Accord for Kaine and Pence: A More Assertive U.S.
Stand on Syria," *New York Times*, October 6, 2016, https://www.nytimes
.com/2016/10/06/us/syria-vice-presidential-debate.html.

45. Jennifer Jacobs, "McFarland to Exit White House as McMaster Consolidates
Power," *Bloomberg News*, April 9, 2017, https://www.bloomberg.com/news
/articles/2017-04-09/mcfarland-to-exit-white-house-as-mcmaster
-consolidates-power.

46. Fredrick Kunkle, "Trump Aide Was among Record Numbers Taking a Gun through TSA Checkpoint Last Year, Police Say," *Washington Post*, January 27, 2017, https://www.washingtonpost.com/news/tripping/wp/2017/01/27/trump -aide-was-among-record-numbers-taking-a-gun-through-tsa-checkpoint-last -year/.

47. Donald J. Trump, Twitter, March 4, 2017, 7:02 a.m., https://twitter.com /realDonaldTrump/status/837996746236182529.

48. Henry Farrell, "Sean Spicer Just Suggested That Obama Used British Intelligence to Spy on Trump. Britain Isn't Happy," *Washington Post*, March 16, 2017, https://www.washingtonpost.com/news/monkey-cage/wp/2017 /03/16/sean-spicer-just-suggested-that-obama-used-british-intelligence-to -spy-on-trump-not-so-much/?utm_term=.be9a4cea4416.

49. Deirdre Walsh, "Justice Department: No Evidence Trump Tower Was Wiretapped," *CNN.com*, September 2, 2017, http://www.cnn.com/2017 /09/02/politics/justice-department-trump-tower-wiretap/index.html. NSD refers to the National Security Division within the FBI.

50. "Text of Havel's Speech to Congress," *Washington Post*, February 22, 1990, A28, https://www.washingtonpost.com/archive/politics/1990/02/22/text-of -havels-speech-to-congress/df98e177-778e-4c26-bd96-980089c4fcb2/.

CHAPTER 9: AUTOIMMUNE DISORDER

1. Michael Isikoff, "How the Trump Administration's Secret Efforts to Ease Russia Sanctions Fell Short," *Yahoo News*, June 1, 2017, https://www.yahoo .com/news/trump-administrations-secret-efforts-ease-russia-sanctions-fell -short-231301145.html.

2. Greg Miller, Adam Entous, and Ellen Nakashima, "National Security Adviser Flynn Discussed Sanctions with Russian Ambassador, Despite Denials, Officials Say," *Washington Post*, February 9, 2017, https://www .washingtonpost.com/world/national-security/national-security-adviser -flynn-discussed-sanctions-with-russian-ambassador-despite-denials -officials-say/2017/02/09/f85b29d6-ee11-11e6-b4ff-ac2cf509efe5_story .html.

3. Daniel Dale, "Six Months of Spelling Mistakes from the Trump White House: Analysis," *Toronto Star*, July 19, 2017, https://www.thestar.com/news /world/2017/07/19/six-months-of-spelling-mistakes-from-the-trump-white -house-analysis.html.

4. Heather Nauert, Twitter, October 1, 2017, 11:26 a.m., https://twitter.com /statedeptspox/status/914557115645202432.

5. Natasha Bertrand, Twitter, February 13, 2017, 8:25 a.m., https://twitter.com /natashabertrand/status/831177597165920257.

6. 8 U.S. Code 1182. Sec. 212(f).

7. *Kerry v. Din*, 576 U.S. ___ (2015), https://www.supremecourt.gov/opinions/14pdf/13-1402_e29g.pdf.

8. Order Granting Mot. TRO, *Hawai'i v. Trump*, No. 17-00050 DKW-KSC (D. Haw. Mar. 15, 2017). For PDF, see http://www.politico.com/f/?id=0000015a-d421-db68-a97b-d5e934210000. See also "Highlights from Court Ruling Halting Trump's Revised Travel Ban," *New York Times*, March 16, 2017, https://www.nytimes.com/2017/03/15/us/politics/highlights-immigration-ruling.html.

9. Order, *Trump v. Hawaii*, No. 16-1540 (U.S. July 19, 2017), https://www.supremecourt.gov/orders/courtorders/071917zr_o7jp.pdf.

10. Associated Press, "Sessions Taps Former Army General to Lead Federal Prison System," *ArmyTimes*, August 1, 2017, http://www.armytimes.com/news/your-army/2017/08/01/sessions-taps-former-army-general-to-lead-federal-prison-system/.

11. Philip Rucker, "Trump Friend Says Priebus Is 'In Way over His Head,'" *Washington Post*, February 12, 2017, https://www.washingtonpost.com/news/powerpost/wp/2017/02/12/trump-friend-says-priebus-is-in-way-over-his-head/.

12. Alan Rappeport, "Exxon Is Fined for Violating U.S. Sanctions," *New York Times*, July 21, 2017, A18, https://www.nytimes.com/2017/07/20/us/politics/exxon-mobil-fined-russia-tillerson-sanctions.html.

13. Noah Daponte-Smith, "The State Department in Crisis," *National Review Online*, July 6, 2017, http://www.nationalreview.com/article/449267/state-department-crisis-staffing-cuts-incompetent-leaders-threaten-american-diplomacy.

14. Nicole Lewis and Kristine Phillips, "The Trump White House Keeps Mixing Up the Names of Asian Countries and Their Leaders' Titles," *Washington Post*, July 10, 2017, https://www.washingtonpost.com/news/the-fix/wp/2017/07/08/white-house-press-office-misidentifies-japanese-prime-minister-abe-as-president/.

15. Mike Pence, speech at the U.S. Naval Academy Commencement Ceremony, Annapolis, MD, May 26, 2017, https://www.whitehouse.gov/the-press-office/2017/05/26/remarks-vice-president-us-naval-academy-commencement-ceremony.

16. *Little v. Barreme*, 6 U.S. 170 (1804), https://supreme.justia.com/cases/federal/us/6/170/case.html.

17. Michael R. Gordon, "Trump Gives Mattis Authority to Send More Troops to Afghanistan," *New York Times*, June 14, 2017, A13, https://www.nytimes.com/2017/06/13/world/asia/mattis-afghanistan-military.html.

18. Dexter Filkins, "James Mattis, a Warrior in Washington," *New Yorker*, May 29, 2017, http://www.newyorker.com/magazine/2017/05/29/james-mattis-a-warrior-in-washington.

19. Josh Dawsey, Twitter, August 9, 2017, 11:45 a.m., https://twitter.com/jdawsey1 /status/895310022502219776.

20. Joshua Berlinger, Zachary Cohen, and Angela Dewan, "Tillerson Dials Back Rhetoric after Trump's North Korea 'Fire and Fury' Threats," *CNN.com*, August 9, 2017, http://www.cnn.com/2017/08/09/politics/north-korea -donald-trump/index.html.

21. "Statement by Secretary of Defense Jim Mattis," Release No: NR-286-17, August 9, 2017, https://www.defense.gov/News/News-Releases/News -Release-View/Article/1273247/statement-by-secretary-of-defense-jim -mattis/.

22. The Reagan Battalion, Twitter, August 25, 2017, 1:49 p.m., https://twitter .com/ReaganBattalion/status/901184752094457856/video/1.

23. *The Records of the Federal Convention of 1787*, vol. 3, ed. Max Farrand (New Haven, CT: Yale University Press, 1911), 251, http://oll.libertyfund.org/titles /1787#Farrand_0544-03_787.

24. *The Records of the Federal Convention of 1787*, rev. ed., vol. 2, ed. Max Farrand (New Haven, CT: Yale University Press, 1937), 154, http://press-pubs.uchicago .edu/founders/print_documents/a1_2_5s7.html.

CHAPTER 10: RESENTMENTS

1. *Meet the Press*, NBC, July 24, 2016, https://www.nbcnews.com/meet-the-press /meet-press-july-24-2016-n615706.

2. Sopan Deb, "Trump celebrates big Michigan, Mississippi wins amid branded products," *CBS News*, March 8, 2016, http://www.cbsnews.com/news/trump -celebrates-big-michigan-mississippi-wins-amid-branded-products/.

3. Republican presidential debate, Cleveland, OH, August 6, 2015.

4. Reuters video, 2:13, December 10, 2015, http://www.reuters.com/video /2015/12/11/trump-we-cant-worry-about-being-politica?videoId=366641534.

5. Louis Nelson, "Trump: Clinton, Obama Protecting Terrorists to Be 'Politically Correct,'" *Politico*, June 13, 2016, http://www.politico.com/story /2016/06/donald-trump-muslim-ban-224272.

6. Donald Trump, speech at Iowa Events Center, Des Moines, IA, December 8, 2016. See "President-Elect Donald Trump Victory Rally in Des Moines, Iowa," C-SPAN video, 58:12, https://www.c-span.org/video/?419792-1 /presidentelect-donald-trump-holds-rally-des-moines-iowa.

7. "D. L. Hughley Defends Debbie Reynolds Death Joke | TMZ," YouTube video, 1:55, posted by "TMZ," January 3, 2017, https://www.youtube.com /watch?v=I3wxRkXMQcY.

8. "Why I Voted for Donald Trump," *Washington Post*, November 13, 2016, A12, last modified November 23, 2016, https://www.washingtonpost.com /graphics/opinions/trump-supporters-why-vote/.

9.   Andrew Klavan, "Why I'll Vote for Donald Trump," *PJ Media*, November 6, 2016, https://pjmedia.com/andrewklavan/2016/11/06/why-ill-vote-for -donald-trump/.

10. Andrew Klavan, "Be Thankful for What Trump Is Not," *PJ Media*, June 4, 2017, https://pjmedia.com/andrewklavan/2017/06/04/what-trump-is-not/.

11. Chris Jones, "'Straight White Men': Young Jean Lee Asks Audience, Herself to See Both Sides," *Chicago Tribune*, February 12, 2017, http://www .chicagotribune.com/entertainment/theater/reviews/ct-straight-white-men -review-ent-0213-20170212-column.html.

12. "Young Voters Supported Obama Less, but May Have Mattered More," *Pew Research Center*, November 26, 2012, http://www.people-press.org/2012 /11/26/young-voters-supported-obama-less-but-may-have-mattered-more/.

13. Jean-Claude Lupis, "The State of Traditional TV: Updated with Q1 2017 Data," *Marketing Charts*, July 26, 2017, http://www.marketingcharts.com /featured-24817.

14. J. M. Berger, "Nazis vs. ISIS on Twitter: A Comparative Study of White Nationalist and ISIS Online Social Media Networks," George Washington University Program on Extremism, September 2016, https://cchs.gwu.edu /sites/cchs.gwu.edu/files/downloads/Nazis%20v.%20ISIS%20Final_0.pdf.

15. Jack Holmes, "Are Young, White Males Being Radicalized Online?," *Esquire*, November 9, 2016, http://www.esquire.com/news-politics/news/a50513 /young-trump-voters-undercover/.

16. Lydia Saad, "Fewer Young People Say I Do—to Any Relationship," *Gallup News*, June 8, 2015, http://www.gallup.com/poll/183515/fewer-young-people -say-relationship.aspx.

17. Camila Domonoske, "For First Time in 130 Years, More Young Adults Live with Parents Than with Partners," *NPR*, May 24, 2016, http://www.npr.org /sections/thetwo-way/2016/05/24/479327382/for-first-time-in-130-years -more-young-adults-live-with-parents-than-partners.

18. Jean M. Twenge, Ryne A. Sherman, and Brooke E. Wells, "Sexual Inactivity During Young Adulthood Is More Common Among U.S. Millennials and iGen: Age, Period, and Cohort Effects on Having No Sexual Partners after Age 18," *Archives of Sexual Behavior* 46, no. 2, February 2017: 433-40: https://doi.org/10.1007/s10508-016-0798-z.

19. Richard Fry, "For First Time in Modern Era, Living with Parents Edges Out Other Living Arrangements for 18- to 34-Year-Olds," *Pew Research Center*, May 24, 2016, http://www.pewsocialtrends.org/2016/05/24/for-first-time-in -modern-era-living-with-parents-edges-out-other-living-arrangements-for-18 -to-34-year-olds/.

20. Ana Swanson, "Why Amazing Video Games Could Be Causing a Big Problem for America," *Washington Post*, September 23, 2016, https://www

.washingtonpost.com/news/wonk/wp/2016/09/23/why-amazing-video-games
-could-be-causing-a-big-problem-for-america/ (citing US Census data).
Women are significantly less likely to play video games at all, and they play
fewer hours on average. Those women who do play heavily skew much older
than male heavy gamers. See http://essentialfacts.theesa.com.

21. Justin McCarthy, "One in Eight U.S. Adults Say They Smoke Marijuana,"
Gallup News, August 8, 2016, http://www.gallup.com/poll/194195/adults-say
-smoke-marijuana.aspx.

22. "Celebrating 10 Years of Porn . . . and Data!," *Pornhub*, May 25, 2017,
https://www.pornhub.com/insights/10-years.

23. Milo Yiannopoulos, "FULL TEXT: MILO On How Feminism Hurts Men
and Women," *Breitbart*, October 7, 2016, http://www.breitbart.com/milo
/2016/10/07/full-text-milo-feminism-auburn.

24. Peter Beinart, "Fear of a Female President," *Atlantic*, October 2016, https://
www.theatlantic.com/magazine/archive/2016/10/fear-of-a-female-president
/497564/.

25. Philip Bump, "White Male Democrats Have Disproportionately Voted
against Hillary Clinton for Eight Years Running," *Washington Post*, May 5,
2016, https://www.washingtonpost.com/news/the-fix/wp/2016/05/05/white
-male-democrats-have-disproportionately-voted-against-hillary-clinton-for
-eight-years-running/.

26. Ibid.

27. Ross Douthat, "A Playboy for President," *New York Times*, August 14, 2016,
http://www.nytimes.com/2016/08/14/opinion/sunday/a-playboy-for
-president.html.

28. Dale Beran, "How the 'Isolated Man-Boys' of 4chan Turned a Meme into
the President of the United States," *Quartz*, February 17, 2017, https://
qz.com/914142/how-the-isolated-man-boys-of-4chan-turned-a-meme-into
-the-president-of-the-united-states/.

29. Daniel Lombroso and Yoni Appelbaum, "'Hail Trump!': White Nationalists
Salute the President-Elect," *Atlantic*, November 21, 2016, https://www.the
atlantic.com/politics/archive/2016/11/richard-spencer-speech-npi/508379/.

30. *The Daily Show with Jon Stewart*, "Ken Salazar" (Season 14, Episode 63),
Comedy Central, May 7, 2009, http://www.cc.com/video-clips/iknvhd/the
-daily-show-with-jon-stewart-white-in-america---the-children.

31. Emily Badger, "Americans Vastly Overestimate How Diverse the Country
Really Is," *CityLab*, October 22, 2013, https://www.citylab.com/equity
/2013/10/americans-vastly-overestimate-how-diverse-country-really/7320/.

32. Jonathan Swan, "Trump to Protesters: All Lives Matter," *Hill*, February 29,
2016, http://thehill.com/blogs/ballot-box/presidential-races/271159-trump
-to-protesters-all-lives-matter.

33.   *Hannity*, Fox News Network, December 6, 2016.

34.   "Donald Trump: We'll All Be Saying 'Merry Christmas' Again!," YouTube video, 0:46, posted by "American Born Republic," November 23, 2015, https://www.youtube.com/watch?v=k9W-_El6GMc.

35.   Donald J. Trump, Twitter, December 25, 2016, 4:46 a.m., https://twitter .com/realDonaldTrump/status/813003030186622976.

36.   American Foundation for Suicide Prevention, "Suicide Statistics," https:// afsp.org/about-suicide/suicide-statistics (citing data from the Centers for Disease Control and Prevention Data & Statistics Fatal Injury Report for 2015).

37.   Henry J. Kaiser Family Foundation, "Opioid Overdose Deaths by Race/ Ethnicity," http://www.kff.org/other/state-indicator/opioid-overdose-deaths -by-raceethnicity/ (citing data from the Centers for Disease Control and Prevention).

38.   Jeanna Smialek, "'Deaths of Despair' Are Surging Among the White Working Class," *Bloomberg News*, March 23, 2017, https://www.bloomberg.com /news/articles/2017-03-23/white-working-class-death-rate-to-be-elevated-for -a-generation.

39.   Tami Luhby, "Working Class White Men Make Less than They Did in 1996," *CNN.com*, October 5, 2016, http://money.cnn.com/2016/10/05/news /economy/working-class-men-income/index.html.

40.   W. Bradford Wilcox, Andrew J. Cherlin, Jeremy E. Uecker, and Matthew Messel, "No Money, No Honey, No Church: The Deinstitutionalization of Religious Life Among the White Working Class," *Research in the Sociology of Work* 23 (2012): 227–50, https://dx.doi.org/10.1108% 2FS0277-2833(2012)0000023013.

41.   Ronald Brownstein, "The White Working Class: The Most Pessimistic Group in America," *Atlantic*, May 27, 2011, https://www.theatlantic.com /politics/archive/2011/05/the-white-working-class-the-most-pessimistic -group-in-america/239584/.

42.   Author's own search at *NYTimes.com*.

43.   *Rush Limbaugh Show*, June 3, 2015, https://www.rushlimbaugh.com /daily/2015/06/03/jenner_declares_i_m_the_new_normal/.

44.   Selena Zito, "Taking Trump Seriously, Not Literally," *Atlantic*, September 23, 2016, https://www.theatlantic.com/politics/archive/2016/09/trump-makes -his-case-in-pittsburgh/501335/.

45.   *Hannity*, Fox News Network, May 12, 2017, http://insider.foxnews.com/2017 /05/12/judge-jeanine-donald-trump-interview-preview-sean-hannity-main stream-media.

46.   Matt Young, "Gavin McInnes, Man Who Criticised Waleed Aly, Releases Strange Video in Tel Aviv, Forced to Respond," *News.com.au*, March 19,

2017, http://www.news.com.au/technology/online/gavin-mcinnes-man-who
-criticised-waleed-aly-releases-strange-video-in-tel-aviv-forced-to-respond
/news-story/743cd1c0b821bdad5c00d09bacea8927.

47. Publius Decius Mus [pseud.], "The Flight 93 Election," *Claremont Review of Books*, September 5, 2016, http://www.claremont.org/crb/basicpage/the
-flight-93-election/.

48. Ibid.

49. Ibid.

CHAPTER 11: BELIEVERS

1. Emily Karl, "Just 20% of Americans under 30 Approve of Trump: Poll," *Axios*, August 29, 2017, https://www.axios.com/trumps-approval-among
-people-under-30-reaches-new-low-2479223836.html.

2. Omarosa Manigault, interview by Jim Gilmore, *Frontline*, PBS, June 23, 2016, http://www.pbs.org/wgbh/frontline/article/the-frontline-interview
-omarosa-manigault/.

3. Bob Woodward and Robert Costa, "Transcript: Donald Trump Interview with Bob Woodward and Robert Costa," *Washington Post*, April 2, 2016, https://www.washingtonpost.com/news/post-politics/wp/2016/04/02
/transcript-donald-trump-interview-with-bob-woodward-and-robert-costa/.

4. "Famous Quotes by Vince Lombardi," VinceLombardi.com © 2017 Family of Vince Lombardi c/o Luminary Group LLC, http://www.vincelombardi
.com/quotes.html.

5. Justin Baragone, "'I'm Pissed!' Sean Hannity Absolutely Loses It Over 'Never Trumper Jerks' and Evan McMullin," *Mediaite*, October 26, 2016, https://
www.mediaite.com/online/im-pissed-sean-hannity-absolutely-loses-it-over
-never-trumper-jerks-and-evan-mcmullin/.

6. *Hannity*, Fox News Network, November 9, 2016.

7. *The Kelly File*, Fox News Network, August 18, 2016.

8. Anthony Scaramucci, Twitter, August 18, 2016, 6:13 p.m., https://twitter
.com/scaramucci/status/766442965724192777.

9. William McGurn, "The Cheap Moralizing of Never Trump," *Wall Street Journal*, October 17, 2016, https://www.wsj.com/articles/the-cheap
-moralizing-of-never-trump-1476745922.

10. David Limbaugh, "The Ongoing Frustration of Trump's Conservative Critics," *Townhall*, July 7, 2017, https://townhall.com/columnists/david
limbaugh/2017/07/07/the-ongoing-frustration-of-trumps-conservative
-critics-n2351540.

11. Barack Obama, speech at the 2004 Democratic National Convention, Boston, MA, July 27, 2004.

12. Ingrid Melander, "France's Le Pen Launches Election Bid with Vow to Fight

Globalization," Reuters, February 5, 2017, http://www.reuters.com/article /us-france-election-fn/frances-le-pen-launches-election-bid-with-vow-to-fight -globalization-idUSKBN15K0R1.

13. Gabriel Gatehouse, "Marine Le Pen: Who's Funding France's Far Right?," *BBC.com*, April 3, 2017, http://www.bbc.com/news/world-europe-39478066.

14. "Election 2016: Exit Polls," *New York Times*, November 8, 2016, https://www .nytimes.com/interactive/2016/11/08/us/politics/election-exit-polls.html.

15. Philip Bump, "Donald Trump Got Reagan-like Support from Union Households," *Washington Post*, November 10, 2016, https://www.washington post.com/news/the-fix/wp/2016/11/10/donald-trump-got-reagan-like-support -from-union-households/.

16. Amanda Sakuma, "Trump Did Better with Blacks, Hispanics Than Romney in '12: Exit Polls," *NBC News*, November 9, 2016, https://www.nbcnews.com /storyline/2016-election-day/trump-did-better-blacks-hispanics-romney-12 -exit-polls-n681386.

17. Tara Golshan, "The Women Who Helped Donald Trump Win," *Vox*, January 21, 2017, https://www.vox.com/policy-and-politics/2017/1/20 /14061660/women-march-washington-vote-trump.

18. Gabriella Paiella, "6 Women on Why They're Not Voting in This Election," *The Cut*, October 19, 2016, https://www.thecut.com/2016/10/women-who -are-not-voting-2016-election.html.

19. Pew Research Center, "The Generation Gap and the 2012 Election," November 3, 2011, http://assets.pewresearch.org/wp-content/uploads/sites/5 /legacy-pdf/11-3-11%20Generations%20Release.pdf.

20. Ibid.

21. Ibid.

22. Ibid.

23. Ibid.

24. Ibid.

25. Ibid.

26. Ibid.

27. Teresa Ghilarducci, "Our Ridiculous Approach to Retirement," *New York Times*, July 22, 2012, https://www.nytimes.com/2012/07/22/opinion /sunday/our-ridiculous-approach-to-retirement.html.

28. "41hh I Am Concerned about the Government Becoming Too Involved in Health Care," American Values Survey Question Database, *Pew Research Center*, accessed September 28, 2017, http://www.people-press.org/values-questions /q41hh/concerned-government-becoming-too-involved-in-health-care/#age.

29. Vanessa Williamson, Theda Skocpol, and John Coggin, "The Tea Party and the Remaking of Republican Conservatism," *Perspectives on Politics* 9, no. 1 (March 2011): 33, doi:10.1017/S153759271000407X.

30. Glenn Beck, "We Surround Them," accessed September 29, 2017, http://www.glennbeck.com/content/articles/article/198/21018/.

31. David Frum, *Why Romney Lost* (Newsweek e-book, 2012), chap. 2.

32. Ibid.

33. Robert D. Putnam, "*E Pluribus Unum*: Diversity and Community in the Twenty-first Century, the 2006 Johan Skytte Prize Lecture," *Scandinavian Political Studies* 30, no. 2 (June 2007): 137, doi:10.1111/j.1467-9477.2007.00176.x.

34. Ed O'Keefe, "Jeb Bush Announces Presidential Bid: 'We Will Take Command of Our Future Once Again,'" *Washington Post*, June 15, 2015, https://www.washingtonpost.com/news/post-politics/wp/2015/06/15/jeb-bush-to-formally-launch-presidential-campaign/.

35. "Transcript: Ted Cruz's speech at Liberty University," *Washington Post*, March 23, 2015, https://www.washingtonpost.com/politics/transcript-ted-cruzs-speech-at-liberty-university/2015/03/23/41c4011a-d168-11e4-a62f-ee745911a4ff_story.html; "Full text of Marco Rubio's 2016 presidential campaign announcement," *Washington Post*, April 13, 2015, https://www.washingtonpost.com/news/post-politics/wp/2015/04/13/full-text-of-marco-rubios-2016-presidential-campaign-announcement/.

36. George Gao, "Biggest Share of Whites in U.S. Are Boomers, but for Minority Groups It's Millennials or Younger," *Fact Tank* (blog), *Pew Research Center*, July 7, 2016, http://www.pewresearch.org/fact-tank/2016/07/07/biggest-share-of-whites-in-u-s-are-boomers-but-for-minority-groups-its-millennials-or-younger/.

37. Emma Green, "It Was Cultural Anxiety That Drove White, Working-Class Voters to Trump," *Atlantic*, May 9, 2017, https://www.theatlantic.com/politics/archive/2017/05/white-working-class-trump-cultural-anxiety/525771/.

38. Abraham Lincoln, "Response to a Serenade," November 10, 1864, in *The Language of Liberty: The Political Speeches and Writings of Abraham Lincoln*, ed. Joseph R. Fornieri (Washington, DC: Regnery, 2003), 682.

CHAPTER 12: HOPE

1. Chris Ariens, "MSNBC Wins Its First Week Ever in Prime Time," *Ad Week*, May 22, 2017, http://www.adweek.com/tvnewser/for-1st-time-in-17-years-fox-news-was-3rd-in-prime-time-demo/329902.

2. Theodore Roosevelt, *History as Literature* (New York: Charles Scribner's Sons, 1913), 187.

3. John F. Kennedy, "Radio and Television Report to the American People on Civil Rights," June 11, 1963. Online by Gerhard Peters and John T. Woolley, *The American Presidency Project*, http://www.presidency.ucsb.edu/ws/?pid=9271.

4. Timothy Synder, Facebook, November 15, 2016, 6:57 p.m., https://www
.facebook.com/timothy.david.snyder/posts/1206636702716110.

5. Matthew Reade, "Students Demand Administrators 'Take Action' Against
Conservative Journalists," *Claremont Independent*, April 17, 2017, http://
claremontindependent.com/students-demand-administrators-take-action
-against-conservative-journalists/.

6. Michel Foucault, *The Foucault Reader*, ed. Paul Rabinow (New York:
Pantheon Books, 1984), 74.

7. Maria Konnikova, "Trump's Lies vs. Your Brain," *Politico Magazine*, January/
February 2017, http://www.politico.com/magazine/story/2017/01/donald
-trump-lies-liar-effect-brain-214658.

8. Eric Oliver and Thomas Wood, "A New Poll Shows 52% of Republicans
Actually Think Trump Won the Popular Vote," *Washington Post*, December
18, 2016, https://www.washingtonpost.com/news/monkey-cage/wp/2016
/12/18/a-new-poll-shows-an-astonishing-52-of-republicans-think-trump
-won-the-popular-vote/.

9. Michael Wolff, "A Conversation with Kellyanne Conway: 'I'm the Face of
Trump's Movement,'" *Hollywood Reporter*, January 26, 2017, http://www
.hollywoodreporter.com/features/a-conversation-kellyanne-conway-im-face
-trumps-movement-968579.

10. Gary Langer, "6 Months In, a Record Low for Trump, with Troubles from
Russia to Health Care (POLL)," *ABC News*, July 16, 2017, http://abcnews
.go.com/Politics/months-record-low-trump-troubles-russia-health-care
/story?id=48639490.

11. "Czeslaw Milosz—Nobel Lecture," *Nobelprize.org*, Nobel Media AB 2014,
https://www.nobelprize.org/nobel_prizes/literature/laureates/1980/milosz
-lecture.html.

12. "U.S. Voters Say 68–27% Let Transgender People Serve, Quinnipiac
University National Poll Finds; Voters Disapprove 5–1 of GOP Handling of
Health Care," Quinnipiac University Poll, August 3, 2017, https://poll
.qu.edu/national/release-detail?ReleaseID=2477.

13. Yael Bame, "21% of Americans Believe That Being Transgender Is a Mental
Illness," *YouGov*, May 17, 2017, https://today.yougov.com/news/2017/05/17
/21-americans-believe-identifying-transgender-menta/.

14. Jennifer Senior, "A Book from 1998 Envisioned 2016 Election," *New York
Times*, November 21, 2016, https://www.nytimes.com/2016/11/21/books
/richard-rortys-1998-book-suggested-election-2016-was-coming.html,
quoting Richard Rorty, *Achieving Our Country: Leftist Thought in
Twentieth-Century America* (Cambridge, MA: Harvard University Press,
1998), 89–90.

15. Peggy Noonan, "Trump Is Woody Allen Without the Humor," *Wall Street Journal*, July 29, 2017, https://www.wsj.com/articles/trump-is-woody-allen-without-the-humor-1501193193.

16. Greg Miller, Ellen Nakashima, and Adam Entous, "Obama's Secret Struggle to Punish Russia for Putin's Election Assault," *Washington Post*, June 23, 2017, https://www.washingtonpost.com/graphics/2017/world/national-security/obama-putin-election-hacking/.

17. David Frum, "The Dangers of the Putin-Trump Relationship," *Atlantic*, September 21, 2016, https://www.theatlantic.com/politics/archive/2016/09/trump-and-putins-relationship/500852/.

18. Roberto Stefan Foa and Yascha Mounk, "The Democratic Discontent," *Journal of Democracy* 27, no. 3 (July 2016): 7–8, http://www.journalofdemocracy.org/sites/default/files/Foa%26Mounk-27-3.pdf.

19. Jacob Poushter, "40% of Millennials Ok with Limiting Speech Offensive to Minorities," *Fact Tank* (blog), *Pew Research Center*, November 20, 2015, http://www.pewresearch.org/fact-tank/2015/11/20/40-of-millennials-ok-with-limiting-speech-offensive-to-minorities/.

20. "Limited Sovereignty in the United States," *Atlantic Monthly*, February 1879, 186, quoted in Alexander Keyssar, *The Right to Vote: The Contested History of Democracy in the United States* (New York: Basic Books, 2000), 79. By "universal suffrage," the unknown author meant "universal male suffrage."

21. Bernie Sanders, presidential campaign announcement, May 26, 2015, https://berniesanders.com/bernies-announcement/.

22. David Frum, "The Conservative Case for Voting for Clinton," *Atlantic*, November 2, 2016, https://www.theatlantic.com/politics/archive/2016/11/dont-gamble-on-trump/506207/.

INDEX

ABOUT THE AUTHOR

David Frum is a senior editor at the *Atlantic* and the author of nine books, including the *New York Times* bestseller *The Right Man*. From 2001 to 2002, he served as a speechwriter and special assistant to President George W. Bush. He and his wife, Danielle Crittenden Frum, live in Washington, DC, and Wellington, Ontario. They have three children.